EU GENERAL DATA PROTECTION REGULATION

EU GENERAL DATA PROTECTION REGULATION

A Guide to the New Law

James Castro-Edwards

The Law Society

Crown copyright material is reproduced with the permission of the Controller of Her Majesty's Stationery Office

ISBN-13: 978-1-78446-077-8

Published in 2017 by the Law Society
113 Chancery Lane, London WC2A 1PL

Typeset by Columns Design XML Ltd, Reading
Printed by CPI Antony Rowe, Chippenham, Wilts

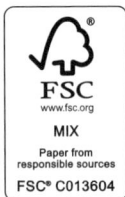

CONTENTS

APPENDICES

FOREWORD

For me, the end game in the data protection field is always about increasing public trust and confidence in how their personal data is used.

This is fundamental. Innovation relies on consumer trust. The digital economy depends on the trust of consumers to engage with it. Trust in both privacy and Freedom of Information regulation is fundamental to democracy.

The way our personal information is handled has never been more important.

We have a digital infrastructure that was unimaginable when the current Data Protection Act was forged 20 years ago.

Technology is moving so fast. The law needed to move with it. And the GDPR does that.

Because while the new law builds on the previous legislation, it provides more protections for consumers, and more privacy considerations for organisations. It brings a more 21st century approach to the processing of personal data.

The GDPR gives specific new obligations for organisations, for example around reporting data breaches and transferring data across borders.

But the real change for organisations is understanding the new rights for consumers.

Consumers and citizens will have stronger rights to be informed about how organisations like yours use their personal data. They'll have the right to request that personal data be deleted or removed if there's no compelling reason for an organisation to carry on processing it, and new rights around data portability and how they give consent.

The new law equals bigger fines for getting it wrong. That's the obvious headline here. If your organisation can't demonstrate that good data protection is a cornerstone of your business policy and practices, you're leaving your organisation open to enforcement action that can damage both public reputation and bank balance. That makes data protection a boardroom issue.

But there's a carrot here as well as a stick, and as regulators we actually prefer the carrot. Get data protection right, and you can see a real business benefit.

Accepting broad accountability for data protection encourages an upfront investment in privacy fundamentals, but it offers a payoff down the line, not just in better legal compliance, but a competitive edge. Whether that means attracting more customers or more efficiently meeting pressing public policy needs, I believe there is a real opportunity for organisations to present themselves on the basis of how they respect the privacy of individuals. Over time this can play a real role in consumer choice.

Now is the time to act.

Elizabeth Denham
UK Information Commissioner
July 2017

PREFACE

It is difficult to imagine anyone or any organisation that will not be affected by the General Data Protection Regulation (GDPR). The GDPR grants enhanced rights to individuals, giving them choice and visibility over the way organisations use their information. In turn, operators in the public, private and charitable sectors will be subject to more stringent obligations than under the preceding law. Some organisations in the UK and Europe, whose core activities fall outside the ambit of the Data Protection Act 1998, will find themselves subject to the GDPR. While some businesses that do not even have a presence in the European Union will need to comply with the new regulation, thanks to its extra-territorial reach.

The GDPR marks a sea change in data protection law. To date, many businesses have used individuals' personal information on the assumption that if an activity is not expressly prohibited, they have free rein to do as they please. However, the GDPR is intended to turn the tables, in favour of the citizen. Businesses, public authorities and charities will be put to task as to how they collect, use and share personal information. In particular, many current practices that purport to be justified on the basis of individuals' consent, perhaps most notably in the realm of digital marketing, will become outlawed.

Many organisations will be required to appoint a dedicated data protection professional, to promote and oversee compliance with the new law. At the same time, principles such as privacy by design and privacy by default are intended to embed data protection into the bases of their operations. The cumulative effect is likely to be a quantum leap in awareness of data protection, as well as a dramatic expansion in the ranks of data protection professionals.

Any organisation that chooses to ignore the GDPR will be pursuing a high-risk strategy. One of the European Commission's aims when it proposed the new law as a draft was to escalate data protection to a corporate board level topic, which it seeks to achieve by imposing heavy fines for noncompliance. The GDPR also includes detailed provisions requiring data protection authorities to work together, enabling more efficient and effective enforcement. At the same time, the UK data protection regulator has announced plans to increase its staff by 40 per cent, to manage the increased workload that will be generated by the new law. This combination looks set to increase the volume and magnitude of enforcement action.

The enhanced regulation of data protection has not occurred in a vacuum. Widespread sharing of individuals' personal information is increasing at an exponential rate, making the need for protecting citizens' data readily apparent. Stories of data breaches affecting health trusts, cyber attacks compromising retailers' customer databases, and deliberate misuse of individuals' details regularly make news headlines. However, many prevailing data handling practices are so complex that ordinary citizens have little chance of understanding them, let alone protecting themselves. The GDPR aims to address this.

This is an exciting time to be practising in data protection, as the field takes a leap in significance, underpinned by the game-changing GDPR. This textbook is intended to provide a practical guide to the new law for private practice and in-house solicitors, whether experienced or new to the field, as well as non-legally qualified data protection practitioners.

James Castro-Edwards
Partner and head of data protection
Wedlake Bell LLP
June 2017

ACKNOWLEDGEMENTS

Special thanks to Francesca Mansell for all her assistance in writing this text.

INTRODUCTION

The EU General Data Protection Regulation (GDPR) was drafted in response to longstanding calls for reform of existing data protection law, enshrined in Directive 95/46/EC of the European Parliament and of the Council of 24 October 1995 on the protection of individuals with regard to the processing of personal data and on the free movement of such data (the Directive), often referred to as the Data Protection Directive. While the Directive may have been largely adequate, since its adoption in 1995 the world has changed dramatically in the way information is used.

The beginning of the new millennium has seen an explosion in the use of technology by the public at large, both in terms of the ever-increasing popularity of constantly evolving technology such as smartphones, tablet computers, wearables and connected devices, and the way in which such technology is used through the internet, in particular social media. In the light of this 'information revolution' and the increasing globalisation of businesses, the weaknesses of the Directive have become all too apparent. Its successor, the GDPR, is a significant evolution, addressing technological developments, clarifying individuals' rights, clarifying organisations' obligations and extending the powers of regulators to monitor compliance and impose heavy penalties upon those who fail to discharge their responsibilities.

In the intervening two decades between the adoption of the Directive and the conception of the GDPR, data protection has become a significantly more important field to both the general public and organisations in the private, public and third sectors. Individuals have become more conscious of privacy through factors such as the increased use of social networking and exposure to constant reminders of the need for data protection, with data breaches, cyber attacks and identity theft making the news almost daily. In response, organisations have increasingly devoted resources to the issue, resulting in an emerging field of dedicated data protection and privacy professionals. This field looks set to expand further as the GDPR imposes the requirement for many organisations – according to some estimates tens of thousands – to appoint an experienced, professional data protection officer (or DPO). Of course, there are organisations that fail to comply with their obligations and make headlines as they receive significant fines under the current law. The GDPR will almost certainly accentuate this with its enormous fines. It is difficult to imagine any single piece of legislation introduced in recent years with such far reaching consequences, or any individual or organisation that is not directly affected by this legislation, either through enhanced rights or more stringent obligations.

Data protection has come of age, with a new generation of law, an expanding field of experienced professionals, a general public that increasingly values its privacy and understands when it has been infringed, and more sophisticated and powerful data protection authorities. The decades following the introduction of the GDPR are likely to be characterised by the embedding of data protection and privacy as a corporate board level topic within organisations. For data protection and privacy professionals, whether external advisers or internal specialists, a thorough understanding of the GDPR will be a fundamental necessity.

Overview

The GDPR consists of 99 Articles, divided into 11 Chapters and 173 Recitals, running to a length of 88 pages of text, over four times the length of the Directive and significantly more prescriptive. It has been described as a 'regulation of recitals' and while the recitals may not have the legal force of the articles, they are essential for an understanding of its operative provisions.

The chapters of the GDPR cover the following:

■   Chapter I describes the subject matter and objectives of the GDPR, and defines the terms.

■   Chapter II sets out the principles, the requisite conditions for establishing valid consent and the rules for processing sensitive personal data.

■   Chapter III establishes the rights of data subjects.

■   Chapter IV sets out the obligations upon data controllers and data processors.

■   Chapter V contains the rules on data transfers.

■   Chapter VI establishes the role, responsibilities and powers of supervisory authorities.

■   Chapter VII explains the cooperation and consistency rules for supervisory authorities.

■   Chapter VIII sets out the remedies, liabilities and penalties under the GDPR.

■   Chapter IX provides for specific data processing situations.

■   Chapter X sets out the rules on delegated acts and implementing legislation.

■   Chapter XI contains the final provisions.

This text mirrors the structure of the GPDR.

TABLE OF CASES

TABLE OF STATUTES

TABLE OF STATUTORY INSTRUMENTS

—

TABLE OF INTERNATIONAL LEGISLATION

ABBREVIATIONS

APEC	Asia Pacific Economic Cooperation
BCRs	binding corporate rules
Board	European Data Protection Board
Charter	Charter of Fundamental Rights of the European Union
CISPE	Cloud Infrastructure Service Providers in Europe
CJEU	Court of Justice of the European Union
COM(2017) 7	Communication from the Commission to the European Parliament and the Council: Exchanging and Protecting Personal Data in a Globalised World (Brussels, 10 January 2017, COM(2017) 7 Final)
Directive	Directive 95/46/EC
DPA 1998	Data Protection Act 1998
DPIA	data protection impact assessment
DPO	data protection officer
EDPS	European Data Protection Supervisor
EEA	European Economic Area
EU	European Union
FEDMA	Federation of European Direct Marketing
GDPR	General Data Protection Regulation
HR	human resources
ICO	Information Commissioner's Office
IT	information technology
RFID	radio-frequency identification
SCC	standard contractual clauses
TEC	Treaty Establishing the European Community

TEU	Treaty on European Union
TFEU	Treaty on the Functioning of the European Union
WP 242	Article 29 Data Protection Working Party Guidelines on the right to data portability
WP 243	Article 29 Data Protection Working Party Guidelines on Data Protection Officers
WP 244	Article 29 Data Protection Working Party Guidelines for identifying a controller or processor's lead supervisory authority
WP 248	Article 29 Data Protection Working Party Guidelines on Data Protection Impact Assessment (DPIA) and determining whether processing is 'likely to result in a high risk' for the purposes of Regulation 2016/679

1 SUBJECT MATTER, MATERIAL AND TERRITORIAL SCOPE, AND DEFINITIONS

Chapter I of the General Data Protection Regulation (GDPR) sets out the aim and scope of the GDPR, establishing its geographical reach and specifying the types of organisation that will be subject to its provisions. Significantly, the GDPR seeks to protect individuals' personal data as an overarching, fundamental human right, in contrast to other legal systems which may protect some aspects of privacy by regulating specific sectors. The scope of the GDPR is substantially extended beyond that of the EU Data Protection Directive (Directive 95/46/EC; 'the Directive') as a result of its extra-territorial reach and its application to a wider range of organisations.

The final Article of Chapter I sets out the definitions used in the GDPR, which build on those of the Directive. All of the definitions from the Directive can be found in the GDPR, with some minor changes, although the latter introduces a number of new concepts. The GDPR builds on the preceding legislation and as such amounts to an evolution of the Directive. Accordingly, data protection and privacy practitioners who are familiar with the existing rules should find at least some of the GDPR not entirely new.

1.1 SUBJECT MATTER AND OBJECTIVES

The GDPR establishes a set of rules that aim to protect individuals' personal information, while allowing its free movement. Its objectives are:

(a) to protect individuals' fundamental rights and freedoms, in particular their right to the protection of personal data; and

(b) to allow the free movement of personal data between Member States.

These stated objectives are virtually identical to those of the Directive (Directive, Article 1).

The Recitals help to explain the rationale underlying the provisions of the GDPR and provide insight as to how the Articles should be interpreted. The first of the Recitals explains the legal basis for the protection of individuals in the context of the processing of their personal data, enshrined in the Charter of Fundamental Rights of the European Union ('the Charter') and the Treaty on the Functioning of the European Union (TFEU).

The Charter, which became legally binding in the EU with the entry into force of the Treaty of Lisbon in December 2009, sets out the fundamental rights that are protected in the EU. Article 8(1) of the Charter states:

> Everyone has the right to the protection of personal data concerning him or her.

Articles 8(2) and 8(3) further provide, respectively:

> Such data must be processed fairly for specified purposes and on the basis of the consent of the person concerned or some other legitimate basis laid down by law. Everyone has the right of access to data which has been collected concerning him or her, and the right to have it rectified.

and:

> Compliance with these rules shall be subject to control by an independent authority.

The TFEU (formerly known as the EC Treaty, the Treaty of Rome or the Treaty establishing the European Community (TEC)) sets out organisational and functional details of the EU. Article 16(1) of the TFEU provides:

> Everyone has the right to the protection of personal data concerning them.

The wording of Article 8(1) of the Charter and Article 16(1) of the TFEU are virtually identical. The effect of these provisions is to establish an explicit right to data protection.

The GDPR seeks to protect individuals regardless of their nationality and wherever they are located in the world, not just in the EU. Organisations established in, or who use equipment located in, the EU should be aware of this and not overlook the fact that they may process information relating to individuals who may live outside Europe, but who nevertheless enjoy the right to protection of their personal data.

The GDPR is intended to help promote European economic development, an aim shared with other jurisdictions outside the EU which have also adopted data protection laws. The GDPR is not just intended to promote trade; it is also intended to protect a fundamental human right (Recital 3). However, the right conferred upon individuals, namely to have their personal data protected, is not absolute and must be balanced with wider considerations (Recital 4). Rights conferred upon individuals, such as the right to be forgotten and the right to erasure, for example, are not absolute and should be balanced with broader considerations such as the public interest.

Technological developments such as smartphones, tablet computers, connected devices, the internet and social media, and the way individuals, as well as organisations in the private, public and third sectors, use such technology have resulted in huge volumes of personal data being shared within the EU and around the globe. The GDPR recognises that technology should enable the free flow of personal data, but that such information must also be protected (Recital 6). It aims to address the data protection risks associated with these new technologies and their widespread use by imposing more stringent obligations, in a more uniform, consistent manner. To this end, the heavy penalties for breaches of the GDPR are intended to escalate the importance of data protection to a corporate board level topic, and embed the concept into organisations in the private, public and third sectors from the top down.

Before delving further into the provisions, it is important to recognise the significance of the GDPR's status as a regulation rather than an EU directive. Its predecessor, the Directive, took effect in Member States by way of national implementing legislation, for example the Data Protection Act 1998 (DPA 1998) in the UK. It is widely acknowledged that the Directive has not been implemented uniformly by Member States; national laws differ and data protection authorities have adopted diverging approaches. This lack of uniformity has given rise to uncertainty, particularly for multinational and online businesses, and has a detrimental economic effect. Differing national approaches have meant that pan-European operators have had to negotiate their way through the differing requirements of individual Member States, which can be both costly and time-consuming. As a European regulation, the GDPR takes direct effect without the need for national implementing legislation, in an attempt to harmonise data protection laws within Europe.

The uniform application of data protection law within the EU is essential for the protection of individuals' rights and the free movement of personal data. However, the GDPR allows Member States scope to tailor its application to accommodate national legal requirements, public interest considerations or the exercise of official authority. It allows Member States some leeway in its application, for example around the processing of sensitive personal data. Arguably this flexibility conferred upon Member States defeats one of the fundamental aims of the GDPR, afflicting it with a potential lack of uniform application, a weakness from which the Directive suffered. However, this reflects a legal reality commented upon by observers during its lengthy evolution, namely that the GDPR could never operate uniformly across Europe, given the differences between the legal systems of Member States (see for example, Recital 151). This means that the GDPR is unlikely to ever apply completely homogenously across Europe, and multinational operators may still be thwarted in trying to adopt a 'one size fits all' approach (Recital 10). Nonetheless, the GDPR steps significantly closer to the goal of 'one continent, one law' than the Directive.

To ensure effective protection of individuals' personal data throughout the EU, the GDPR strengthens data subjects' rights and sets them out in detail. The obligations upon organisations that process such data are clearly specified and data protection authorities are empowered to monitor and ensure compliance with data protection rules and to impose significant sanctions for infringements (Recital 11). This is consistent with Article 16(2) TFEU, which mandates the European Parliament and the European Council to enact data protection laws, and provides:

> The European Parliament and the Council, acting in accordance with the ordinary legislative procedure, shall lay down the rules relating to the protection of individuals with regard to the processing of personal data by Union institutions, bodies, offices and agencies, and by the Member States when carrying out activities which

fall within the scope of Union law, and the rules relating to the free movement of such data. Compliance with these rules shall be subject to the control of independent authorities.

The rules adopted on the basis of this Article shall be without prejudice to the specific rules laid down in Article 39 of the Treaty on European Union.

The Lisbon Treaty amended the TFEU, introducing Article 16(2), on 1 December 2009.

The GDPR aims to provide consistent protection for citizens, legal certainty for organisations (including micro, small and medium-sized enterprises) and consistency as to how supervisory authorities monitor and enforce the law. However, a derogation exists for the benefit of organisations with fewer than 250 employees. Supervisory authorities within Member States are specifically required to take into account the needs of micro, small and medium-sized enterprises in the application of the GDPR. This addresses concerns that its provisions could place an excessive burden on small and medium-sized enterprises which may have limited resources to address compliance and could otherwise be placed at a competitive disadvantage (Recital 13).

The GDPR grants individuals a range of data protection rights regardless of their nationality or location. Any individual whose personal data is processed by an organisation subject to the GDPR benefits from the same rights of protection, whether they are located in the EU or elsewhere. These rights extend to 'natural persons', in other words, living individuals. The GDPR expressly excludes application to both the deceased (Recital 27) and undertakings established as legal persons (Recital 14), i.e. corporate entities, which is consistent with the aim of protecting a fundamental human right.

1.2   MATERIAL SCOPE

1.2.1   Fully automated, partly-automated and manual processing

The GDPR governs processing personal data by automated and partly automated means, as well as manually, using a 'filing system', which is defined later at **1.4**, although it will not apply to unstructured files. The GDPR is, by design, technology neutral in order to avoid becoming obsolete.

Whilst current guidance may of course be superseded after the GDPR comes into effect, structured manual filing systems are considered in guidance published by the UK Information Commissioner's Office (ICO), which illustrates the concept, with the proviso that other Member States may take a different approach to the UK. In the UK, structured data is considered by reference to a 'relevant filing system'.[1] ICO guidance provides that manual files which refer to individuals' names, but

---

[1]   Relevant filing systems are defined in s.1 of the DPA 1998, which in turn stems from Article 2(c) of the Directive.

where each individual file contains multiple categories of information, constitute 'unstructured files'.[2] Conversely, where a file contains only a single category of information, such as an individual's complaint, his or her account, or personnel records, this is likely to constitute a 'structured file'.

The ICO guidance suggests a useful rule of thumb to apply in determining whether a filing system is structured or not. The 'temp test' considers whether a reasonably competent temporary administrative assistant, after a short induction, explanation and/or operating manual on the particular filing system in question would be able to extract specific information about an individual from a set of manual records without any particular knowledge of the data controller's type of work, and without having to search through all of the records to find the information needed. If a system consists of files relating to named individuals, sub-divided into specific categories (such as annual leave, training history, sickness absence), this constitutes a structured system.

Notwithstanding that the GDPR applies to fully and partly automated processing, as well as manual processing using structured files, the Recitals provide a number of specific situations where the GDPR does not apply, including the following:

■ Member States' processing of personal data for national security purposes (including EU foreign and security policy) (Recital 16).
■ Processing personal data by EU institutions themselves, which is currently governed separately by Regulation (EC) 45/2001 on the protection of individuals with regard to the processing of personal data by the Community institutions and bodies and on the free movement of such data (Community Processing Regulation) (Recital 17).
■ Processing personal data by 'competent authorities' for the purposes of prevention, investigation, detection or prosecution of criminal offences and execution of criminal penalties, which is regulated separately.[3] However, where competent authorities process personal data for other non-crime related purposes (e.g. public security), processing will be subject to the GDPR. In such cases, Member States should be able to introduce more specific provisions to adapt the application of the GDPR to accommodate processing by private sector organisations, allowing for the restriction of rights and obligations where doing so is in the public interest. For example, in the context of anti-money laundering or forensic laboratories (Recital 19).
■ Processing personal data by an individual for purely personal or household purposes, provided these are not connected to a professional or commercial activity. Exempted personal or household activities could include correspondence, keeping addresses and social networking. The specific mention of social

---

[2] *Frequently asked questions and answers about relevant filing systems* V2.0, May 2011, available from the Information Commissioner's website (**ico.org.uk**).
[3] Directive (EU) 2016/680 of the European Parliament and of the Council of 27 April 2016 on the protection of natural persons with regard to the processing of personal data by competent authorities for the purposes of the prevention, investigation, detection or prosecution of criminal offences or the execution of criminal penalties, and on the free movement of such data, and repealing Council Framework Decision 2008/977/JHA.

networking can be considered a development of the household exemption found in the Directive.

Courts and other judicial bodies are subject to the GDPR; however, in order to safeguard their independence, courts and judicial bodies acting in their judicial capacity should not be subject to the competence of the supervisory authority. Instead, the GDPR specifies that there should be a separate supervisory body within the judiciary. It applies to courts' and judicial authorities' processing activities, although Member States may specify their processing operations and procedures in local law (Recital 20).

The GDPR expressly does not alter the application of the E-Commerce Directive 2000/31/EC, which takes effect in the UK as the Electronic Commerce (EC Directive) Regulations 2002, SI 2002/2013 and applies to providers of information society services (which includes online traders) (Recital 21).

1.3   TERRITORIAL SCOPE

A significant change introduced by the GDPR is the extension of its scope to apply to data controllers and data processors established in the EU, as well as those established outside the EU, but who are offering goods or services to individuals within the EU, or who are engaged in profiling the behaviour of individuals in the EU. This includes goods or services offered without charge, so could include, for example, social networking sites. The extra-territorial reach only operates where a data controller demonstrates an intention to offer goods and services to EU citizens, as opposed to where such goods and services are merely accessible from the EU. Such an intent may be inferred from factors such as the use of local language or currency, for example (Recital 23).

Organisations that conduct monitoring of EU citizens' behaviour will be subject to the GDPR in relation to any behaviour which takes place within the EU. Evidence that monitoring is being conducted includes online tracking and profiling in order to take decisions about a data subject or to predict personal preferences, behaviours and attitudes. Online behavioural analysis, such as the collection of information about websites visited in order to identify shopping preferences, is likely to constitute monitoring (Recital 24).

Further clarification as to the territorial scope can be found in the Recitals (Recital 22), which provide:

- where a data controller or processor established in the EU processes personal data, the GDPR will apply, even if the processing itself did not take place within the EU (for example where it was carried out by a group company or sub-contractor located in a third country); and
- whether or not there is an 'establishment' within the EU depends upon the actual substance of an arrangement, rather than its legal form. For example, an entity which *de facto* directs data processing activities will be subject to the GDPR notwithstanding that the data controller may seek to rely on the location

of a registered office elsewhere in an attempt to avoid being subject to the GDPR. This is similar to the position under the Directive, which states (Directive, Recital 19):

> Whereas establishment on the territory of a Member State implies the effective and real exercise of activity through stable arrangements; whereas the legal form of such an establishment, whether simply branch or a subsidiary with a legal personality, is not the determining factor in this respect.

Stable arrangements were considered in the 2015 European Court of Justice Case *Weltimmo* v. *Nemzeti Adatvédelmi és Információszabadság Hatóság* (C-230/14), which concerned a company, Weltimmo s.r.o., registered in Slovakia, but which had a representative (an owner of the company) in Hungary and used internet servers installed in Germany or Austria. Weltimmo s.r.o. did not carry out any activity from its registered office in Slovakia. However, it had a bank account in Hungary and a Hungarian post box for the management of its everyday business affairs. Its websites were exclusively in the Hungarian language and one owner lived in Hungary. The location of the activity (i.e. Hungary) was the decisive factor in determining whether there was a 'stable arrangement' within the EU, and not the location of the registered office, nor the location of the affected data subjects.

Notwithstanding that *Weltimmo* pre-dates the new law, it follows that, under the new regime, an organisation that is legally established outside the EU, but in practice consists of one person who regularly works from within a Member State, would in principle be subject to the GDPR. If the reality of the arrangement is that the corporate entity is no more than a registered address, the GDPR is likely to apply to the establishment in the Member State.

Note that where Member State law applies through the operation of public international law, the GDPR may also apply. For example, a data controller established outside the EU, such as the diplomatic office or consulate of a Member State, should be subject to its provisions (Recital 25).

1.4   DEFINITIONS

The GDPR, like the Directive before it, relies upon a number of fundamental concepts, in particular, personal data, data controller, data processor and processing, which are defined in Article 2 of the Directive. The definitions from the Directive are all found in the GDPR, having largely been directly transposed, although with some material changes explained at **1.4.1**. The GDPR also introduces a number of completely new definitions, which are also explained at **1.4.2**.

1.4.1   Definitions adopted from the Directive

Article 4 sets out the definitions used throughout the GDPR, including those transposed from the Directive (Directive 95/46/EC, Article 2), incorporating the changes explained below.

'**Personal data**' remains materially the same, although the GDPR definition includes name, location data, online identifiers and genetic factors as examples of information by which individuals may be identified.

The GDPR acknowledges in the Recitals that the Directive pre-dated many forms of technology which are now ubiquitous, such as smartphones and tablet computers, and widespread use of the internet and online activities, such as social networking and the creation of user-generated content. The GDPR recognises a broad range of new categories of personal data which the Directive does not explicitly acknowledge, since the technology either did not exist or was not in widespread use at the time of its drafting in the late 1980s. Recital 30 of the GDPR expressly acknowledges identifiers arising from technology such as hardware (for example, smartphones, tablet computers and wearable technology), software, online identifiers (such as internet protocol addresses) and radio-frequency identification (RFID) tags. The GDPR acknowledges that these categories of information may be combined with data subjects' unique identifiers and used for profiling or identification purposes.

The GDPR introduces another category of personal data, not expressly considered by the Directive, in the form of genetic data, which is defined in Article 4(13) as:

> personal data relating to the inherited or acquired genetic characteristics of a natural person which give unique information about the physiology or the health of that natural person and which result, in particular, from an analysis of a biological sample from the natural person in question.

Genetic data is included among the special categories of personal data identified in Article 9. 'Special categories of personal data' is also the term used in Article 8 of the Directive, which is referred to as 'sensitive personal data' in the DPA 1998. Neither special categories of personal data, as defined by the Directive, nor sensitive personal data, as defined by the DPA 1998, includes genetic data.

For practitioners considering the practical implications, the GDPR definition does not appear to materially change the position under the Directive, although it expressly recognises a number of identifiers not mentioned in the Directive, albeit in the context of a non-exhaustive list of examples.

'**Processing of personal data**' (as defined in the Directive) is abbreviated to '**processing**' in the GDPR, although is materially the same as the earlier definition. The GDPR includes 'structuring' as an example of processing and substitutes 'blocking' with 'erasure'. However, processing is purposefully defined broadly in order to capture virtually any permissible use of personal data, so the minor drafting points of the GDPR are unlikely to make any difference in practice.

'**Personal data filing system**' ('**filing system**') (as defined in the Directive) is abbreviated to '**filing system**' in the GDPR but is otherwise identical.

'**Controllers**', '**processors**' and '**third parties**' are defined in both the Directive and the GDPR identically in all material respects.

'**Recipient**' as defined in the GDPR mirrors the definition from the Directive, but clarifies the express exclusion for public authorities that may receive personal data in the context of a particular enquiry by specifying that such disclosure must be in accordance with EU or Member State law, and that such processing must comply with the data protection rules applying to the purposes of the processing. The GDPR further specifies in the Recitals that official requests for personal data should be in writing and with appropriate safeguards in place to protect individuals' rights, and public authorities should process any such personal data in accordance with the principles of the GDPR (Recital 31).

'**Consent**' is more stringently defined in the GDPR and requires the data subject's unambiguous indication of his or her wishes by way of a statement or clear, affirmative action in addition to the requirements from the Directive that consent must be freely given, specific and informed. Consent is discussed in **Chapter 2**.

1.4.2   New definitions

Article 4 of the GDPR includes a number of new definitions not found in the Directive, which are explained below.

'**Restriction of processing**' is defined as:

> [T]he marking of stored personal data with the aim of limiting their processing in the future.

Such a restriction could include the situation where, for example, a data controller holds a customer's personal data in order to continue providing a product or service but the customer has indicated that he or she does not wish to receive marketing communications. Data subjects are granted the right to restrict processing of their personal data by Article 18 of the GDPR, explained further in **Chapter 3**.

'**Profiling**' is defined as:

> [A]ny form of automated processing of personal data consisting of the use of personal data to evaluate certain personal aspects relating to a natural person, in particular to analyse or predict aspects concerning that natural person's performance at work, economic situation, health, personal preferences, interests, reliability, behaviour, location or movements.

While profiling by definition entails automated processing, it differs from the concept of automated decision taking found in Article 15 of the Directive, since it need not necessarily produce legal effects concerning the data subject, nor significantly affect him or her. Nor should profiling be confused with monitoring, which is an important concept since the occurrence of monitoring may trigger the requirement to conduct a data protection impact assessment (GDPR, Article 35(c)), the obligation to appoint a data protection officer (Article 37(1)(b)), or the involvement of the extra-territorial reach provisions (Article 3(2)(b)).

'**Pseudonymisation**' is a new concept not found in the Data Protection Directive, and is defined in Article 4(5) as:

> [T]he processing of personal data in such a manner that the personal data can no longer be attributed to a specific data subject without the use of additional information, provided that such additional information is kept separately and is subject to

technical and organisational measures to ensure that the personal data are not attributed to an identified or identifiable natural person.

Pseudonymisation may be used to help organisations reduce the risks associated with their processing activities; however, it should not be seen as a means by which they can avoid their legal obligations. For example, an organisation could 'key code' employees' data, i.e. identifiers such as the employee's name and date of birth could be separated from other information such as disciplinary or sickness record, by reference to a code number. This would mean that an employees' identity would not be immediately apparent to anyone processing the information as part of their job function, although the records could be pieced together again with relative simplicity. This approach would reduce risk, but the data should still be treated as personal data since it relates to an identifiable individual.

The concept is also considered in Recital 26, which states:

> Personal data which have undergone pseudonymisation, which could be attributed to a natural person by the use of additional information should be considered to be information on an identifiable natural person.

This may at first glance appear to be a self-evident statement since, by definition, pseudonymised data could be attributed to a data subject by reference to additional information. If this was not the case, the affected data would be categorised as anonymised rather than pseudonymised. However, the issue is that a pseudonymised data set may be attributed to a particular data subject by a data controller or processor if he or she has the additional information (such as a key code) which 'unlocks' the data. If this is the case, that controller or processor must treat the pseudonymised data as personal data in accordance with the principles of the GDPR. However, for another controller or processor that is not in possession of the additional information, the pseudonymised data is, in effect, anonymous.

Recital 26 goes on to suggest various factors that should be taken into account in determining whether a natural person is identifiable from pseudonymised data, such as the costs and amount of time required to identify a data subject, and the technology available to enable 're-identification'.

The significance of the distinction between pseudonymised and anonymised data is that information concerning identified or identifiable individuals must be processed in accordance with the principles of the GDPR. Conversely, anonymised data falls outside the scope of the GDPR and thereby enables processing for purposes such as statistics or research. This potentially has positive implications for organisations struggling to establish a legal basis for processing, for example transferring their employees' personal data to an externally-hosted software platform located outside the EU, namely that by anonymising the data this could enable a transfer that would otherwise be prohibited. However, the organisation would have to ensure that the data was truly anonymised, and not simply masked on a temporary basis, as this would make it easily retraceable and hence enable the identification of the underlying data subjects.

Pseudonymisation potentially offers a useful tool for data controllers and processors. It can enable general analysis, which does not identify living individuals at the same time as data processing which does identify specific data subjects and is hence subject to the GDPR. For example, pseudonymisation could enable the same data controller to carry out general analysis such as statistical research where the data used does not identify specific data subjects, at the same time as marketing activity where data subjects are identifiable and the processing activity is carried out in accordance with the principles of the GDPR. The information which ties pseudonymised data to identifiers, for example a numeric code, must be kept separately and securely, only accessible by specific employees of the data controller.

'**Personal data breach**' is defined as:

> a breach of security leading to the accidental or unlawful destruction, loss, alteration, unauthorised disclosure of, or access to, personal data transmitted, stored or otherwise processed

and is integral to a significant new obligation upon data controllers, namely to report personal data breaches to the supervisory authority, pursuant to Article 33, and affected data subjects, pursuant to Article 34, if the personal data breach is likely to result in a high risk to them.

'**Genetic data**' is a category of personal data not expressly considered in the Directive, defined as:

> [P]ersonal data relating to the inherited or acquired genetic characteristics of a natural person which give unique information about the physiology or the health of that natural person and which result, in particular, from an analysis of a biological sample from the natural person in question.

Genetic data is, as explained above, included among the special categories of personal data identified in Article 9.

'**Biometric data**' is defined as:

> [P]ersonal data resulting from specific technical processing relating to the physical, physiological or behavioural characteristics of a natural person, which allow or confirm the unique identification of that natural person, such as facial images or dactyloscopic (i.e. fingerprint) data.

Biometric data is one of the special categories of personal data, when it is used to uniquely identify a living individual (Article 9(1)). The GDPR recognises the possibility that information contained in photographs could potentially constitute biometric data, for example, a photograph could potentially reveal information about a data subject's race or ethnicity, or religious beliefs. However the GDPR states that processing photographs should not necessarily be construed as processing one of the special categories of personal data. The use of photographs would only constitute processing biometric data when it includes the use of specific technical means to allow the identification of a specific individual, for example facial recognition technology. Such processing should not take place unless permitted under the GDPR or the law of a Member State, and any processing must be in accordance with the GDPR (Recital 51).

'**Data concerning health**' is a subset of one of the 'special categories of personal data' (Article 9(1)), and is defined as:

> [P]ersonal data related to the physical or mental health of a natural person, including the provision of health care services, which reveal information about his or her health status.

The GDPR construes this subset very broadly and includes information concerning the data subject's past, present and future health; any identifiers used by a health care provider; examination and test results; samples; diseases, disabilities, disease risk and medical history (Recital 35).

'**Main establishment**' is a fundamental concept for the operation of the so-called 'one stop shop' mechanism, one of the main benefits of the GDPR heralded by the European Commission. The one stop shop enables multinational organisations to report to one supervisory authority (the 'lead supervisory authority') in the Member State of its 'main establishment' (Article 56), rather than the authority of each Member State in which it has a presence.

For data controllers, the main establishment is:

- the place of its central administration within the EU; unless decisions concerning the purposes and means of processing personal data are taken elsewhere within the EU; in which case,
- the establishment where decisions concerning the purposes and means of processing personal data are taken.

For data processors, the main establishment of the processor should be:

- the place of its central administration in the Union; or, if it has no central administration in the EU,
- the place where the main processing activities take place in the EU.

In practice, this would mean that, for example, the main establishment of a multinational provider of cloud hosting services would be the head office from which the company's activities were directed, even if the actual servers were located in a different Member State. The rules around lead supervisory authorities are discussed further in **Chapter 6**.

'**Representative**' is defined as:

> [A] natural or legal person established in the Union who, designated by the controller or processor in writing pursuant to Article 27, represents the controller or processor with regard to their respective obligations under this Regulation.

The role of a representative was also envisaged by the Directive for data controllers established outside the EU but using equipment located in a Member State. The associated responsibilities were limited to providing transparency information to data subjects (Directive, Article 10), and notifying the supervisory authority (Directive, Articles 18 and 19). However, under the GDPR, representatives have a broader range of responsibilities, as well as significant potential liability. The rules on representatives are explained further in **Chapter 4**.

'**Enterprise**' is defined very broadly as:

> a natural or legal person engaged in an economic activity, irrespective of its legal form, including partnerships or associations regularly engaged in an economic activity.

The GDPR includes references to 'micro, small and medium-sized enterprises' (Recital 13).

'**Group of undertakings**' is defined as:

> a controlling undertaking and its controlled undertakings

where a dominant influence exists, for example through ownership, financial participation or governing rules, and includes where an undertaking controls the data processing activities of another affiliate (Article 37).

'**Binding corporate rules**' (commonly known as BCRs) are an 'appropriate safeguard' that enable the transfer of personal data from a Member State to a third country (Article 46), and are defined as:

> [P]ersonal data protection policies which are adhered to by a controller or processor established on the territory of a Member State for transfers or a set of transfers of personal data to a controller or processor in one or more third countries within a group of undertakings, or group of enterprises engaged in a joint economic activity.

The rules on BCRs are explained in Article 47.

'**Supervisory authority**' is the data protection authority established by a Member State pursuant to Article 51. The rules surrounding supervisory authorities are set out in Chapter VI of the GDPR and **Chapter 6**.

'**supervisory authority concerned**' is a supervisory authority other than the lead supervisory authority that is concerned with a data processing activity because:

(a) the controller or processor engaged in the processing is established in the Member State of that supervisory authority;
(b) the processing activity affects data subjects residing in the Member State of the supervisory authority; or
(c) a complaint has been lodged with that supervisory authority.

The lead supervisory authority should co-operate with concerned supervisory authorities (Recital 124), and concerned supervisory authorities, although competent to handle local cases in their territory (for example, local employment matters), must inform the lead supervisory authority promptly. The lead authority may decide to handle the matter or allow the local authority to do so (Recital 127).

'**Cross-border processing**' is defined as either:

(a) processing in multiple Member States by a controller or processor established in more than one Member State; or
(b) processing by a controller or processor established in one Member State, which affects or is likely to affect data subjects in multiple Member States.

Note that the defined term 'cross-border processing' does not refer to processing in countries outside the EU.

'**Relevant and reasoned objection**' is defined as:

> [A]n objection to a draft decision [by a supervisory authority] as to whether there is an infringement of this Regulation, or whether envisaged action in relation to the

controller or processor complies with this Regulation, which clearly demonstrates the significance of the risks posed by the draft decision as regards the fundamental rights and freedoms of data subjects and, where applicable, the free flow of personal data within the Union

The concept is used in the co-operation procedure between lead and concerned supervisory authorities (Article 60), and the dispute resolution procedure (Article 65).

'**Information society service**' is defined by reference to point (b) of Article 1(1) of Directive (EU) 2015/1535 of the European Parliament and of the Council[4] which provides:

'service' means any Information Society service, that is to say, any service normally provided for remuneration, at a distance, by electronic means and at the individual request of a recipient of services.

For the purposes of this definition:

(i)   'at a distance' means that the service is provided without the parties being simultaneously present;

(ii)   'by electronic means' means that the service is sent initially and received at its destination by means of electronic equipment for the processing (including digital compression) and storage of data, and entirely transmitted, conveyed and received by wire, by radio, by optical means or by other electromagnetic means;

(iii) 'at the individual request of a recipient of services' means that the service is provided through the transmission of data on individual request.

An indicative list of services not covered by this definition is set out in Annex I.

Annex I provides as follows:

Indicative list of services not covered by the second subparagraph of point (b) of Article 1(1)

1.   Services not provided 'at a distance'

Services provided in the physical presence of the provider and the recipient, even if they involve the use of electronic devices:

(a)   medical examinations or treatment at a doctor's surgery using electronic equipment where the patient is physically present;

(b)   consultation of an electronic catalogue in a shop with the customer on site;

(c)   plane ticket reservation at a travel agency in the physical presence of the customer by means of a network of computers;

(d)   electronic games made available in a video arcade where the customer is physically present.

2.   Services not provided 'by electronic means'

–   services having material content even though provided via electronic devices:

---

4   Directive (EU) 2015/1535 of the European Parliament and of the Council of 9 September 2015 laying down a procedure for the provision of information in the field of technical regulations and of rules on Information Society services ([2015] OJ L241/1).

     (a)   automatic cash or ticket dispensing machines (banknotes, rail tickets);

     (b)   access to road networks, car parks, etc., charging for use, even if there are electronic devices at the entrance/exit controlling access and/or ensuring correct payment is made,

–   offline services: distribution of CD-ROMs or software on diskettes,

–   services which are not provided via electronic processing/inventory systems:

     (a)   voice telephony services;

     (b)   telefax/telex services;

     (c)   services provided via voice telephony or fax;

     (d)   telephone/telefax consultation of a doctor;

     (e)   telephone/telefax consultation of a lawyer;

     (f)   telephone/telefax direct marketing.

3.   Services not supplied 'at the individual request of a recipient of services'

Services provided by transmitting data without individual demand for simultaneous reception by an unlimited number of individual receivers (point to multipoint transmission):

     (a)   television broadcasting services (including near-video on-demand services), covered by point (e) of Article 1(1) of Directive 2010/13/EU;

     (b)   radio broadcasting services;

     (c)   (televised) teletext.

'International organisation' is defined as:

[A]n organisation and its subordinate bodies governed by public international law, or any other body which is set up by, or on the basis of, an agreement between two or more countries.

2 THE DATA PROTECTION PRINCIPLES

Chapter II sets out the principles of the GDPR, including the rules around consent and processing special categories of personal data. The principles of the GDPR set the standards by which data controllers and data processors must process personal data, and are a development of those set out in the Directive. Article 6 of the Directive provides:

> Member States shall provide that personal data must be:
>
> (a)   processed fairly and lawfully;
> (b)   collected for specified, explicit and legitimate purposes and not further pro-cessed in a way incompatible with those purposes. Further processing of data for historical, statistical or scientific purposes shall not be considered as incompatible provided that Member States provide appropriate safeguards;
> (c)   adequate, relevant and not excessive in relation to the purposes for which they are collected and/or further processed;
> (d)   accurate and, where necessary, kept up to date; every reasonable step must be taken to ensure that data which are inaccurate or incomplete, having regard to the purposes for which they were collected or for which they are further processed, are erased or rectified;
> (e)   kept in a form which permits identification of data subjects for no longer than is necessary for the purposes for which the data were collected or for which they are further processed. Member States shall lay down appropriate safeguards for personal data stored for longer periods for historical, statistical or scientific use.
>
> 2. It shall be for the controller to ensure that paragraph 1 is complied with.

Practitioners familiar with the eight principles of the DPA 1998 will note that the Directive provides five principles, which correspond to the first five principles of the DPA 1998; while the sixth, seventh and eighth principles (i.e. that processing must be in accordance with the rights of data subjects; subject to appropriate security measures; and not transferred outside the European Economic Area (EEA) to third countries that do not ensure adequate protection, respectively) are found elsewhere in the Directive though not expressed as principles.

There are six principles of the GDPR, which are as follows:

■   lawfulness, fairness and transparency;
■   purpose limitation;
■   data minimisation;
■   accuracy;

- storage limitation; and
- integrity and confidentiality.

Each of these principles is now considered in turn.

2.1   LAWFULNESS, FAIRNESS AND TRANSPARENCY

The first principle of the GDPR states that personal data must be processed lawfully, fairly and in a transparent manner in relation to the data subject. The grounds for establishing lawfulness of processing are set out in Article 6, and discussed below. Transparency is explained in Chapter III of the GDPR and is discussed in **Chapter 3**. While not expressly mentioned in Article 6 of the Directive, the transparency requirement appears in the recitals. Recital 38 of the Directive states:

> ...if the processing of data is to be fair, the data subject must be in a position to learn of the existence of a processing operation and, where data are collected from him, must be given accurate and full information, bearing in mind the circumstances of the collection.

As such, the fair and lawful processing principle established by the Directive rather than being extended by the GDPR, is clarified.

While the GDPR expressly sets out the lawfulness and transparency requirements, it does not define or further explain what is meant by 'fairness', so a prudent approach is to construe the term in accordance with its ordinary meaning. In practice, in ascertaining whether the requirement of fairness has been met, data controllers or processors should consider whether an affected data subject might reasonably feel that the processing in question was unfair. A useful rule of thumb is that processing is likely to be unfair if the data subject is likely to feel that it is 'sneaky, creepy or dishonest'.

Article 6 of the GDPR permits processing where one or more of the following six legal grounds have been established:

- consent;
- performance of a contract;
- compliance with a legal obligation;
- vital interests of the data subject;
- public interest; and
- the legitimate interests of the data controller.

These six legal grounds are addressed in the following sections.

2.1.1   Consent

Consent is probably the best known of the legal grounds for processing and one of the most widely relied upon. In circumstances where particularly sensitive processing is contemplated, consent is likely to be preferable to the other potential grounds (which are discussed in more detail below). However, generally speaking, the other grounds that are available to justify lawful processing should not be overlooked.

Article 7 sets out the requirements necessary to establish valid consent (though the definition is set out in Article 4, as explained in **Chapter 1**). The changes to consent introduced by the GDPR have been the subject of widespread discussion, and adapting to the new rules will present a significant challenge for organisations. The GDPR builds on the concept of consent introduced by the Directive by addressing deficiencies that have become apparent over the subsequent 20 years, such as reliance on pre-ticked boxes, the practice of inferring data subjects' consent from the mere absence of their objection, and making access to a product or service conditional upon the data subject's consent (Recital 32). However, the stringent requirements of the GDPR will in practice drive significant changes around the way organisations manage consent.

The Directive defines consent in Article 2(h) as:

> ...any freely given specific and informed indication of his wishes by which the data subject signifies his agreement to personal data relating to him being processed.

The GDPR introduces the requirement that data controllers must obtain an unambiguous indication from the data subject, citing written or oral statements and electronic tick-boxes as examples of valid indications of data subjects' consent. However, practices such as inferring consent from an absence of any objection by the data subject, or a pre-ticked box should not constitute valid consent. Further, practices relied upon by organisations such as the reliance on one indication of consent to enable a variety of processing activities should not be used, in favour of separate consent for each individual use (Article 7(2)).

Where a data controller obtains consent using a written declaration concerning another matter, for example within the terms and conditions of a contract, the controller must make the data subject aware that it has obtained consent and clarify the extent of such consent (Recital 42).

Recital 42 further specifies that any pre-formulated declaration of consent shall comply with the requirements of Council Directive 93/13/EEC of 5 April 1993 on unfair terms in consumer contracts, which provides *inter alia* (Article 3(1)):

> A contractual term which has not been individually negotiated shall be regarded as unfair if, contrary to the requirement of good faith, it causes a significant imbalance in the parties' rights and obligations arising under the contract, to the detriment of the consumer.

To be informed, consent must at least identify:

- the data controller; and
- the purposes of the processing.

Consent cannot be freely given if the data subject:

- has no real choice; or
- is unable to refuse or withdraw consent without suffering detriment.

The GDPR expressly states that consent must be capable of withdrawal by the data subject at any time and that withdrawing consent must be as simple as giving consent (Article 7(3)).

Consent cannot be valid where there is a clear imbalance between the data controller and the data subject, such that consent was not freely given. Recital 43 refers to an imbalance between data controller and data subject in a situation where the data controller is a public authority, stating that it is unlikely that consent, in such circumstances, would be freely given. In the negotiation of the Regulation, the employee/employer relationship was also cited as a likely imbalance.

A data controller cannot rely on one blanket consent to conduct various processing activities if these are separate in nature and, in such a situation, separate consents would be more appropriate. Nor can consent in the context of a contract be valid if the performance of the contract depends upon consent being given but such consent is not in fact necessary for performance (Recital 43).

A further development of the GDPR is that it clarifies that the burden of proof lies with the data controller and not the data subject. In practice this means that, in the event of a dispute, the organisation would have to prove that it validly obtained consent rather than the data subject having to prove that he or she did not consent to a particular activity (Article 7(1)).

Data controllers may rely on generic consent from data subjects to allow the use of their personal data for scientific research purposes, since it may be difficult to specify the exact process. As a safeguard, however, data subjects should be able to consent to the use of their data in relation to particular areas of scientific research, while potentially withholding consent in relation to others. This is likely to be of particular relevance to operators in the health and pharmaceutical sectors (Recital 33).

The GDPR specifies that children must be aged at least 16 to be able to consent to the provision of 'information society services' (defined in Article 4; see 1.4.2), and parental consent is required for children any younger; however, it provides that Member States may specify a lower age, subject to a minimum of 13 (Article 8(1)). The GDPR also specifies that data controllers must make reasonable efforts to verify parental consent, i.e. that any purported parental consent upon which they rely is actually from the parent and not the child.

The ICO has published draft guidance on establishing consent under the GDPR (ICO Consent Guidance).[1] While, at the time of writing, the guidance has not been finalised, it is useful in aiding understanding of the practical implications of the changes the GDPR will introduce vis-à-vis consent. The ICO Consent Guidance observes that the GDPR sets a high standard for consent, and that organisations will need to check their consent practices and existing consents to ascertain whether they meet the GDPR standard. It goes on to specify that consent will require a positive opt-in, must be specific and granular, and capable of withdrawal easily. The ICO Guidance also specifies that organisations and third parties who will be relying on consent must be named, and that even precisely defined categories of third party

---

[1]   Information Commissioner's Office Consultation: GDPR Consent Guidance (start date 2 March 2017, end date 31 March 2017).

organisations will not be acceptable.[2] It observes that, while the GDPR does not specify a lifespan, consent is likely to degrade over time and its longevity will depend upon the context and the individual's expectations. To address this, organisations should regularly review and refresh the consent they have obtained. If in doubt, the ICO Consent Guidance recommends that organisations should consider refreshing consent every two years.[3] The guidance implies that organisations should consider offering a 'privacy dashboard' to enable data subjects to actively manage consent, which represents a significant departure from widespread current practices.

The changes around consent are likely to have far-reaching consequences for businesses, many of which will need to revisit their databases to evaluate whether they meet with the new enhanced requirements. Given the rigorous criteria necessary for establishing valid consent under the GDPR, organisations are likely to find that in many cases they will no longer be able to rely on consent and will have no choice but to rely on alternative grounds.

2.1.2   Performance of a contract

The GDPR provides a legal basis for processing that is necessary for the performance of a contract to which the data subject is a party, or where processing is necessary in order to 'take steps' at the request of the data subject prior to entering into a contract (Article 6(1)(b)). The GDPR, like the Directive before it (Directive, Article 7(b)), is silent as to the meaning of 'take steps', but these could include sending sales literature to an enquiring data subject, for example. Note that a processing activity may be in the interests of the data controller or processor in the context of the performance of a contract, though it may not be necessary *per se*. For example, a controller may choose to outsource processing activities to a data processor (or a processor may choose to sub-contract to a sub-processor) for cost saving reasons, though this would not be necessary for the performance of a contract. In such circumstances, the controller or processor would not be able to rely on this lawfulness ground.

2.1.3   Compliance with a legal obligation

Processing may be necessary for compliance with a legal obligation to which the controller is subject. The recitals provide some clarity on the point, stating that where the GDPR refers to a legal basis or a legislative measure, this does not necessarily require a legislative act, but the legal basis relied upon must be clear and precise, and its application foreseeable in accordance with the case law of the Court of Justice of the European Union (CJEU) and the European Convention on Human Rights (Recital 41). Further, any processing carried out in accordance with a legal obligation of the data controller must have a basis in the law of that Member State,

---

[2]   See ICO Consent Guidance, 'What are the key changes to make in practice?' and 'Specific and informed'.
[3]   See ICO Consent Guidance, 'How should you manage consent?'.

or the EU. A data controller established in a Member State could not therefore rely on a non-European law, for example US legislation (Recital 45).

2.1.4   Vital interests

The GDPR permits processing that is necessary to protect the vital interests of the data subject or another natural person. Recital 46 provides further clarification; the processing must be necessary to protect an interest which is essential for the life of the data subject or another natural person. 'Vital interests' are generally interpreted as a life-or-death situation, where processing may serve both individual and public interest purposes. Examples include processing necessary for humanitarian purposes, such as monitoring epidemics and their spread or in situations of humanitarian emergencies, in particular in situations of natural and man-made disasters.

2.1.5   Public interest or exercise of official authority

Processing is lawful where it is necessary for the performance of a task carried out in the public interest or in the exercise of official authority vested in the controller. In either case, the processing should have a basis in EU or Member State law (though there need not be a specific law for each individual processing activity) (Recital 45). An example is the use of individuals' personal data by a tax authority for the collection of income tax.

2.1.6   Legitimate interests of the data controller

The 'legitimate interests' ground provides a lawful justification for processing where the interests of the data subject, and their fundamental rights and freedoms, are not overridden. This depends on the data subject's relationship with the data controller and the data subject's reasonable expectations. Whether or not a legitimate interest exists requires careful consideration and an evaluation of the data subject's expectations at the time the personal data were collected. If a processing activity would be outside the data subject's expectations, the legitimate interests ground is unlikely to be available to the data controller. Note that there are specific situations where data controllers cannot rely on legitimate interests as a ground for establishing lawful processing: Public authorities are expressly prohibited from relying upon this ground (Article 6(1)), and the data controller's interests will always be overridden where the data subject is a child (Article 6(1)(f)).

The GDPR provides examples of where the legitimate interests ground may be appropriate. Multinational organisations, for instance, may have a legitimate interest in sharing personal data relating to their employees or customers, such as in the context of a centralised human resources (HR) software system or client management database. Any transfers of personal data to third countries would remain subject to the data transfer rules, explained in **Chapter 5** (Recital 48). Further, it may be in a data controller's legitimate interests to process personal data for network and/or information security purposes, for example to maintain cyber-security (Recital 49). Processing activities that are strictly necessary for the prevention of fraud also constitute a legitimate interest of the data controller, as would processing personal data for marketing purposes (Recital 47).

In practice, the legitimate interests ground may often be overlooked. However, with more stringent requirements necessary to establish valid consent as a ground for processing, organisations may increasingly need to rely on alternatives such as this. Provided the data subject's rights and freedoms are not overridden and subject to the circumstances where reliance on legitimate interests is inappropriate, namely in circumstances involving public authorities or children, this ground will frequently provide a convenient basis for establishing lawful processing.

2.1.7   Other points to consider

Member States have discretion to introduce or maintain more specific provisions to adapt the application of some of the GDPR's provisions (Article 6(2)). This discretion is in relation to processing that is necessary for compliance with a legal obligation to which the data controller is subject (Article 6(1)(c)), and processing that is necessary for the performance of a task carried out in the public interest or in the exercise of official authority vested in the controller (Article 6(1)(e)). The basis of any processing justified on either of these two grounds must be laid down by EU or Member State law (Article 6(3)). A practical implication of this is that the application of the legal obligation ground, and the public interest or exercise of public authority ground, will vary between Member States. Multinational operators will need to be mindful of this variation where they rely on either of these two legal bases for establishing lawfulness of processing.

Note that, where a data controller relies on the legal grounds of the processing being in the public interest, or in the exercise of official authority, or in the data controller's legitimate interests, a data subject has the right to object to the processing of his or her data. In such an instance, the data controller bears the burden of proving that its legitimate interest overrides the rights and freedoms of the data subject (Recital 69).

2.2   PURPOSE LIMITATION

The purpose limitation principle states (Article 5(1)(b)) that personal data must be:

> [C]ollected for specified, explicit and legitimate purposes and not further processed in a manner that is incompatible with those purposes.

The purposes for which personal data are to be processed must be expressed in the information provided to data subjects, pursuant to the principle of transparency, which requires the provision of certain 'fair processing information' and is discussed in more detail in **Chapter 3**. In practice, organisations typically provide transparency information by way of a website privacy notice, though it may be provided in other ways such as by way of wording on a paper form or by oral statement, for instance a pre-recorded message in the context of a telephone call. The crucial point is that the purpose (or purposes) for which personal data are to be processed must be specified to the data subject. Any further purposes for which personal data may be processed that are not specified explicitly in the transparency language are likely to fall outside the principle.

Where personal data is collected and processed for one purpose, it may only be processed for a further purpose if that processing is compatible with the first purpose. If the new purpose is compatible, the data controller does not need to establish a new legal basis for processing. Moreover, if the further processing activity is in the public interest, or in connection with the exercise of the data controller's official authority, this constitutes compatible and lawful processing, as would processing for archiving purposes in the public interest, or for scientific or historical research purposes.

In evaluating whether a further purpose is compatible with the original purpose for which personal data was collected, in the absence of consent or a legal basis for processing the data controller, having met all of the criteria for establishing lawful processing for the original purpose, should consider the following factors:

- any link between the original purpose(s) and the purposes of the intended further processing;
- the context in which the personal data have been collected, in particular the reasonable expectations of data subjects based on their relationship with the controller as to their further use;
- the nature of the personal data;
- the consequences of the intended further processing for data subjects; and
- the existence of appropriate safeguards in both the original and intended further processing operations (Recital 50 and Article 6(4)).

The purpose limitation principle is virtually identical to the principle that personal data must be collected for specified, explicit and legitimate purposes as expressed in the Directive (Directive, Article 6(1)(b)). However, the GDPR is more prescriptive than the Directive in relation to personal data processed for archiving purposes in the public interest, scientific or historical research purposes, or statistical purposes, and refers to specific safeguards to ensure appropriate technical and organisational measures are in place, in particular pseudonymisation and anonymisation (Article 89(1)). See **2.6** for an explanation as to what is deemed 'appropriate'.

2.3   DATA MINIMISATION

The data minimisation principle of the GDPR provides (Article 5(1)(c)) that personal data should be:

> [A]dequate, relevant and limited to what is necessary in relation to the purposes for which they are processed.

This is a development from the equivalent principle in the Directive, which provides that personal data should be 'adequate, relevant and not excessive' (Directive, Article 6(1)(c)).

Currently, organisations may frequently collect more data than is strictly necessary, particularly in a marketing context in connection with activities such as developing a 'single customer view'. An internet retailer, for example, may collect information on a purchaser's financial circumstances and interests. Such data may not be necessary for the transaction, but it is still valuable to the retailer for marketing purposes. The collection of this excess data would *prima facie* be in breach of the data minimisation principle, giving a disgruntled customer a more readily available ground for complaint than may have been the case under the Directive.

In practice, the data minimisation principle could have a significant effect upon organisations' data collection practices, since it is likely to be easier for a data subject to establish that the collection of particular data fields was not necessary for the immediate purpose than it would be to establish that the collection was excessive.

2.4   ACCURACY

The accuracy principle of the GDPR is largely the same as that of the Directive (Directive, Article 6(1)(d)), specifying that personal data must be accurate and kept up to date where necessary and deleted or corrected if inaccurate (Article 5(1)(d)). However, the accuracy principle as espoused by the GDPR adds the requirement that any erasure or rectification must be without delay although, unlike the Directive, it does not include the obligation to erase or rectify incomplete data. Such erasure or rectification should have regard to the purpose or purposes for which personal data are processed. Organisations should consider the potential risks arising from inaccurate personal data: For example, a person's name spelled incorrectly on a membership card may be mildly irritating, but an inaccurate medical record could have potentially life-threatening consequences.

2.5   STORAGE LIMITATION

The storage limitation principle of the GDPR (Article 5(1)(e)) is largely similar to that of the Directive (Directive, Article 6(1)(c)). As with the purpose limitation principle, the GDPR is more prescriptive than the Directive in relation to personal data processed for archiving purposes in the public interest, scientific or historical research purposes or statistical purposes, and refers to specific safeguards to ensure appropriate technical and organisational measures are in place, in particular pseudonymisation and anonymisation (Article 89(1)).

According to the storage limitation principle, personal data should not be kept in a form which permits the identification of data subjects for longer than is necessary.

In practice, this frequently precipitates the question 'How long is necessary?', the answer to which will depend on the specific legal or business reasons underlying the retention of information. Categories of information, relating for example to employees, ex-employees, unsuccessful job candidates, customers, enquirers and suppliers will each have different factors driving retention and should be considered on a case-by-case basis. As a general comment, it will rarely be justifiable to hold personal data in a form that permits the identification of individual data subjects for an unlimited period.

2.6   INTEGRITY AND CONFIDENTIALITY

The GDPR imposes security obligations upon organisations that process personal data through the integrity and confidentiality principle (Article 5(1)(f)), in contrast with the Directive, which sets out the security obligations in a dedicated article (Directive, Article 17). The integrity and confidentiality principle specifies that personal data must be:

> [P]rocessed in a manner that ensures appropriate security of the personal data, including protection against unauthorised or unlawful processing and against accidental loss, destruction or damage, using appropriate technical or organisational measures.

As with the Directive, the GDPR does not prescribe specific security measures which, given the speed of technological developments, would be likely to become obsolete in a short space of time, thereby requiring further legislation. Instead, organisations are required to implement 'appropriate' measures. Note that the requirement is for both technical and organisational measures; while the former encompasses information technology (IT) hardware and software, the latter is more broad and could include non-technical measures such as pass card systems to control entry to an organisation's premises; a clear desk policy with documents stored in lockable cabinets; restricting staff access to personal data on a 'need to know' basis and employee vetting, training and monitoring processes. The requirement for 'appropriate' measures indicates that the measures will differ depending on the type and sensitivity of data collected and therefore implies that more stringent means of protection should be adopted for higher risk data.

The GDPR differs significantly from the Directive in its approach to data processors. Under the Directive, appointment of a data processor is subject to organisational security measures, namely conducting appropriate due diligence on the service provider to establish whether it could provide adequate guarantees, and then binding it by way of a written contract (Directive, Article 17(2), (3)). Such a contract is necessary since the provisions of the Directive do not apply directly to data processors. However, the GDPR applies to both data controllers and data processors, though it still imposes the obligation upon data controllers to engage processors by way of an engagement contract (Article 28). The rules relating to data processors are explained in **Chapter 4**.

2.7   ACCOUNTABILITY

The GDPR introduces the principle of accountability (Article 5(2)), which is absent among the principles of the Directive, though it is implicit in its provisions. The Directive requires data controllers to ensure personal data is processed in accordance with its principles (Directive, Article 6(2)), whereas the GDPR contains an additional requirement that data controllers are able to demonstrate compliance with the principles. The fact that the accountability principle is expressly stated in the GDPR indicates the importance of having demonstrable measures in place to ensure compliance. In practice, demonstrable measures may include:

■   having an appropriate data protection policy;
■   maintaining records of processing activities (see **2.8**);
■   appointment of a data protection officer (see **Chapter 4**);
■   data protection training for staff;
■   data protection audits;
■   data protection impact assessments (see **Chapter 4**); and
■   evidence of incorporation of the principles of privacy by design and by default (see **Chapter 4**).

2.8   PROCESSING SPECIAL CATEGORIES OF PERSONAL DATA

Article 9(1) establishes a general prohibition on processing 'special categories of personal data', which are personal data revealing the following types of information about individuals:

■   racial or ethnic origin;
■   political opinions;
■   religious or philosophical beliefs;
■   trade union membership;
■   genetic data;
■   biometric data for the purpose of uniquely identifying a natural person;
■   data concerning health; and
■   data concerning a natural person's sex life or sexual orientation.

The 'special categories of personal data' under the GDPR are the same as those under the Directive, with the addition of genetic data and biometric data. The GDPR also clarifies the meaning of 'data concerning health'. The aforementioned terms are all explained in **Chapter 1**. Article 9(4) specifies that Member States may introduce further conditions relating to genetic data, biometric data or data concerning health.

Article 9(2) provides a list, similar to that of the Directive, of circumstances in which the general prohibition on processing the special categories of personal data may be lifted. A summary of each of these grounds is set out below, along with a comparison against their equivalent provision from the Directive (to the extent that any comparison is possible):

- **Consent**: The data subject has given explicit consent to the processing, unless such consent is prohibited by EU or Member State law. This is identical to the ground set out in Article 8(2)(a) of the Directive.
- **Employment**: The processing is necessary for carrying out the obligations and exercising specific rights of the data controller or data subject in the field of employment and social security and social protection law. This extends the provisions of Article 8(2)(b) of the Directive, which referred to the field of employment, though not to the fields of social security or social protection.
- **Vital interests**: Processing is necessary to protect the vital interests of the data subject or another natural person where the data subject is physically or legally incapable of giving consent. This is identical to the ground set out in Article 8(2)(c) of the Directive.
- **Not-for-profit**: Processing members' (and former members') personal data by a not-for-profit body for political, philosophical or religious aims. This is equivalent to Article 8(2)(d) of the Directive.
- **Made public**: The processing relates to personal data made public by the data subject. This is materially identical to Article 8(2)(e) of the Directive.
- **Legal claims**: The processing is necessary for establishing, exercising or defending legal claims. This is effectively the same as Article 8(2)(e) of the Directive, though the GDPR ground expressly extends to courts acting in their judicial capacity.
- **Public interest**: Processing is necessary for reasons of substantial public interest, based on EU or Member State law. A similar provision appears as Article 8(4) of the Directive.
- **Health**: The processing is necessary for:
  - preventative or occupational medicine;
  - assessment of the working capacity of the employee;
  - medical diagnosis;
  - the provision of health or social care or treatment; or
  - the management of health or social care systems and services; and

  the processing is carried out by a professional subject to an obligation of professional secrecy (Article 9(3)).

  This is similar to Article 8(3) of the Directive.
- **Public health**: Processing is necessary for reasons of public interest in the area of public health, for example protecting against serious cross-border threats to health, or ensuring quality and safety standards for health care, medical products or medical devices. Recital 34 of the Directive addresses the same issue.

  The GDPR specifically recognises that processing personal data relating to health may be necessary for public health reasons without the data subject's consent. The GDPR refers to the definition of 'public health' from Regulation (EC) No 1338/2008 of the European Parliament and of the Council (Article 3(c)) namely:

> [A]ll elements related to health, namely health status, including morbidity and disability, the determinants having an effect on that health status, health care needs, resources allocated to health care, the provision of, and universal access to, health care as well as health care expenditure and financing, and the causes of mortality.

However, the GDPR does specify that personal data relating to health should not be processed for other purposes by third parties such as employers, insurance or banking companies (Recital 54).

- **Archiving, research and statistics**: Processing is necessary for archiving purposes in the public interest, scientific or historical research purposes or statistical purposes, subject to appropriate safeguards to ensure appropriate technical and organisational measures are in place (in particular minimisation and potentially pseudonymisation and anonymisation) (Article 89(1)). The Directive includes similar provisions in relation to secondary uses of personal data (Article 6(1)(b)), though not the special categories of data. Accordingly, the GDPR extends the available grounds in the Directive to include establishing lawful processing of the special categories of personal data.

Processing personal data relating to criminal convictions or offences is addressed in Article 10, which requires that processing must be under the control of an official authority with appropriate safeguards provided under EU or Member State law. This is virtually identical to Article 8(5) of the Directive.

Where a data controller processes personal data in such a way that does not identify a data subject, the GDPR does not require the controller to process additional information for the sole purpose of complying with its provisions and as such, the data subjects' rights of access, rectification, erasure, restriction of processing and portability (see **Chapter 3**) do not apply (Article 11 and Recital 57). However, if a data subject provides additional information which has the effect of making him or her identifiable to the data controller, the controller must observe the data subject's rights. Data controllers cannot refuse to accept such additional information which would have the effect of making the data subject identifiable simply to avoid having to comply with the data subject's rights.

3   DATA SUBJECTS' RIGHTS

The GDPR extends the rights of data subjects in a number of ways, most notably with the introduction of the right to erasure (so-called 'right to be forgotten') and the right to data portability. Data subjects' rights are set out in Chapter III of the GDPR and are as follows:

- the right to transparency;
- the right to information and access to personal data;
- the right to rectification;
- the right to erasure ('right to be forgotten');
- the right to restriction of processing;
- the right to data portability;
- the right to object to processing; and
- rights in relation to automated decision taking.

These rights are considered individually below.

3.1   THE RIGHT TO TRANSPARENCY

The right to transparency is an integral part of the lawfulness, fairness and transparency principle explained in the previous chapter. The transparency provisions of the GDPR are significantly more prescriptive than those of the Directive (Directive, Articles 10 and 11), and in practice organisations will need to review their privacy notices to ensure they comply with the new rules.

The recitals provide that data subjects should be informed of processing activities concerning their personal data, particularly where the activity includes profiling, in which case the subjects should be informed of its potential consequences (Recital 60). Individuals should be informed whether they are obliged to provide personal data and of the consequences of not doing so. Information should be provided clearly, including icons where appropriate, and may be in electronic form. This is particularly relevant where the processing activity is complex due to the technology used and the numerous parties involved in processing an individual's personal data, for instance, in the case of online advertising (Recital 58). Data controllers should provide the prescribed transparency information at the point in time when personal data is collected from the data subject. Where personal data is legitimately disclosed to other recipients or processed for additional purposes beyond the original purpose of collection, data subjects must be informed (Recital 61).

However, transparency information need not be provided where:

(a) the data subject is already aware of the processing activity;
(b) the recording or disclosure of personal data is expressly permitted by law; or
(c) providing the information to the data subject would be impossible or involve a disproportionate effort (e.g. public interest archiving, or scientific or historical research, taking into account the number of data subjects, the age of the data and any safeguards taken) (Recital 62).

Data controllers must provide the following information in a concise, transparent, intelligible and easily accessible form, using clear and plain language (in particular when addressing a child):

1. the identity and contact details of the data controller (or its representative);
2. the contact details of the data protection officer (if applicable);
3. the purpose of the processing and its legal basis;
4. where processing is based on the data controller's legitimate interests (as per Article 6(1)(f)), the legitimate interests pursued by the data controller or a third party;
5. any recipients or categories of recipient of the personal data;
6. details of any transfers to third countries and means of safeguarding;
7. the period for which personal data will be stored or the criteria used for determining such storage period;
8. the existence of the right for data subjects to request from the controller the following in relation to their personal data:

    (a) access;
    (b) rectification;
    (c) erasure (the 'right to be forgotten');
    (d) restriction; and
    (e) portability;

9. where the processing is based upon the data subject's consent, the data subject's right to withdraw his or her consent at any time, without affecting the lawfulness of the processing based upon such consent prior to its withdrawal;
10. the right to complain to the supervisory authority;
11. whether the provision of personal data is a statutory or contractual require-ment, or is necessary to enter into a contract, and whether the data subject is obliged to provide such personal data and the consequences of failure to do so;
12. the existence of automated decision making (including profiling) and the logic involved behind such decision; and
13. any further processing activities beyond the initial purpose, including the information described in points 7–12 (above) (Article 13).

Where personal data are collected other than directly from the data subject, i.e. from a third party or other source such as a public register, the data subject must be provided with all of the information described above and the following, further information:

- The categories of personal data concerned; and
- the source of the personal data and whether this was publicly accessible (Article 14).

The above-mentioned transparency information must be provided to the affected data subject promptly. Where personal data are collected other than directly from the data subject, the GDPR specifies that the above-mentioned transparency information must be provided within a reasonable period but, at the latest, within one month of collection (Article 14(3)). If the personal data are to be used for communication with the data subject, the prescribed transparency information must be provided at the time of the first communication with the data subject at the latest, and, if the personal data are disclosed to a new recipient, at the latest when the data are first disclosed. Where a data controller uses personal data for further processing, beyond that of its original purpose of collection, the data subject must be informed prior to the commencement of the secondary processing activity (Article 14(4) and Recital 61).

The GDPR recognises a number of situations where the provision of the above-mentioned transparency information may not be appropriate, namely where:

- the data subject already has the information;
- providing the information would involve a disproportionate effort;
- obtaining or disclosing the personal data is pursuant to EU or Member State law; and
- the personal data must be kept confidential for professional secrecy reasons (Article 14(5)).

3.2   THE RIGHT TO INFORMATION AND ACCESS TO PERSONAL DATA

In common with the Directive (Directive, Article 12), the GDPR grants data subjects a right of access to information held about them by a data controller (Article 15). Both sets of legislation require that data controllers confirm whether or not they are processing personal data about a data subject and, if so, that data subject has a right of access to the personal data and the data controller must provide the following information:

- the purpose of the processing;
- the categories of personal data concerned; and
- the recipients of personal data or categories of recipient.

The GDPR extends the right of access conferred upon data subjects by the Directive, granting a right to the following information, in addition to that described above:

- whether any recipients or categories of recipient are located in third countries;
- where possible, the period for which data will be stored, or if not possible, the criteria used to determine the retention period;

- the existence of the data subject's right to rectification, erasure, and restriction of processing and the right to object to processing;
- the data subject's right to complain to the supervisory authority;
- where data are not collected from the data subject, any information available as to their source;
- the existence of automated decision taking and the logic involved; and
- details of any transfers to third countries and safeguards implemented in respect of the data transferred.

The GDPR specifies that the data controller must provide a copy of the personal data subject to the processing (Article 15(3)). Data subjects should be able to easily access their personal data (including health data) at reasonable intervals and, where possible, data controllers should provide data subjects with direct access to their own data via a secure, remote system. The right of access should not, however, prejudice the rights owed by the data controller to any third parties, for example, intellectual property rights (Recital 63). Controllers must use all reasonable measures to verify the identity of individuals requesting information to their personal data (Recital 64).

Under the Directive, data controllers may charge a fee for dealing with subject access requests and this is implemented by individual Member State legislation.[1] Consequently, the potential maximum fee (if a fee is permitted at all) and statutory period for responding to a request (to the extent that this is specified) varies according to the Member State.[2] Under the GDPR, data controllers may not charge a fee for dealing with a request for access, but where a data subject requests further copies, the controller may charge a reasonable fee, based on administrative costs, for such copies (Article 15(3)).

A further, significant development concerns the prescribed period in which data controllers must respond to requests for access and information (as well as requests for rectification, erasure, restriction of processing, data portability, and the exercise of rights in relation to automated decision taking and objections). The GDPR specifies that data controllers must respond to such a request promptly and, in any event, within one month of receiving the request (including requests for the exercise of any other right) (Article 12(3)). The period may be extended by a further two months for complex or numerous requests, although the controller must inform the data subject of the extension and reason for the delay. Where the data controller does not take any action, it must inform the data subject why this is the case, and inform the data subject of his or her right to lodge a complaint with the data protection authority.

With respect to unfounded or excessive requests for access and information, and for the exercise of any other data subject rights, the GDPR gives data controllers

---

[1]   Directive 95/46/EC, Article 12 provides 'Member States shall guarantee every data subject the right to obtain from the controller…without excessive delay or expense'.
[2]   For example, under the DPA 1998 data controllers may charge a fee up to a maximum of £10, and must respond to requests within 40 days.

discretion to charge either a reasonable fee or refuse to comply with the request (Articles 15 to 22). However, the data controller bears the burden of proving that the request was unfounded or excessive.

3.3   THE RIGHT TO RECTIFICATION

Article 16 grants data subjects the right to rectification of any inaccurate personal data held about them by a data controller, which in effect mirrors the accuracy principle explained above (Article 5(12)(d)). Article 16 further confers on data subjects a right to have incomplete data completed, taking into account the purpose of the processing, including by means of a supplementary statement.

Where the controller has shared incorrect personal data with third parties, it must inform the recipients of any rectification of such personal data, unless doing so proves impossible or would involve a disproportionate effort (Article 19).

3.4   THE RIGHT TO ERASURE ('RIGHT TO BE FORGOTTEN')

The right to erasure, more commonly known as the right to be forgotten (Article 17), is one of the most widely publicised changes introduced by the GDPR, and was heralded by the European Commission as a significant expansion of data subjects' rights. It has been the subject of widespread debate, with concerns voiced by data controllers wondering how they will comply with erasure requests from data subjects, and by freedom of expression proponents concerned about the possibility of public figures being able to erase an embarrassing past. Equally, given the explosion in use of social media, members of the public will welcome the right to erase information that they may have youthfully 'over shared'.

As explained below, the right to erasure is not absolute; data subjects have a right to be forgotten where their personal data is no longer necessary for the purposes for which it was collected, particularly in an online context where the data subject is a child. However, the right to erasure does not apply where there is a lawful reason for continued processing (Recital 65).

Article 17 imposes an obligation upon data controllers to erase personal data concerning a data subject without delay in the following circumstances:

- the personal data are no longer required for the purpose for which they were requested;
- the data subject withdraws consent and there is no other legal basis for processing;
- the data subject objects to the processing pursuant to the right expressed in Article 21 (explained below);
- the personal data have been unlawfully processed;
- the personal data must be erased pursuant to a legal obligation to which the data controller is subject;

- the personal data have been collected in relation to the offer of 'information society services' to a child.

Where data controllers have disclosed personal data to other controllers, they should notify them of requests relating to the right to be forgotten, and should inform such controllers to erase any links or copies of such data (Recital 66). Article 17(2) requires controllers to erase personal data they have made public and to take reasonable steps, taking into account the available technology and cost, to inform other controllers that are also processing the personal data, of the request of erasure of any links to, or copy or replication of, such personal data.

Article 17(3) includes a number of exemptions to the right to erasure, where the processing is necessary for:

- exercising the right to freedom of expression and information;
- compliance with a legal obligation to which the controller is subject or for the performance of a task in the public interest;
- any reason of public interest in the area of public health;
- archiving purposes in the public interest, scientific or historical research purposes or statistical purposes; or
- for the establishment, exercise or defence of legal claims.

As a practical matter, organisations will have to ensure that they have appropriate processes in place to deal with requests, which will have to be documented to comply with the accountability principle.

Where the controller has shared personal data with third parties, it must inform the recipients of the personal data of the right to erasure, unless doing so proves impossible or would involve a disproportionate effort (Article 19).

3.5   THE RIGHT TO RESTRICTION OF PROCESSING

The GDPR introduces another new right, namely the right to restrict processing (Article 18), which grants data subjects a right to restrict the processing of their personal data in the following circumstances:

- where the data subject contests the accuracy of his or her personal data, processing can be restricted for a period enabling the controller to verify whether the personal data is accurate;
- the processing is unlawful and the data subject opposes erasure of the data and instead requests restriction of processing;
- the controller no longer needs the personal data for the purpose of its processing, but the data subject requires the personal data for establishing, exercising or defending legal claims; or
- where the data subject has exercised the right to object to processing pursuant to Article 21(1) (explained below), processing may be restricted for the period necessary to ascertain whether the controller's legitimate grounds override those of the data subject (Article 18(1)).

Where a data subject exercises the right, other than for storage, the affected personal data may only be processed:

■ with the data subject's consent;
■ for establishing, exercising or defending legal claims;
■ for the protection of another natural or legal person's rights; or
■ for reasons of important public interest of the Union or a Member State (Article 18(2).

The controller must inform the data subject before lifting the restriction of processing (Article 18(3)).

Recital 67 provides some guidance as to how the right to restriction of processing might operate in practice, suggesting that affected data could be temporarily moved to another processing system, made temporarily unavailable to users or making published data temporarily unavailable from a website. It further suggests that personal data in an automated filing system should not be further processed, should not be changed and should be marked as restricted in the system.

Where the controller has shared personal data with third parties, it must inform the recipients of the personal data subject to the right to restriction of processing, unless doing so proves impossible or would involve a disproportionate effort (Article 19).

3.6   THE RIGHT TO DATA PORTABILITY

The right to data portability is a new right introduced by the GDPR, and gives data subjects a right to receive their information from the data controller, and to re-use it with other service providers. It has been the cause of some consternation among data protection practitioners, given the practical challenges organisations are likely to face when they implement measures to fulfil their obligations. This uncertainty appears to have been recognised at a European level, as the Article 29 Working Party adopted an opinion on the subject, as set out below.[3]

The right to data portability applies only to data processing by automated means that is necessary for the performance of a contract, or to personal data processed on the basis of the data subject's consent (Article 20(1)). It is not available for data processing based on any of the other conditions for processing, for example, where the processing is based upon a legal obligation of the data controller, or the vital interests of the data subject or another person. The right to data portability allows a data subject to instruct a data controller to transmit his or her personal data to another controller, where it is technically feasible to do so (Article 20(2)). For example, a data subject could instruct his or her bank supplier to transfer his or her information to a new bank.

---

[3]   Article 29 Data Protection Working Party Guidelines on the right to data portability (WP 242), adopted on 13 December 2016.

The right to data portability is without prejudice to the data subject's right to erasure (right to be forgotten) (Article 20(3)). It does not apply where data are processed for the performance of a task in the public interest or in the exercise of the data controller's official authority (Article 20(3)), and must not affect the rights and freedoms of others (Article 20(4)).

The GDPR provides that data controllers are encouraged to develop interoperable formats that enable data portability. However, it clarifies that the right to data portability does not create an obligation for data controllers to maintain or adopt technically compatible systems (Recital 68).

WP 242 explains the nature and scope of the right to portability and provides guidance on how the right should be interpreted and implemented, with practical examples. It observes that:

> the primary aim of data portability is to facilitate switching from one service provider to another…[and enabling]…the creation of new services in the context of the digital single market strategy.
>
> (WP 242, Part I)

In other words, the right seeks to empower consumers and create opportunities for innovative data sharing between data controllers.

In particular, WP 242 clarifies the following issues:

1. The right to portability is a right

    > for data subjects to receive the personal data which they have provided to a data controller, in a structured, commonly used and machine-readable format, and to transmit those data to another data controller without hindrance.(WP 242, Part I)

2. The right of data portability consists of two elements, namely:

    (a)   a right to receive personal data; and
    (b)   a right to transmit personal data from one data controller to another (WP 242, Part II).

3. The right to data portability does not require a data controller to retain personal data for longer than is necessary for the purpose for which it is processed. In other words data controllers are not required to retain personal data after their processing activities concerning that personal data have ceased for the sole purpose of being able to comply with a portability request, should one arise (WP 242, Part II).

4. A receiving data controller becomes a new data controller itself with respect to the portable data and as such bears responsibility for compliance with the principles of the GDPR. In particular, the new controller must ensure the portable data are relevant and not excessive for the purpose of the new processing (WP 242, Part II).

5. The right to portability is without prejudice to other data subjects' rights; a data subject may continue to receive a data controller's services after exercising the right to portability and any other rights (such as the right to erasure). The right to portability cannot be used as a reason for not complying with such a right (WP 242, Part II).

6. The right only applies to personal data provided by the data subject to the data controller (which would include 'observed data' arising by virtue of the data subject's use of the service, such as search history). Anonymous data or personal data pertaining to another data subject falls outside the scope of the right to data portability, as would personal data 'inferred' by the data controller, such as a credit score or health assessment (WP 242, Part III).

7. The right to portability should not adversely affect the rights and freedoms of others. For example, in the context of a mobile phone subscription, an individual's personal data may include the data subject's contacts' names and telephone numbers, which could be within the scope of a portability request, provided the data controller does not try to use such contact information for other purposes, such as sending marketing communications. The rights and freedoms of others are not confined to rights in respect of privacy, and could refer to trade secrets and intellectual property rights (WP 242, Part III).

8. WP 242 confirms that controllers must provide the requested portable data within one month of receipt of the request (or a maximum of three months in complex cases). It suggests that the circumstances in which a fee may be charged, or a data portability request refused are likely to be rare (WP 242, Part IV).

9. Regarding the requirement that portable data must be provided 'in a structured, commonly used and machine-readable format', WP 242 acknowledges that the GDPR does not impose specific recommendations on the format, and that the most appropriate format may differ between sectors. However, formats should generally be selected on the basis of enabling interpretability, and where applicable, include appropriate metadata (for example, a PDF of an email inbox would be inappropriate, since it is unlikely to include the contents of emails and any metadata). The Article 29 Working Party strongly encourages co-operation between industry stakeholders and trade associations in order to develop common standards and formats, thus enabling interoperability and delivering the right to data portability (WP 242, Part V).

10. Finally, WP 242 observes two potential security risks, arising from the right to data portability; the risk of a data breach in transmission, including where portable data is transmitted to the wrong recipient; and the data security risk arising where an individual stores portable data in a less secure environment than that of the data controller (WP 242, Part V).

The Opinion provides some clarity on the nature of the right to data portability and guidance on how organisations may comply with the requirements in practice. However, it seems likely that practitioners seeking further clarity on interoperability standards may have to wait for sector-specific guidance to emerge.

3.7   THE RIGHT TO OBJECT TO PROCESSING

The GDPR grants data subjects a right to object to certain types of processing in a number of specific circumstances (Article 21). In each of the circumstances, the right operates differently, particularly with regard to the data controller's ability to refuse. In each case, the data controller must respond to the request within one month, with a potential two-month extension for complex or numerous requests (Article 12(3) and Recital 59).

The circumstances where the right to object arises are as follows:

■   processing based on the data controller's legitimate interests or performance of a task carried out in the public interest or exercise of official authority;
■   processing for the purpose of direct marketing; and
■   processing for scientific or historical research purposes, or statistical purposes.

Each of these circumstances is now considered in more detail.

Data subjects may object to processing, including profiling, that is necessary for the public interest, or for the exercise of the data controller's official authority, or where it is based on the data controller's legitimate interests (Articles 6(1)(e) or (f) and 21(1)). Upon receiving an objection, the data controller must cease processing unless it is able to demonstrate that its legitimate interests override those of the data subject, or that the processing is necessary for establishing, exercising or defending legal claims (Article 21(1)).

Data subjects may object to processing for direct marketing purposes, which includes profiling for the purpose of direct marketing. Upon receiving a request, the data controller must cease processing (Article 21(2) and (3)). Note that, in the case of direct marketing, there are no grounds for a data controller to refuse to comply with such a request.

Data controllers must bring the rights explained above to the data subject's notice, clearly and separately from any other information, by the time of the first communication with that data subject, at the latest (Article 21(4)). Where a data controller operates online (i.e. provides information society services) it must provide data subjects with an online means of objecting (Article 21(5).

Where personal data are processed for scientific or historical research, or statistical purposes, the data subject may object to processing, based on his or her individual circumstances. The data controller must comply with the request, unless the processing is in the public interest.

3.8   RIGHTS IN RELATION TO AUTOMATED DECISION TAKING

The GDPR, like the Directive (Directive, Article 15), includes rights for individuals who are subject to automated decisions, i.e. decisions made entirely by technological means, without human intervention (Article 22). These rights exist where an automated decision could have a serious effect on a data subject.

Individuals have the right not to be subject to a decision based solely on automated processing, including profiling, where the processing results in a legal, or similarly significant effect. Automated decision taking includes 'profiling', i.e. any form of automated processing for the purpose of evaluating individuals, for example the data subject's performance at work, or his or her economic situation, health, personal preferences or interests, reliability or behaviour, location or movements.

An exemption to this right exists where:

- the processing is necessary for entering into, or the performance of, a contract between the data subject and a data controller;
- the controller is authorised by Member State or EU law (and has implemented appropriate safeguards), for example, for the purpose of preventing fraud or tax evasion; or
- the data subject has given explicit consent to the automated processing.

In any of these situations, the data controller must safeguard the data subject's rights and freedoms, and must at least give the data subject the right to human intervention, to express his or her point of view and to contest the automated decision. However, the exemptions do not apply where the data subject is a child (Recital 71), nor do they apply to decisions based on special categories of personal data, unless the data subject has consented to automated decision making, or the processing is for reasons of substantial public interest (Article 22(4)).

3.9   RESTRICTIONS

Article 23 permits the EU and Member States to enact legislative measures that restrict the rights conferred upon data subjects by the GDPR for various public interest reasons (these grounds are set out in Article 23(1)(a)–(j)), provided such legislative measures include specific provisions to address certain data protection considerations (set out in Article 23(2)(a)–(h)).

The data subjects' rights that may be supressed by EU or Member State law are set out in Articles 12 to 22 (these are the rights to transparency, access, rectification, erasure, restriction of processing, notification (of rectification, erasure or restriction of processing), portability, to object and the rights in relation to automated decision making) and Article 34 (the right to be informed of a personal data breach concerning him or her) and Article 5 (the rights conferred upon data subjects by way of the data protection principles).

4 CONTROLLERS AND PROCESSORS, BREACH NOTIFICATION AND DPOs

Chapter IV of the GDPR sets out the responsibilities of data controllers and data processors, and introduces significant new requirements, such as the obligation to appoint a data protection officer (DPO) to notify data protection breaches to the supervisory authority and affected data subjects, and to conduct data protection impact assessments. One of the game-changing developments of the GDPR is its application to data processors as well as controllers. As well as imposing new obligations, Chapter IV also promotes the use of codes of conduct and certification mechanisms.

4.1 DATA CONTROLLERS' RESPONSIBILITIES

The GDPR recognises that processing personal data creates a wide range of risks, of varying likelihood and severity, to individuals' rights and freedoms (Recital 75).

Article 24 requires data controllers to implement appropriate technical and organisational measures to ensure and be able to demonstrate compliance with the GDPR (Article 24(1) and Recital 74). The requirement that data controllers must not only comply with the provisions of the GDPR, but must also be able to demonstrate that they do so is known as the Accountability Principle. Data controllers may demonstrate compliance by way of data protection policies, where this is proportionate to the processing activities (Article 24(2)). The GDPR promotes the use of approved codes of conduct, certifications and guidelines (which are explained in more detail later in this chapter) provided by the European Data Protection Board ('Board') or an indication provided by the DPO (Recital 77). Adhering to a code of conduct or a certification scheme may also help demonstrate compliance with the GDPR (Articles 40 and 42).

4.2 DATA PROTECTION BY DESIGN AND BY DEFAULT

The GDPR promotes the principles of data protection by design and by default. Data controllers are required to implement appropriate measures to ensure the principles of the GDPR are integrated into their processing activities. In other words, the GDPR requires organisations to ensure that data protection principles are designed into their processes as a matter of course. To establish 'appropriate' technical and organisational measures, data controllers should take into account the state of the art in terms of technology and security etc., the cost of implementation, the nature, scope, context and purposes of processing, and the likelihood and severity of the risks to data subjects (Article 25(1)).

The principle of data protection by default requires that controllers must implement technical and organisational measures to ensure that, by default, only personal data that is necessary for the specific purpose for which it was collected is processed. This principle extends to the quantity of personal data collected, the extent of processing of such data, the period of storage of such data, and accessibility to such data. The provisions specifically state that, by default, personal data should not be made accessible to an indefinite number of people without the data subject's intervention (Article 25(2)). This appears to address the widespread and frequently misleading practice of relying on privacy statement wording, such as 'we will only share your personal data with carefully-selected third parties', to license unchecked data sharing.

Data controllers should adopt internal policies and measures that meet the principles of data protection by design and by default, including minimisation, pseudonymisation and transparency. Producers of products, services and applications should consider the right to data protection during their design and development to enable controllers and processors to fulfil their obligations. In particular, data protection by design and by default should be taken into consideration in the context of public tenders (Recital 78). The GDPR advocates the use of certification mechanisms to demonstrate compliance with the principles of data protection by design and default (Article 25(3)).

4.3   JOINT CONTROLLERS

Where two or more data controllers jointly determine the purposes and means of processing, they must, in a transparent manner, clearly allocate their respective responsibilities for compliance with the provisions of the GDPR. In particular, joint controllers must be clear as to which controller is responsible in relation to the exercise of data subjects' rights and the provision of transparency information (Article 26 and Recital 79). Joint controllers must have an arrangement between themselves to apportion responsibilities, the essence of which must be made available to data subjects (Article 26(1) and (2)). However, regardless of any arrangement, data subjects may exercise their rights under the GDPR against each of the data controllers (Article 26(3)).

4.4   DATA PROTECTION REPRESENTATIVES

Organisations that are not established in the EU but are nonetheless subject to the GDPR may need to appoint a data protection representative. The role of the external data protection representative is not a new concept, as the requirement also exists under the Directive. Article 4(2)) of the Directive requires the appointment of a representative where the data controller is established outside the EU, but uses equipment located in an EU Member State.

The Directive further specifies that the representative's role includes the following:

- providing the transparency information specified in Article 10 to data subjects;
- if appointed, notification to the supervisory authority;

in practice, a representative may also deal with ad hoc data protection queries.

However, it is a requirement of which many organisations located outside the EU may not necessarily be aware. Given the extra-territorial reach of the GDPR and the heavy penalties for breaches of its provisions, the role of the data protection representative seems likely to assume a higher profile when the new law takes effect.

Under the GDPR, a 'representative' is defined as:

> a natural or legal person established in the Union who, designated by the controller or processor in writing…represents the controller or processor with regard to their respective obligations under this Regulation.
>
> (Article 4(17))

Data controllers or processors that are established outside the EU but are offering goods or services to EU citizens, or monitoring the behaviour of EU citizens must designate a representative in writing. No representative is required where the processing activity is low risk (Article 27).

Where one is appointed, the data protection representative's responsibilities include maintaining a record of the controller's or processor's data processing activities, and co-operating with the supervisory authority when required (Articles 30 and 31). The representative may be approached by, and must co-operate with, European supervisory authorities in relation to compliance matters, and must be appointed to be addressed, either in addition to or instead of the controller or processor, by supervisory authorities or data subjects, in particular (Article 27(4)). Where a representative is appointed, data subjects must be informed as part of the transparency principle (Articles 13 and 14).

The appointment of a representative is without prejudice to legal actions which could be initiated against the controller or processor (Article 27(5)). However, the recitals provide that:

> The designated representative should be subject to enforcement proceedings in the event of non-compliance by the controller or processor.
>
> (Recital 80)

This is confusing since it appears to contradict the operative provisions of the GDPR (explained above); however, it could be taken into account by the CJEU and/or the Board. As such, there is a risk, albeit apparently remote, that a representative could, in principle, be subject to enforcement action by the supervisory authority.

4.5   DATA PROCESSORS

A major development of the GDPR is the extension of its scope to include data processors, which were not directly subject to the provisions of the Directive. For many organisations, it may appear counterintuitive that, under the Directive, in the event of a data breach by their third party processor, it is the controller rather than the service provider that bears the responsibility for complying with data protection law, and hence risks regulatory action from the data protection authority. This anachronism is at least in part a hangover from the prevailing computing practices at the time the Directive was drafted. The GDPR addresses this issue by including data processors within its scope. Some of the most significant changes that businesses will need to accommodate concern the status of data processors under the GDPR. In practice, most businesses will have to review their arrangements with data processors, to ensure compliance with the requirements of the new law.

The GDPR, like the Directive before it, stipulates that where a data controller requires the processing of personal data by a third party acting on its behalf, it may only use a data processor able to offer sufficient guarantees to implement technical and organisational security measures to ensure that the processing meets the requirements of the GDPR and ensures the protection of the rights of the data subjects (Directive, Article 17(2)). Adherence to an approved code of conduct or certification scheme may help demonstrate such sufficient guarantees (Article 28(5)).

Processors may sub-contract their responsibilities subject to obtaining prior authorisation from the data controller (Article 28(2)). This may be prior, specific or general written authorisation, provided the processor notifies the controller of any change in sub-processing arrangements, so that the controller has the option to object to such changes. Where a processor does appoint a sub-processor, it must bind the sub-processor with contractual provisions equivalent to those by which the processor itself is bound. In the event of a breach by the sub-processor, the processor remains fully liable to the data controller (Article 28(4)).

A data processor, and any other person authorised by the data controller or by the data processor, shall only process personal data on the instructions of the data controller, unless required to do so by EU or Member State law (Article 29). Where a processor, in breach of the GDPR, determines the purposes and means of processing, it will be deemed to be the data controller in respect of such processing, and hence liable for any breach (Article 28(10)).

Having satisfied the due diligence requirements explained above, where a data controller does appoint a data processor, it must do so by way of a written contract, which may be in electronic form, and may be in a standard contractual form, as prescribed by the European Commission (Article 28(6), (7) and (9)). Such contract must include the following provisions:

- the subject matter, duration, nature and purpose of the processing; and

- the type of personal data, categories of data subjects and obligations and rights of the data controller.

The processor will:

- process personal data only on documented instructions from the controller (including in relation to transfers to third countries or international organisations), unless the processing is required by EU or Member State law, in which case the processor will inform the controller;
- ensure persons authorised to process the personal data (i.e. its workers) are bound by appropriate confidentiality obligations;
- implement appropriate security measures (as required by Article 32, and discussed at 4.7);
- observe the provisions relating to the appointment of sub-processors, i.e. obtain prior authorisation and ensure any sub-processors are bound by equivalent obligations as those imposed upon the data processor by the data controller (per Article 28(2) and (4));
- assist the controller in dealing with the exercise of affected data subjects' rights;
- assist the controller in complying with its security and breach notification obligations; its obligations to conduct privacy impact assessments, and any prior consultation with the supervisory authority that may be necessary in the case of proposed high-risk activities;
- at the end of the provision of services, either delete or return (at the data controller's option) all the personal data processed under the arrangement to the data controller; and
- provide all such information to the data controller as may be necessary to demonstrate compliance with its obligations (as set out in Article 28), and allow audits and inspections by the data controller (or its nominated auditor) (Article 28(3)).

Many organisations will be familiar with the requirements imposed by the Directive *vis-à-vis* the appointment of data processors. These are that the controller must engage the processor by way of a written contract that obliges the processor to only act in accordance with the data controller's instructions, and to implement security measures equivalent to those imposed on the data controller by the operation of national data protection law (Directive, Article 17(3)). However, the requirements of the GDPR are significantly more prescriptive, and are likely to require considerably more thought than a simple, standard clause. In particular, in complex processing situations, the GDPR requirement of a specific description of the processing activity (described in the first two bullet points above) is likely to render insufficient the widespread practice of relying upon wording such as 'to the extent that the client is a data controller and the service provider is a data processor'. In practice, organisations will need to review their processing arrangements with third-party processors, and ensure the applicable contractual provisions accurately and specifically reference the processing in order to ensure compliance with the new law.

4.6   RECORDS OF PROCESSING ACTIVITIES

A significant new obligation under the GDPR is the requirement for data controllers, data processors, and, where applicable, their representatives to maintain a register of their data processing activities (Article 30(2)). The register must be in writing, which includes in electronic form, and must also be made available to the supervisory authority upon request in order to assist the supervisory authority to monitor the processing operations (Article 30(3) and (4)).

There is an exception to the requirement to keep a record of processing activities for organisations that employ fewer than 250 people, that are not engaged in high-risk activities, and where the processing is only occasional and does not include any of the special categories of data or details of criminal convictions and offences (Article 30(5)).

The record must include the following information:

For data controllers

■   the name and contact details of the data controller (including any joint controllers and representatives) and the DPO;
■   the purposes of the processing;
■   a description of:

    (a)   the categories of data subjects; and
    (b)   the categories of personal data;

■   the categories of recipients to which data have or will be disclosed (including those in third countries and international organisations);
■   details of any transfers to a third country or international organisation, and the documentation of suitable safeguards where the transfer is not based on an adequacy decision (pursuant to Article 45), any of the prescribed appropriate safeguards (pursuant to Article 46), or binding corporate rules (per Article 47). The transfer must also fulfil the following criteria:

    (a)   it is not repetitive;
    (b)   it concerns only a limited number of data subjects;
    (c)   it is pursuant to the data controllers' compelling legitimate interests (which the data controller must explain to the affected data subjects) and does not override the interests, rights or freedoms of the affected data subjects;
    (d)   the controller has assessed all the circumstances of the transfer and implemented appropriate safeguards to protect the personal data;
    (e)   the controller has informed the supervisory authority; and
    (f)   the controller has informed the affected data subjects (Article 49(1));

■   the duration for which categories of personal data will be held prior to erasure (where possible); and
■   a general description of the applicable technical and organisational security measures (Article 30(1)).

For data processors

■   the name and contact details of:

    (a)   the processor(s);
    (b)   each controller on behalf of which the processor is acting;
    (c)   the controller or processor's representative (where applicable); and
    (d)   the DPO;

■   the categories of processing carried out on behalf of each data controller;
■   details of transfers to third countries or international organisations (including the information required for limited, non-repetitive transfers, described above); and
■   a general description of the applicable technical and organisational security measures (Article 30(2)).

4.7   SECURITY MEASURES

Section 2 of Chapter IV imposes a security obligation upon data controllers and data processors, as well as the obligation upon both data controllers and processors to notify the supervisory authority and affected data subjects if they suffer a personal data breach (Articles 32 and 33).

The security obligations under the GDPR, like those of the Directive before it, are generic in nature rather than specific (Article 32(1) and Recital 83, and Directive, Article 17). The level of security should be appropriate to the risk, taking into account the prevailing state of the art in terms of technological developments, the costs of implementation, and the severity and likelihood of risk to affected data subjects. Accordingly, organisations engaged in privacy intrusive activities, involving sensitive information, would be expected to adopt more stringent measures than those engaged in low-risk processing activities, involving limited information that, for example, is widely available in the public domain. Appropriate security measures may be technical, including, for example, encryption and password protection, and organisational, which could include layered access to information on a 'need to know' basis, a clear-desk policy, and data protection training.

In assessing the appropriate level of security, the potential risks in processing should be taken into account, such as the risks arising from accidental or unlawful destruction, loss, alteration, unauthorised disclosure of, or access to personal data in the course of transmission, storage or other processing (Article 32(2)), in particular, those that could lead to physical, material or non-material damage (Recital 83). The GDPR advocates the use of approved codes of conduct and approved certification schemes in demonstrating appropriate security measures (Article 32(3)).

The security requirements of the GDPR differ materially from those of the Directive as they apply to both data controllers and data processors. This will have significant implications for data processors, which hitherto have enjoyed the benefits of falling outside the scope of the Directive, and must instead be bound by a contract with the data controller (Directive, Article 17(3)). Under the Directive, data breaches arising as a result of the data processor's failure could result in the data controller being prosecuted by the data protection authority. The controller would then have to pursue a contractual remedy with the processor. However, the GDPR imposes security obligations directly upon the data processor (Article 32(1)).

The GDPR suggests a number of potential security measures which may be appropriate, such as: pseudonymisation and encryption; the ability to ensure ongoing confidentiality, integrity, availability and resilience of processing systems and services; the ability to restore personal data in a timely manner following an incident; and ongoing testing and evaluation of security measures. The GDPR also specifies that controllers and processors must take steps to ensure that any individuals accessing personal data under their authority (for example, workers) only do so in accordance with the controller's or processor's instructions (or as may be required by EU or Member State law) (Article 32(4)). In practice, controllers and processors will have to implement an appropriate policy to meet this requirement, together with measures such as data protection training.

4.8   MANDATORY DATA BREACH NOTIFICATION – TO THE SUPERVISORY AUTHORITY

A major change under the GDPR is the introduction of mandatory breach notification. The GDPR acknowledges that a data breach which is not addressed in a timely manner creates a variety of risks to the data subject. The risks to individuals include physical, material and non-material damage, such as the individual's loss of control over his or her personal data, limitation of the individual's rights, discrimination, identity theft, fraud, financial loss, unauthorised reversal of pseudonymised data, damage to reputation and loss of confidentiality of personal data protected by professional secrecy (for example, medical records). The GDPR seeks to address those risks by imposing a reporting obligation upon data controllers (Recital 85). Data processors are under an obligation to notify the data controller, but not the supervisory authority.

Data controllers, on becoming aware that they have suffered a data breach, must report this to the supervisory authority and, where the breach is high risk, the affected data subjects. This is a significant responsibility, since organisations will be forced to bring themselves to the supervisory authority's attention, potentially alerting the authority to their non-compliance. As a result, many organisations are likely to consider appointing a DPO voluntarily (i.e. those organisations that fall outside the mandatory appointment requirement) (per Article 37(1)) to ensure that breaches are promptly detected and reported, as well as to benefit from the experience of a DPO accustomed to liaising with the supervisory authority.

Controllers must ensure that they have systems in place to immediately establish whether a data breach has taken place; for example, technical measures such as breach detection software, as well as organisational measures such as a data breach response policy and training (Recital 87). Data breach policies should respond to the nature of the breach and risks arising from it, taking into account law enforcement authorities' interests where early disclosure could hamper an investigation (Recital 88). Where there has been a breach, the supervisory authority must be promptly informed, and it should be established whether the data breach was in fact promptly notified, considering its nature and gravity. Data controllers should be aware that notification of a breach may result in intervention by the supervisory authority, and the potential exercise of its powers, including the issue of a penalty (Recital 87).

Upon becoming aware of a personal data breach, data controllers must notify the supervisory authority without undue delay and, where feasible, within 72 hours. The obligation does not apply where the breach is unlikely to result in a risk to the affected data subjects. Where the controller fails to notify the supervisory authority within 72 hours, it must account to the authority for the delay (Article 33(1)).

For a data controller that is only established in one jurisdiction, the competent supervisory authority is most likely to be that of the country in which the controller is established. However, for a controller established in multiple jurisdictions, the position may be less straightforward. The rules regarding competent supervisory authorities for multinational organisations are explained in **Chapter 6**.

A personal data breach is defined as:

> a breach of security leading to the accidental or unlawful destruction, loss, alteration, unauthorised disclosure of, or access to, personal data transmitted, stored or otherwise processed.
>
> (Article 4(12))

The definition is broad and could potentially include the loss or theft of a mobile device, a hacking attack, a sensitive letter sent to the wrong address, or an email sent to recipients in copy (i.e. 'cc all') who should have been blind copied instead.

Where a data processor becomes aware of a breach, it must inform the controller without undue delay (Article 33(2)). The processor itself should be bound by a contract that requires it to assist the controller in ensuring compliance with its security and breach notification obligations (Article 28(3)(f)). It seems likely that, in practice, data controllers will impose a contractual obligation upon data processors to notify the controller of a breach (as is frequently the case in existing data processing contracts), with the result that a data processor that fails to promptly report a breach to the data controller risks not only enforcement action from the supervisory authority, but also contractual remedies from the affected data controller.

The notification to the supervisory authority must include the following information:

■   the nature of the personal data breach, including (where possible):

(a)   the categories and approximate number of data subjects concerned; and
(b)   the categories and approximate number of data records concerned;

- the name and contact details of the DPO or other contact point in the event that further information is required;
- the likely consequences of the personal data breach;
- the measures taken, or to be taken by the data controller to address the breach, including any mitigation measures (Article 33(3)).

Where the controller is not able to provide all of the prescribed information at the same time, it may be provided in phases, without undue delay (Article 33(4)). In order to enable the supervisory authority to verify the data controller's compliance with its breach notification obligations, the data controller must also document any breaches it sustains, explaining the facts related to the breach, its effects and any remedial action taken (Article 33(5)).

4.9   MANDATORY DATA BREACH NOTIFICATION – TO THE DATA SUBJECT

Where a personal data breach is likely to result in a high risk to the data subject, the data controller must notify the data subject of the breach without delay (Article 34(1)). The communication must be in clear and plain language, and include the following information:

1. the name and contact details of the DPO or other contact point in the event that further information is required;
2. the likely consequences of the personal data breach; and
3. the measures taken, or to be taken by the data controller to address the breach, including any mitigation measures (Article 34(2)).

However, the controller does not need to inform data subjects of a breach in the following circumstances:

1. the personal data was subject to security measures that rendered it unintelligible to anyone not authorised to access it, such as encryption;
2. the data controller has taken measures to ensure the high risk to data subjects is no longer likely to materialise; or
3. it would involve a disproportionate effort, in which case there must be a public communication or similar measure instead, whereby data subjects are informed in an equally effective manner (Article 34(3)).

Where a data controller has not already communicated the breach to the affected data subjects, the supervisory authority may direct it to do so if the authority perceives the breach as resulting in a high risk to the rights and freedoms of the affected data subjects. Alternatively, the supervisory authority may form the view that the affected data subjects do not need to be informed, as one of the sets of circumstances above has been established (Article 34(4)).

The GDPR advocates close co-operation with the supervisory authority, and any guidance it may have produced, as well as any relevant guidance produced by other

authorities such as law enforcement bodies (Recital 86). In practice, a data controller that has suffered a data breach, at the time it informs the supervisory authority,
may wish to consider seeking advice from the authority regarding the notification
to data subjects. However, this approach is not without risk, since it would involve
inviting the authority's scrutiny.

4.10   DATA PROTECTION IMPACT ASSESSMENTS

Data protection impact assessments (DPIAs), also known as privacy impact assessments (PIAs), do not expressly feature in the Directive, though they are currently
recognised as good practice.[1] A DPIA aims to identify and evaluate the likely data
protection risks arising from a new activity that involves processing personal data.
Identified risks may then be avoided altogether, mitigated, or accepted. Draft
guidance from the Article 29 Working Party (WP 248)[2] describes a DPIA as:

> a process designed to describe the processing, assess the necessity and proportional-
> ity of a processing and to help manage the risks to the rights and freedoms of natural
> persons resulting from the processing of personal data (by assessing them and
> determining the measures to address them).

WP 248 provides that DPIAs are important tools for accountability, as they help
controllers to comply with the requirements of the GDPR, and to demonstrate that
appropriate measures have been taken to ensure compliance (WPA 248, Section 1).

Typical situations where a DPIA may be appropriate include the implementation of
an employee monitoring system, or the gathering of public social media profiles by
private companies generating profiles for contact directories. A DPIA may also be
appropriate where an organisation is considering commencing a new business
activity, such as using online analytics in the context of selling goods or services
online. In the context of corporate acquisitions or disposals, privacy and data
protection considerations may be overlooked, although a DPIA may be necessary
where, for example, an organisation plans to acquire a target company for its
customer database, which it intends to use for its own marketing activities, or where
during the due diligence process, a target company is required to disclose details of
its workforce to the potential acquirer headquartered in a third country outside the
EEA.

The GDPR acknowledges that the general obligation to notify the supervisory
authority, as imposed under the Directive (Directive, Article 18), generates an
administrative and financial burden, although it does not in all cases contribute to
improving the protection of personal data. To address this, the GDPR abolishes the
notification requirement and proposes its replacement with mechanisms that focus
on processing activities that create a significant risk. Types of processing that

---

[1]   However, Article 20 of the Directive advocates 'prior checking' before commencing
       processing activities that present specific risks to data subjects.
[2]   Article 29 Data Protection Working Party Guidelines on Data Protection Impact Assess-
       ment (DPIA) and determining whether processing is 'likely to result in a high risk' for the
       purposes of Regulation 2016/679 (WP 248) adopted on 4 April 2017.

require such consideration may include operations that involve the use of new technologies, activities of a new kind that have not previously been assessed by the controller for their impact upon the protection of personal data, or processing operations where an assessment becomes necessary as a result of the time that has elapsed since the initial processing took place (Recital 89).

The GDPR requires that data controllers must carry out a DPIA prior to processing that is likely to result in a high risk to the rights and freedoms of individuals (Article 35(1)). A DPIA should take into account the nature, scope, context and purposes of the proposed processing, and assess its impact on the protection of personal data. It should include measures, safeguards and mechanisms to mitigate any risks that have been identified, ensure the protection of personal data and demonstrate compliance with the GDPR (Recital 90). Where a DPO has been appointed, he or she should be involved in carrying out the assessment (Article 35(2)). Data controllers should, where necessary, conduct a review to assess whether processing has been carried out in accordance with the DPIA, in particular where there is a change in the risk created by the processing activities (Article 35(11)).

Activities that, in particular, require a DPIA to be conducted include the following (Article 35(3) and Recital 91):

- any automated processing, including profiling, that produces legal or similarly significant effects concerning the data subject;
- large-scale processing of special categories of personal data, or personal data concerning criminal convictions or offences (including decision making based on profiling). However, a DPIA is not required for processing of patients' or clients' personal data by an individual physician or lawyer (Recital 91);
- large-scale, systematic monitoring of a publicly accessible area (especially by optic-electronic devices);
- large-scale processing operations which aim to process a considerable amount of personal data at a regional, national or a supranational level, and which could affect a large number of data subjects; and are likely to result in a high risk; and
- processing activities that are considered to be high risk by the supervisory authority. The supervisory authority must publish a list of these high-risk processing activities (Article 35(4)), together with a public list of processing activities that do not require an assessment (Article 35(5)).

In practice, organisations may be uncertain as to whether a DPIA is necessary or not. WP 248 specifically states:

> The GDPR does not require a DPIA to be carried out for every processing operation which may result in risks for the rights and freedoms of natural persons.

However, where it is not clear whether a DPIA is necessary, WP 248 suggests conducting one.

WP 248 suggests the following processing operations constitute a 'high risk':

- evaluation or scoring (including profiling or predicting);

- automated decision making with legal or similar significant effects;
- systematic monitoring;
- processing sensitive data;
- processing on a large scale;
- matching or combining data sets;
- processing data concerning vulnerable data subjects;
- innovative use or applying technological or organisational solutions;
- data transfers outside the EU; or
- where the processing prevents data subjects from exercising a right or from using a service or a contract.

As a rule of thumb WP 248 proposes that a processing operation meeting less than two of the above criteria would not need a DPIA. However, it recognises that there may be circumstances where only one of the criteria are met, but the processing is sufficiently high risk to warrant a DPIA, and conversely, a processing operation may meet at least two of the criteria but still not be high risk. However, in the latter case, WP 248 recommends thoroughly documenting a decision not to conduct a DPIA.

WP 248 confirms that a DPIA is not necessary for the following processing activities:

- where the processing is not likely to result in a high risk;
- where the nature, scope, context and purposes of the processing are very similar to the processing for which a DPIA has already been carried out;
- where the processing has a legal basis in EU or Member State law (and is subject to legal safeguards); and
- where the processing is included on a list of activities for which a DPIA is not necessary (WP 248, section III(B)).

In some circumstances it may be appropriate for one DPIA to be broader than a single project; for example, where private or public sector operators plan to implement a common application or platform, or where a number of controllers plan to introduce a common application or processing environment across an industry sector.

A DPIA should include at least the following:

- a description of the proposed processing activity, the purposes of the processing and, where applicable, the legitimate interests pursued by the data controller;
- an assessment of the necessity and proportionality of the processing in relation to the purpose;
- an assessment of the risks to the rights and freedoms of the affected data subjects; and
- the measures proposed to address the risks, including safeguards, security measures and mechanisms to ensure the protection of personal data and compliance with the requirements of the GDPR, taking into account the data subjects' rights and freedoms (Article 35(7)).

Data controllers and processors may take into account their compliance with relevant approved codes of conduct in assessing the potential impact of their processing operations, for the purposes of conducting a DPIA (Article 35(8)). Where appropriate, controllers and processors should also seek the views of affected data subjects and their representatives. However, such consultation should be without prejudice to the controller or processor's commercial interests, the public interest or the security of the processing operations in issue (Article 35(9)).

A processing operation may be necessary for compliance with a legal obligation to which the data controller is subject, or necessary for the performance of a task carried out in the public interest, or in the exercise of official authority vested in the data controller. Where such processing has a legal basis in EU or Member State law to which the controller is subject, and a general assessment was carried out in adoption of that law, a DPIA will not be necessary. Notwithstanding the foregoing, Member States may make conducting a DPIA a legal requirement prior to the commencement of any processing (Article 35(10)).

4.11   PRIOR CONSULTATION

An effective data protection impact assessment should identify and evaluate risks to data subjects, and propose strategies to address any risks that have been identified. The outcome will generally be that the identified risks may be avoided altogether, or, more likely, mitigated. However, in some circumstances, the risk to individuals may be unavoidable, and, in some cases, immitigable.

Where processing activities would, in the absence of safeguards, result in a high risk to data subjects that, in the opinion of the data controller, cannot reasonably be mitigated (in terms of available technologies and the costs of implementation of such technologies) the controller must consult with the supervisory authority prior to commencing the proposed processing activity. Processing activities may present a high risk because of their nature, frequency or extent. As part of the consultation process, the data controller should provide the outcome of any data protection impact assessment carried out, in particular any mitigation measures proposed to address the risk (Article 36 and Recital 94).

The prior consultation process allows the supervisory authority a period of eight weeks following the receipt of a request for consultation (per Article 36(2)) to exercise any of its powers (as set out in Article 58), including issuing a ban on processing (per Article 58(2)(f)). The eight-week period may be extended by a further six weeks in complex cases, subject to the supervisory authority informing the controller (and processor, where applicable) within one month of receiving the request for consultation, along with the reasons for the delay. The prescribed periods may be suspended until the authority has all the information requested for the purpose of the consultation.

A data controller seeking a consultation with the supervisory authority must provide the following:

- where applicable, the respective responsibilities of the controller, joint controllers and processors involved in the processing, in particular for processing carried out within a group of undertakings;
- the purpose and means of the intended processing;
- the measures and safeguards provided to protect data subjects' rights under the GDPR;
- the contact details of the DPO (where applicable);
- the data protection impact assessment conducted in relation to the proposed processing; and
- any other information requested by the supervisory authority (Article 36(3)).

Member States proposing to enact legislation or regulations that provide for the processing of personal data must also consult with the supervisory authority (Article 36(4) and Recital 96). For example, legislation around a government identity card scheme, a toll road system, or perhaps more pertinently, government surveillance legislation (in the light of the adoption of the controversial Investigatory Powers Act 2016), would be likely to require consultation. Further, Member State law may also require prior authorisation by the controller for the performance of a task carried out in the public interest, including social protection and public health (Article 36(5)).

4.12   DATA PROTECTION OFFICERS

The European Commission claimed that one of the benefits of the GDPR for business was the abolition of the requirement to notify the data protection authority. Notification can be particularly onerous for multinational organisations with multiple operations in each Member State. Multinational operators potentially face the challenge of maintaining a large number of filings across Europe, with each data protection authority imposing different requirements. However, the GDPR recognises that despite the administrative and financial burden it imposes, notification may do little to protect the underlying personal data (Recital 89).

The GDPR abolishes the requirement to notify, and instead imposes the obligation to appoint a DPO. The appointment of a DPO will be central to demonstrating compliance for many organisations, facilitating adherence to the provisions of the GDPR. According to the Article 29 Working Party, which issued guidelines on DPOs in December 2016 (WP 243),[3] the DPO is a 'cornerstone of accountability'.[4] The requirement to appoint a DPO is not completely new, with mandatory appointment generally required in Germany,[5] and in France and Sweden organisations may benefit from notification exemptions if they appoint voluntarily. In the

---

[3]   Article 29 Data Protection Working Party Guidelines on Data Protection Officers (DPOs) (WP 243) adopted on 13 December 2016.
[4]   WP 243, Section 1 (paragraph 5).
[5]   Pursuant to Section 4f(1) of the Federal Data Protection Act (Bundesdatenschutzgesetz), which implements the Directive in Germany.

UK, there is no legal requirement to appoint a DPO, though, in practice, many large organisations engaged in high-risk processing do so voluntarily.

The criteria triggering the mandatory appointment obligation have changed as the GDPR has evolved into its final form, and had originally included enterprises with 250 employees or more, and those processing personal data relating to more than 500 data subjects over a 12-month period. However, the final version of the GDPR provides that the following types of organisation, whether they are a data controller or processor, must appoint a DPO:

■   public authorities (except for courts acting in their judicial capacity);
■   organisations whose core activities require regular and systematic monitoring on a large scale; and
■   organisations whose core activities involve processing special categories of data and personal data relating to criminal convictions and offences, on a large scale (though note the comments in relation to the use of 'or' rather than 'and', below).

Considering each of these categories in more detail:

1.   **Public authorities**
      The GDPR does not define 'public authorities', which will instead be determined by Member State laws, and will include national, regional and local authorities. However, public tasks may also be carried out by natural or legal persons, for example in public transport, water and energy supply, road infrastructure, public service broadcasting, public housing or disciplinary bodies for regulated professions (according to Member State law). In such cases, data subjects may be in a similar position as when their personal data is processed by a public authority; the data subject has little choice as to how his or her data may be processed, and hence requires the additional protection of a DPO. In these situations, the Article 29 Working Party recommends that private organisations that carry out public tasks should appoint a DPO. The Working Party also recommends that, in the interests of good practice, the DPO should cover all the organisation's activities, i.e. not just the public function, but ancillary activities also such as processing an employee database, managing the organisation's IT system, or payroll (WP 243, Section 2.1.1).

2.   **Organisations whose core activities require regular and systematic monitoring on a large scale**
      In relation to data controllers in the private sector, 'core activities' relate to the primary activity of an organisation, and not its ancillary activities. The Article 29 Working Party opines '"Core activities" can be considered as the key operations necessary to achieve the controller's or processor's goals'. It observes that the core activity of a hospital is in providing healthcare, of which processing health data is an inextricable part, and, hence, the hospital must appoint a DPO (WP 243, Section 2.1.2). However, a data controller in the private sector that processes sensitive personal data because it has a substantial workforce and as a result its HR department holds information about employees' health, would not appear to trigger the appointment requirement (Recital 97).

Unless it is obvious that an organisation is not required to appoint a DPO, the Article 29 Working Party recommends that controllers and processors document the analysis they carry out in determining whether or not designation of a DPO is necessary (WP 243, Section 2.1).

The GDPR does not define 'large scale', although it does refer to processing operations that 'process a considerable amount of personal data at regional, national or supranational level and which could affect a large number of data subjects and which are likely to result in a high risk' (Recital 91). However, it specifically excludes processing of patients' health data or clients' personal data relating to criminal convictions or offences by an individual physician, other healthcare professional or lawyer.

The Article 29 Working Party proposes a consideration of the following factors in determining whether a particular processing activity is 'large scale':

(a)   the number of data subjects concerned, either as a specific number or a proportion of the relevant population;
(b)   the volume of data and/or the range of the different data items being processed;
(c)   the duration or permanence of the data processing activity; and
(d)   the geographical extent of the processing activity (WP 243, Section 2.1.3).

The Article 29 Working Party provides a number of examples of large-scale processing, including:

(a)   processing patient data in the regular course of business by a hospital;
(b)   processing of data relating to travel of individuals using a city's public transport system (e.g. tracking via travel cards);
(c)   processing of real time geo-location data of customers of an international fast food chain for statistical purposes by a processor specialised in providing these services;
(d)   processing of customer data in the regular course of business by an insurance company or a bank;
(e)   processing of personal data for behavioural advertising by a search engine; and
(f)   processing of data (content, traffic, location) by telephone or internet service providers.

The GDPR does not define regular and systematic monitoring of data subjects, though it does mention 'monitoring the behaviour of data subjects' in the Recitals, citing online tracking and profiling to predict preferences, behaviours and attitudes (Recital 24), which would include activities such as online behavioural advertising. However, the Article 29 Working Party cautions that the concept of monitoring is not confined to the online environment. It goes on to clarify that 'regular' means ongoing, or occurring at particular intervals for a particular period; recurring or repeated at fixed times; or constantly or periodically taking place. The Working Party interprets 'systematic' as meaning occurring according to a system, pre-arranged, organised or methodical, taking place as part of a general plan for data collection, or carried out as part of a strategy (WP 243, Section 2.1.4).

The Article 29 Working Party provides the following non-exhaustive list as examples of regular and systematic monitoring: operating a telecommunications network; providing telecommunications services; email retargeting; profiling and scoring for purposes of risk assessment (e.g. for purposes of credit scoring, establishment of insurance premiums, fraud prevention, detection of money laundering); location tracking (e.g. by mobile apps); loyalty programs; behavioural advertising; monitoring of wellness, fitness and health data via wearable devices; closed circuit television; connected devices (e.g. smart meters), smart cars, and home automation (WP 243, Section 2.1.4).

3. **Organisations whose core activities involve processing special categories of data and personal data relating to criminal convictions and offences, on a large scale**

   The third category of organisation that must appoint a DPO refers to those that process special categories of data and those that process personal data relating to criminal convictions (Article 37(1)(c)). The Article 29 Working Party observes that, while the provision uses the word 'and', there is no policy reason for the two criteria having to be applied simultaneously, and the text should be construed as meaning 'or' (WP 243, Section 2.1.5).

For all three categories, both the controller and the processor are potentially required to appoint a DPO. In practice, the mandatory designation requirement may only apply either to the controller or the processor, or to both, depending on the circumstances. The Article 29 Working Party provides the following examples to illustrate the point:

■ A small family business that sells household appliances locally in a small town uses a processor whose core activity is the provision of website analytics services. The family appliance business does not process personal data on a large scale, only limited activities affecting a small number of people. The website analytics processor provides similar services for a large number of small family businesses, which taken together amount to 'large-scale processing'. The processor would be required to appoint a DPO, since its core activities consist of systematic monitoring (of website users) on a large scale, though not the family business.

■ A medium-size tile manufacturer subcontracts its occupational health function to an external processor, which has a large number of similar clients. The external processor would need to appoint a DPO, as its core activities consist of processing special categories of data on a large scale, though the manufacturer would not need to appoint a DPO (WP 243, Section 2.2).

Where a processor does appoint a DPO, the Article 29 Working Party recommends that, as a matter of good practice, the DPO also oversees the processor's activities where the processor is also a controller in its own right (i.e. its HR, IT and logistics activities).

Groups of undertakings may appoint a single DPO provided he or she is easily accessible from each establishment (Article 37(2)). This could potentially allow a single DPO to cover establishments in different countries, provided that the data subjects' ease of access would not be inhibited by conflicting time zones or a language barrier, and the DPO can co-operate with the supervisory authority. In the context of public authorities, a single DPO may be designated for multiple authorities or bodies, where the structure and size of the organisation permits (Article 37(3)). The GDPR also allows a DPO to represent associations or other bodies that represent categories of data controllers or processors (Article 37(4)).

The DPO must have appropriate expert knowledge of data protection law and practices, including an in-depth understanding of the GDPR, and must be able to fulfil the tasks for which it is responsible (explained below) (Article 37(5)). 'Expert knowledge' is not expressly defined in the GDPR, but must be commensurate to the sensitivity, complexity and quantity of data processed by the organisation, as well as whether personal data is transferred out of Europe routinely or only occasionally (WP 243, Section 2.4). The DPO may be a member of staff of the data controller or processor, or the role may be fulfilled by way of a service contract (Article 37(6)). This a useful option as it allows the controller or processor to outsource the role to an external third party, such as a law firm. In Germany, where appointment is mandatory for many organisations, outsourcing the DPO role to an external provider is common practice. Given the likely shortage of potential candidates with expertise in data protection law and practice, the ability to outsource the DPO function is likely to be an attractive and cost-effective alternative to hiring a full-time employee.

Where the DPO function is outsourced to an external team (as opposed to an individual), the Article 29 Working Party recommends clearly allocating tasks within the team, assigning a single individual as the lead contact point for each client (and specifying these points in the service contract) (WP 243, Section 2.4). The Working Party also observes that an organisation providing external DPO services would need to fulfil the same requirements as an individual DPO, for example, ensuring no one in the external team has a conflict of interests.

The DPO is not personally responsible for non-compliance with the GDPR, which makes it clear that the controller or processor is responsible for demonstrating adherence to its provisions (Article 24(1)). However, organisations must ensure the DPO is involved properly and in a timely manner in all issues involving the processing of personal data (Article 38(1)), which would include ensuring the DPO is regularly invited to meetings involving senior and middle management, and ensuring he or she is present when decisions concerning the processing of personal data are made. Early inclusion of the DPO, and ensuring that he or she is included and consulted at the outset regarding any activity that concerns personal data will enable compliance with the GDPR, and hence should be a standard procedure within an organisation's governance (WP 243, Section 3.1).

The DPO's opinion should be given due weight, and where the controller or processor takes a decision that is incompatible with that of the DPO, the DPO should be able to make his or her dissenting opinion clear to such controller or processor (WP 243, Section 3.3). As a matter of good practice, the organisation should document situations where it chooses not to follow the DPO's advice. The DPO must also be informed of any data breaches or other occurrences (WP 243, Section 3.1).

Organisations must support the DPO in performing his or her tasks, by providing appropriate resources, access to personal data and providing resources to allow the DPO to maintain his or her expert knowledge (Article 38(2)). This includes providing active support from senior management, and allowing the DPO sufficient time to fulfil his or her duties, which will be of particular relevance where this forms part of an employee's role. Where an employee's job function includes other responsibilities in addition to the DPO role, a potential conflict exists which could result in the DPO function being neglected. Generally, organisations involved with more complex and/or sensitive processing activities will need to provide greater resources to the DPO (WP 243, Section 3.2).

Controllers and processors must publish the contact details of the DPO (i.e. postal address, telephone number, and email address) and inform the supervisory authority of such details (Article 37(7)), though the DPO need not be named personally and may instead simply be referred to as 'The Data Protection Officer'. The purpose of making the DPO's contact details public is to enable data subjects within and outside the organisation to easily, directly and confidentially contact the DPO without having to contact any other part of the organisation.

The DPO must also report to the controller or processor's highest management level. In practice, this is likely to be the board of directors, which suggests that the DPO will be a senior role. The DPO must be bound by an obligation of secrecy or confidentiality regarding the performance of his or her tasks (Article 38(5)). Data controllers and processors are specifically prohibited from instructing the DPO regarding the exercise of his or her tasks (Article 38(3)), as a measure to ensure the DPO is able to perform the role with a sufficient degree of autonomy. The prohibition on giving the DPO instructions would prevent, for example, data controllers and/processors giving instructions on what result should be achieved, how to investigate a complaint, or whether to consult with the supervisory authority. Nor should the DPO be instructed to take a specified view of an issue relating to data protection law, for example, a particular interpretation of the law. However, the DPO's autonomy does not extend beyond his or her tasks as set out in the GDPR (WP 243, Section 3.3).

As a further means of reinforcing the DPO's autonomy, organisations may not dismiss or otherwise penalise the DPO for performing his or her tasks (Article 38(3)). For example, a DPO could not be dismissed for obstructing proposed marketing activities that were in breach of applicable rules. Penalties could include actual or threatened absence or delay of promotion, prevention of career advancement, and denial of benefits that other employees receive. However, the prohibition on dismissal or other penalties only exists in relation to the DPO's tasks under the GDPR, and does not provide complete immunity from sanctions for other reasons, such as theft, physical, psychological or sexual harassment, or other gross misconduct.

The position need not necessarily be full time, since the DPO may perform other tasks, provided they do not result in a conflict of interest (Article 38(6)). A conflict of interest would be likely to arise if the DPO also holds a position within the organisation which requires him or her to decide the purposes for which and the manner in which personal data are processed. The potential for a conflict of interest arises with many roles within an organisation, and the following positions may be incompatible with the role of DPO:

- chief executive officer, Director, Corporate Administrators, or other managerial positions that are legally or statutorily compulsory;
- head of IT/IT Administrator;
- head of HR;
- head of Marketing;
- head of Sales;
- head of Legal; and
- executives of corporate units processing massive or sensitive personal data.[6]

The conflict of interests point has already lead to regulatory action. In October 2016, the Bavarian Data Protection Authority took action against an organisation that appointed its IT manager as the DPO, because the DPO would be required to monitor whether his activities in his capacity as an IT manager were in accordance with applicable data protection law.[7] It seems likely that under the GDPR, there will be more regulatory intervention where organisations appoint a DPO who has a conflict of interests. Accordingly, organisations should take steps to avoid any such potential conflicts of interest.

The GDPR states that the DPO shall have at least the following tasks (Article 39):

1. Informing and advising the organisation and its employees, who carry out the processing, of their obligations to ensure compliance with the GDPR and other applicable data protection laws.
2. Monitoring compliance with the GDPR and other EU or Member State data protection provisions, and the policies of the controller or processor. This includes assigning responsibilities, raising awareness and training of staff involved in data processing, and conducting related audits.
3. Monitoring compliance could also include collecting information to identify processing activities, analysing the compliance of such activities, and issuing recommendations to the controller or the processor. However, this does not mean that the DPO is personally responsible for instances of non-compliance (WP 243, Section 4.1). The responsibility for compliance with the GDPR sits with the data controller or data processor.
4. Advising the data controller on DPIAs; in particular, whether to carry one out,

---

[6]   'Data Protection Officers According to German Law', Blog article published by Peter Fleischer, Chief Privacy Officer for Google (though writing in a personal capacity) 27 August 2007 (**peterfleischer.blogspot.co.uk/2007/08/data-protection-officers-according-to.html**).

[7]   The Bavarian State Commissioner for Data Protection ('BayLDA') announcement of 20 October 2016.

the approach to follow and whether to use internal or external resources to perform the assessment. The DPO can recommend safeguards to mitigate the risks to data subjects, and advise whether a DPIA has been carried out correctly, and whether its conclusions are valid. However, the DPO's role is advisory; the data controller is responsible for carrying out DPIAs, and may choose to disregard the DPO's recommendations, although where a controller does disregard such recommendations, it should document the decision process (WP 243, Section 4.2).

5.   Co-operating with the supervisory authority.
6.   Acting as the point of contact for the supervisory authority in relation to issues concerning processing, including prior consultations (per Article 36), and consulting, where appropriate, with regard to any other matters.

In performing these tasks, the DPO should take a risk-based approach (Article 39(2)). In practice, this means the DPO should focus primarily on the issues that present the higher data protection risks. This approach would assist the DPO, for example, in advising the controller on the appropriate methodology for conducting a data protection impact assessment, which areas of the organisation require an internal or external audit, the appropriate level of staff training, and which of the organisation's activities should be treated as a priority (WP 243, Section 4.3).

The GDPR states that the DPO should have at least the tasks explained above. However, the Article 29 Working party observes that, while it is the responsibility of the controller or the processor to maintain a register of data processing activities Article 30(1) and (2)), in practice, the task could also be undertaken by the DPO. The DPO will often create data inventories based on information provided by the various departments within the organisation responsible for the data, and hence will be well placed to maintain registers of processing activities (WP 243, Section 4.4).

In practice, the DPO is also likely to assume responsibility for the following activities, particularly in smaller organisations where he or she is the only member of staff with any data protection knowledge:

1.   Dealing with subject access requests and right to be forgotten requests.
2.   Reporting data breaches to affected data subjects.
3.   Implementing and updating policies and procedures.
4.   Dealing with enquiries and complaints from data subjects.

The GDPR does not require all businesses to appoint a DPO. However, given the increased obligations imposed upon data controllers and processors, it may be prudent for many organisations to consider appointing a DPO on a voluntary basis. Indeed, the Article 29 Working Party expressly encourages voluntary appointment (WP 243, Section 1). However, where an organisation does decide to voluntarily designate a DPO, the same provisions that apply to mandatory appointments will bind the controller or processor in relation to a voluntary DPO (the requirements are found in Articles 37 to 39). In particular, this includes the requirement that the DPO has appropriate expertise, must be involved in all issues relating to the protection of personal data, report to the highest level of the organisation's management, be able to operate independently and cannot be dismissed for performing his or her tasks. Accordingly, controllers or processors considering voluntarily appointing a DPO, should be mindful of the potential obligations they could inadvertently assume. In principle, these obligations could arise not only from voluntarily hiring a full-time DPO, but also from hiring a part-time DPO, or training an existing employee to assume the role on a full-time or part-time basis, or even where the role is outsourced to an external provider.

The Article 29 Working Party observes that there is nothing to prevent an organisation that does not wish to voluntarily appoint a DPO, and is not legally required to appoint one, from using an external adviser to provide data protection related services. However, the organisation would have to make it clear in the engagement contract and any communications within or outside the company or to the supervisory authority, that the provider is not the DPO (WP 243, Section 2.1).

4.13   CODES OF CONDUCT AND CERTIFICATION SCHEMES

The GDPR promotes the use of codes of conduct and certification schemes as a means of enabling the proper application of its provisions (Article 40(1)), to enhance transparency and compliance, and to allow data subjects to quickly assess the level of data protection of relevant products and services (Recital 100). The use of codes of conduct is not a novel concept, and can be found in the Directive, which envisaged their use by trade associations and other representative bodies (Directive, Article 27). An example of a code approved under the Directive is the FEDMA (Federation of European Direct Marketing) code of conduct, which was approved by the Article 29 Working Party.[8] More recently, the Cloud Infrastructure Service Providers in Europe (CISPE) code of conduct[9] provides an example of a GDPR compliant code, and is intended to comply with the new law when it comes into force in May 2018. Importantly, the potential scope of codes of conduct and certification schemes is not limited to domestic or even pan-European associations or bodies. A broader aim of the GDPR is the promotion of approved codes of conduct, data protection certification marks and seals as a means of enabling international data transfers to third countries.[10]

The GDPR expressly requires Member States, supervisory authorities, the Board and the European Commission to encourage the adoption of codes of conduct (Article 40(1)). It envisages a tailored approach, which may be executed by associations (for example trade, professional, industry or sector associations) or

---

[8]   Opinion 3/2003, Document WP 77; and Opinion 4/2010, Document WP 174.
[9]   CISPE Data Protection Code of Conduct for Cloud Infrastructure Service Providers, published 27 January 2017.
[10]   Communication from the Commission to the European Parliament and the Council: Exchanging and Protecting Personal Data in a Globalised World (Brussels, 10.1.2017, COM(2017) 7 Final, Section 32.

other representative bodies that are able to recognise the specific characteristics of particular sectors, as well as the needs of micro, small, and medium-sized enterprises. Codes of conduct may be used to calibrate the obligations of controllers or processors in proportion to the risks in the processing they undertake (Recital 98). This could, for example, assist a controller or processor in deciding the appropriate degree of action required to address a low, medium or high risk. The GDPR envisages that associations and representative bodies should engage in consultation with data subjects and other stakeholders in the implementation and maintenance of codes of conduct (Recital 99).

Codes of conduct should address the application of the GDPR, which may include considerations such as:

- fair and transparent processing;
- the legitimate interests of data controllers in specific contexts;
- the collection of personal data;
- the pseudonymisation of personal data;
- the information to be provided to the public and to data subjects;
- the exercise of data subjects' rights;
- the information provided to, and protection of, children, and obtaining parental consent;
- data controllers' responsibilities, including data protection by design and default and security of processing;
- notification of breaches to data subjects and supervisory authorities;
- transfers to third countries and to international organisations; and
- out of court proceedings and dispute resolution processes between data controllers and data subjects (Article 40(2)).

Organisations that are not subject to the GDPR (i.e. that are neither established in the EU, nor offering goods or services within the EU, nor monitoring EU citizens) may also adhere to approved codes of conduct to demonstrate appropriate safeguards in order to enable data transfers to third countries or international organisations. In other words, approved codes of conduct and certification schemes may be used as the basis of a data transfer solution to third countries. Where they rely on approved codes or certification schemes, organisations must make binding and enforceable commitments, using contractual or other legally binding instruments, to apply those safeguards (Article 40(3)). In other words, organisations must ensure the code is legally binding upon them, akin to binding corporate rules.[11]

An approved code of conduct must include mechanisms to enable the representative body or association responsible for developing the code to carry out mandatory monitoring of compliance with its provisions (without prejudice to any competent supervisory authorities' powers) (Article 40(4)). Representative associations or

---

[11] For further explanation, see for example, Article 29 Working Party Working Document: Transfers of personal data to third countries: Applying Article 26(2) of the EU Data Protection Directive to Binding Corporate Rules for International Data Transfers (WP 74), adopted 3 June 2003.

bodies that intend to prepare a code of conduct, or amend or extend an existing one, must submit a draft of that code (or amendment or extension) to the competent supervisory authority for approval. The supervisory authority should then provide an opinion on whether the code complies with the GDPR, and, if it is satisfied that the code contains appropriate safeguards, issue an approval (Article 40(5)). Where the supervisory authority approves a code that does not relate to processing in several Member States, the authority must register and publish the code (Article 40(6)).

Where a code of conduct relates to processing activities in several Member States, the competent supervisory authority must submit the draft code to the Board, in order to apply the consistency mechanism. The Board should then issue an opinion on whether the code of conduct meets the requirements of the GDPR, or, in the case of a code intended to enable data transfers to third countries, issue an opinion as to whether the code provides appropriate safeguards (Article 40(7)). Where a code of conduct meets the requirements of the GDPR, or provides appropriate safeguards, the Board must submit its opinion to the European Commission (Article 40(8)). The Commission may decide, by way of an implementing act, that the approved code of conduct is valid throughout the EU (Article 40(9)), and if so, ensure it is appropriately publicised (Article 40(10)). The Board must collate all approved codes of conduct, amendments and extensions in a public register (Article 40(11)).

Representative associations or bodies may, subject to having appropriate expertise and approval by the supervisory authority, monitor organisations' compliance with approved codes of conduct (Article 41(1)). A representative body may be accredited to monitor compliance with its approved code of conduct if it fulfils the following criteria:

- it is able to demonstrate its independence and expertise in relation to the subject matter to the satisfaction of the competent supervisory authority;
- it has established procedures which allow it to assess the eligibility of controllers and processors concerned to apply the code, to monitor their compliance with its provisions and to periodically review its operation;
- it has established procedures and structures to handle complaints about infringements of the code and the manner in which the code has been or is being implemented by controllers or processors, and to make those procedures and structures transparent to data subjects and the public; and
- it has demonstrated to the satisfaction of the competent supervisory authority that its tasks and duties do not result in a conflict of interests (Article 41(2)).

The competent supervisory authority must submit the draft criteria for accreditation of a representative body or association to the Board, pursuant to the consistency mechanism (Article 41(3)). Without prejudice to the competent supervisory authority's powers, the representative body or association may, subject to appropriate safeguards, take appropriate action in cases of infringement of a code of conduct by a data controller or processor, including suspension or exclusion from the code. The body or association must inform the competent supervisory authority of any such actions and its reasons for taking them (Article 41(4)). Competent supervisory authorities must revoke the accreditation of a body or association that no longer fulfils the criteria for accreditation, or infringes the GDPR (Article 41(5)). Note that these monitoring provisions do not apply to processing carried out by any public authority or body (Article 41(6)).

The GDPR also requires Member States, supervisory authorities, the Board and the European Commission to encourage, in particular at an EU level, data protection certification mechanisms, and data protection seals and marks. These certification mechanisms, seals and marks are intended to demonstrate compliance with the GDPR, and, like approved codes of conduct, should take into account the specific needs of micro, small and medium-sized entities (Article 42(1)). As with approved codes of conduct, organisations not subject to the GDPR (i.e. not established in the EU, nor offering goods or services to EU citizens, nor monitoring citizens' behaviour within the EU), may use certificates, seals or marks to demonstrate appropriate safeguards in the context of international transfers, provided they are legally binding upon the organisation (Article 42(2)).

Certification schemes should be voluntary, and available via a transparent process (Article 42(3)). Such schemes do not absolve a data controller or processor from its obligation to comply with the provisions of the GDPR, nor would adherence to an approved certification scheme limit the supervisory authority's powers (Article 42(4)). A certification may be issued by an accredited certification body, the competent supervisory authority, or the Board. Criteria approved by the Board may result in a common certification, the European Data Protection Seal (Article 42(5)). To obtain such a certification, an organisation must provide the certification body or supervisory authority with all information and access to its processing activities as may be necessary to conduct the certification procedure (Article 42(6)). Certifications may be issued for a maximum three-year period, after which they may be renewed if the certified organisation continues to meet the criteria, or withdrawn by the certification body or competent supervisory authority if they are not (Article 42(7)). The Board must maintain a public register of all certification mechanisms, data protection seals and marks (Article 42(8)).

Certification bodies with appropriate data protection expertise may issue and renew certifications without prejudice and subject to the competent supervisory authority's tasks and powers (Article 43(1)). In particular, the competent supervisory authority may withdraw a certification, or order the certification body to withdraw a certification or refuse to issue a certification if the requirements for certification are not met (Article 58(2)(h)).

Member States must ensure that certification bodies are accredited either by the competent supervisory authority or the national accreditation body (Article 43(1)). In order to be accredited, a certification body must fulfil each of the following criteria:

■   it must be able to demonstrate its independence and expertise in relation to the subject matter of the certification, to the satisfaction of the competent supervisory authority;

- it must undertake to respect the relevant certification criteria approved by the competent supervisory authority or by the Board;
- it must have established procedures for the issuing, periodic review and withdrawal of data protection certificates, seals and marks;
- it must have established structures and procedures to handle complaints about infringements of the certification or the manner in which the certification has been or is being implemented by the controller or processor, and to make those procedures and structures transparent to data subjects; and
- it must be able to demonstrate, to the satisfaction of the supervisory authority, that its tasks and duties do not result in a conflict of interests (Article 43(2)).

Certification bodies may only be accredited on the basis of criteria approved by the competent supervisory authority (i.e. the supervisory authority of the Member State in which the certification body is established or, in the case of a certification body established in more than one Member State, the lead supervisory authority) or the Board, pursuant to the consistency mechanism (Article 43(3)). Approved certification bodies are responsible for the proper assessment leading to certification or its withdrawal, though the data controller or processor remains responsible for compliance with the GDPR (Article 44(4)), and the certification body must provide the competent supervisory authority with the reason for its grant or withdrawal of certification (Article 44(5)).

Supervisory authorities must make public in an easily accessible form their approval requirements for certification bodies. Supervisory authorities must also transmit their requirements and criteria to the Board, which will collate all certification mechanisms and privacy seals in a publicly available register (Article 43(6)). Without prejudice to the supervisory authority's other powers, such supervisory authority, or the relevant national accreditation body may revoke the accreditation of a certification body that does not, or no longer, meets the supervisory authority's or national accreditation body's criteria, or where the certification body's actions infringe the GDPR (Article 43(7)). The European Commission may adopt delegated acts specifying the requirements that must be taken into account in establishing data protection certification mechanisms, seals and marks (Article 43(8)). The European Commission may also adopt implementing acts that specify the technical standards for certification mechanisms, data protection seals and marks, and that promote and recognise such mechanisms, seals and marks (Article 43(9)).

5 DATA TRANSFERS

An initial glance might suggest that the GDPR differs little from the Directive *vis-à-vis* data transfers. Like the Directive,[1] the GDPR generally prohibits the transfer of personal data to 'third countries',[2] i.e. countries outside the EEA,[3] unless personal data are adequately protected. The GDPR recognises a number of specific situations where personal data are adequately protected. These situations are as follows: where an adequacy finding has been made in respect of the destination third country; one of a number of specific situations which give rise to a derogation from the general prohibition on data transfers; and where the recipient data controller or processor in a third country has adopted contractual measures to ensure that personal data is appropriately protected. However, the GDPR has far-reaching ambitions and includes provisions intended to promote itself as a model data protection system, or 'gold standard' to which third countries should aspire.

The European Commission issued a communication on data transfers (COM(2017)7),[4] in which it observes the increasing global recognition of privacy as a fundamental right of individuals, and an opportunity for businesses to gain a competitive advantage through enhancing confidence in their services. COM(2017)7 observes that many legal systems outside Europe are in the process of adopting, or have already adopted, data protection laws, and that greater compatibility between such data protection legislation would facilitate international flows of personal data. The Commission advocates that the EU should seize the opportunity to promote its data protection values and encourage convergence between legal systems (COM(2017)7, Section 1). COM(2017)7 holds the GDPR out as a means of satisfying the dual aims of ensuring the protection of individuals' personal data, while enabling global trade. It asserts that giving individuals control of their data will result in greater trust in the digital economy and goes on to claim that the

---

[1] The data transfer provisions of Directive 95/46/EC are set out in Articles 25 and 26.
[2] The data transfer provisions of the GDPR are set out in Articles 44 to 50.
[3] The EEA (European Economic Area) consists of the EU Member States, Iceland, Liechtenstein and Norway.
[4] Communication from the Commission to the European Parliament and the Council: Exchanging and Protecting Personal Data in a Globalised World (Brussels, 10 January 2017, COM(2017) 7 Final).

EU offers the highest level of protection for individuals, while allowing international data flows. Ambitiously, COM(2017)7 proposes that EU should be 'a hub for data services which require both free flows and trust' (COM(2017)7, Section 2).

COM(2017)7 asserts that the GDPR provides for a single, pan-European set of consistently-applied rules, and claims a levelling of the playing field with third countries by applying the same rules as those applied to countries within the EU to non-European companies doing business with EU citizens (COM(2017)7, Section 2.1). COM(2017)7 explains the mechanism by which non-EU countries can be assessed to establish whether they adequately protect personal data (COM(2017)7, Section 2.2).

The GDPR prohibits the transfer of personal data that is undergoing processing, or intended for processing after transfer, to third countries and international organisations, other than in accordance with its provisions. It also prohibits the onward transfer of personal data to further third countries or international organisations without appropriate safeguards in place to protect personal data (Article 44). Data transfers must be in accordance with the GDPR in order to ensure that flows of data outside the EU should not undermine data subjects' protection (Recital 101).

The GDPR is without prejudice to any existing international agreements that may have been concluded between the EU and third countries regulating the transfer of personal data. Further, Member States may conclude international agreements involving the transfer of personal data to third countries or international organisations, provided such agreements do not contravene the provisions of the GDPR, and the rights of data subjects are adequately protected (Recital 102). However, where a judgment of a court or tribunal, or any decision of an administrative authority of a third country requires a data controller or processor to transfer or disclose personal data, the GDPR expressly provides that such a judgment or decision must be based on an international agreement between the EU or Member State and that third country. For instance, a mutual legal assistance treaty would be an example of such an international agreement (Article 48 and Recital 115).

Under the GDPR, personal data may be transferred to a third country in the following circumstances:

- where an adequacy decision has been made in respect of the destination country;
- where the transfer is subject to appropriate safeguards;
- where the transfer is between members of a group of undertakings or enterprises that have adopted binding corporate rules; and
- in one of the specific situations where a derogation applies.

Each of these grounds for transferring personal data is now considered.

5.1 TRANSFERS ON THE BASIS OF AN ADEQUACY DECISION

The GDPR provides that the European Commission may approve third countries, regions or sectors as providing adequate protection where they meet certain specified criteria (explained below in this section). The effect of such a decision is to enable the free flow of personal data from an EU Member State to a third country without the need for the data exporter having to implement any additional safeguards or obtain any further approval from the competent supervisory authority. Transferring personal data to a country, region or sector that has had an adequacy finding made in its favour is, to all intents and purposes, equivalent to transferring personal data to another EU Member State. As well as making adequacy findings, the Commission may also revoke an adequacy finding provided it gives notice and a full statement setting out the reasons for its decision (Article 45 and Recital 103).

The European Commission may make an adequacy finding in respect of a whole third country, region or sector, or may make a partial adequacy finding. For instance, the US Privacy Shield applies to US organisations that voluntarily adhere to the certification scheme, while Canada has an adequacy finding in respect of private sector organisations that are subject to the Canadian Personal Information Protection and Electronic Documents Act (also known as PIPEDA). The European Commission suggests that adequacy findings could be made for specific sectors in a third country, for instance financial services or IT.

To obtain an adequacy decision, a country must demonstrate a level of protection comparable (or 'essentially equivalent') to that of the EU (COM(2017)7, Section 3.1). An adequacy finding does not require a facsimile of European data protection rules, but the foreign system as a whole must deliver the same level of data protection. Existing adequacy decisions made pursuant to the Directive reflect that the European Commission recognises a diverse range of privacy systems.[5] Diverse as they may be, the Commission observes that those privacy systems share a common core of principles, which are:

- the recognition of privacy as a fundamental right;
- the adoption of overarching data protection legislation;
- the existence of enforceable individual privacy rights; and
- the establishment of an independent supervisory authority (COM(2017)7, Section 3.1).

The Commission observes the proliferation of data protection laws around the world, and recognises the opportunity to further facilitate international data flows, while simultaneously guaranteeing individuals' privacy rights. It takes a surprisingly political approach in relation to deciding with which third countries to pursue a dialogue on adequacy, and cites that relevant considerations may include the following: the extent of commercial relations between the third country and the EU; the extent of personal data flows, reflecting geographical and/or cultural ties; the pioneering role that a third country plays in the field of privacy and data protection that could serve as a model for other countries in the region; and the overall political relationship with the third country in question. The Commission

---

[5]   To date, the European Commission has made adequacy findings in respect of Switzerland, Andorra, Faroe Islands, Guernsey, Jersey, Isle of Man, Argentina, Canada (partial), Israel, the United States (partial), New Zealand and Uruguay.

expresses an intent to engage with Japan, Korea and India, Latin America and the 'European neighbourhood' (COM(2017)7, Section 3.1).

When assessing the adequacy of the protection provided by a third country, the Commission should consider the following elements:

- the rule of law, respect for human rights and fundamental freedoms and access to justice;
- the third country's general and sectoral law, including legislation concerning public security, defence and national security and the access of public authorities to personal data, public order and criminal law and the implementation of such legislation;
- data protection rules, professional rules and security measures, including rules concerning onward transfer to third countries and international organisations, enforceable data subject rights and effective administrative and judicial redress for the data subjects whose personal data are transferred;
- the existence of an effective, independent supervisory authority, with responsibility for ensuring and enforcing compliance with the data protection rules, assisting and advising data subjects in exercising their rights and co-operation with the supervisory authorities of the Member States, as well as adequate enforcement powers; and
- the international commitments that the third country or organisation has entered into, including legally binding conventions or instruments, and participation in regional systems in particular in relation to the protection of personal data (Article 45(2) and Recital 104).

The third country must ensure:

- an adequate level of protection essentially equivalent to that ensured within the EU, in particular where personal data are processed in one or several specific sectors;
- effective independent data protection supervision and provision for co-operation mechanisms with the Member States' data protection authorities; and
- that data subjects are provided with effective and enforceable rights and effective administrative and judicial redress (Recital 104).

The GDPR provides that the European Commission may make an adequacy finding in respect of a third country or international organisation, by way of an implementing act. Implementing acts must provide for a periodic review of the finding at least every four years, and take into account all relevant developments in that third country or organisation. The implementing act must also specify the applicable territory or sector and relevant supervisory authority (Article 45(3)). However, an adequacy finding is in effect a 'living' decision, since the GDPR expressly requires the Commission, on an ongoing basis, to monitor developments in third countries and international organisations that could affect the functioning of an adequacy decision made under the GDPR or under the Directive (Article 45(4) and Recital 106). The ability to revoke an adequacy finding is particularly pertinent, given the annulment of the EU/US Safe Harbour agreement,[6] and the process is likely to see regular use, given the challenges mounted against the US Privacy Shield,[7] and the approved EU model clauses.

Where information reveals that a third country, territory or specified sector (within a third country) in respect of which an adequacy decision has been made no longer ensures an adequate level of protection, the European Commission may repeal, amend or suspend such decision. Any repeal, amendment or suspension may be by way of an implementing act, adopted in accordance with the Committee Procedure as set out in the GDPR. Such acts cannot have a retroactive effect, i.e. cannot apply to data transfers that have taken place before the repeal, amendment or suspension; however, it may be immediately applicable where there is a justified need for urgency (Article 45(5)). The Commission must enter into consultations with the third country in question with a view to remedying the situation (Article 45(6)). Any repeal, amendment or suspension is without prejudice to transfers to that third country made on the basis of other means permitted under the GDPR, including where there are adequate safeguards, binding corporate rules, or where a derogation applies (Article 45(7) and Recital 107). The European Commission is to publish a list in the *Official Journal of the European Union* of those third countries in respect of which adequacy decisions were made, but which no longer guarantee an adequate level of protection (Article 45(8)). Any adequacy decisions made by the European Commission under the Directive remain in force until amended, replaced or repealed in accordance with the requirements of the GDPR (Article 45(9)).

5.2   TRANSFERS SUBJECT TO APPROPRIATE SAFEGUARDS

In addition to an adequacy decision in respect of a country, territory or sector, the GDPR provides a number of alternatives, offering a range of data transfer options to organisations established in the EU. It allows instruments to be developed for specific circumstances, such as standard contractual clauses (SCCs) and binding corporate rules (BCRs). Both of these options exist as data transfer mechanisms under the Directive; however the GDPR offers further data transfer options in the form of approved codes of conduct and accredited third party certifications (explained in **Chapter 4**). These additional data transfer solutions offer organisations additional flexibility and may be tailored to the specific needs of particular industries or sectors. The European Commission envisages the GDPR as providing a 'toolkit for international transfers' and expresses an intent to work with stakeholders to realise its potential. Particular areas of focus for the Commission include priority issues such as developing data processor to data processor SCCs, and promoting convergence between BCRs under European law and the Cross Border

---

[6]   See *Maximillian Schrems* v. *Data Protection Commissioner*, Case C-362/14, 6 October 2015.
[7]   See *Digital Rights Ireland* v. *Commission*, Case T-670/16 and La Quadrature du Net and Others v Commission, Case T-738/16.

Privacy Rules developed by the Asia Pacific Economic Cooperation (APEC) (COM(2017)7, Section 3.2).

In the absence of an adequacy decision, the GDPR provides the following appropriate safeguards to enable data controllers and processors to transfer personal data out of the EEA:

- a legally binding and enforceable instrument between public authorities or bodies;
- BCRs;
- standard data protection clauses adopted by the European Commission;
- standard data protection clauses adopted by a supervisory authority and approved by the Commission;
- an approved code of conduct, together with binding and enforceable commitments of the controller or processor located in the third country to apply the appropriate safeguards, including as regards data subjects' rights; and
- an approved certification, together with binding and enforceable commitments of the controller or processor located in the third country to apply the appropriate safeguards, including as regards data subjects' rights (Article 46(2) and Recital 108).

Data controllers or processors that rely on standard data protection clauses adopted by the Commission or the competent supervisory authority may incorporate such clauses into wider contracts (for instance in a contract between the processor and another processor), or add additional clauses or safeguards, provided that doing so does not prejudice the affected data subjects' rights. The GDPR encourages data controllers and processors to supplement data protection clauses with additional safeguards (Recital 109).

The GDPR also provides that appropriate safeguards may be provided by the following means:

- contractual clauses between the controller or processor and the controller, processor or recipient of personal data in a third country or international organisation; or
- provisions to be inserted into administrative arrangements between public authorities or bodies (such as memoranda of understanding) which include enforceable and effective data subjects' rights.

The safeguards permissible under the GDPR should ensure compliance with the data protection requirements of the GDPR, and the rights of the data subjects appropriate to processing within the EU. They should include the availability of enforceable data subjects' rights and enforceable legal remedies, including conferring upon the data subject the right to obtain effective administrative or judicial redress, and to claim compensation in the EU or the third country concerned. In particular, safeguards should relate to compliance with the general principles relating to the processing of personal data, and data protection by design and by default. Where safeguards provided for in administrative arrangements are not legally binding, the GDPR recommends that authorisation should be obtained from the competent supervisory authority (Recital 108).

Any adequacy decisions made by a Member State in respect of a data controller in a third country, pursuant to Article 26(2) of the Directive, remains valid until amended, replaced or repealed by the competent supervisory authority. Likewise, any SCCs approved by the European Commission, pursuant to Article 26(4) of the Directive will also remain valid until amended, replaced or repealed by the Commission in accordance with the procedure prescribed under the GDPR (Article 46(5)).

5.3   BINDING CORPORATE RULES

BCRs are a set of corporate rules, which allow a group of undertakings, or a group of enterprises engaged in a joint economic activity, to enable the transfer of personal data from within the EU to organisations within the same group of undertakings or group of enterprises, but located outside the EU. The purpose of the BCRs is to ensure that such transferred personal data remains protected by the principles of the GDPR, and the affected data subjects' rights are upheld (Recital 110).

BCRs are not expressly mentioned in the Directive, but are enabled under Article 26(2), which allows Member States to authorise the transfer of personal data if they are satisfied that appropriate safeguards have been adduced. Article 26(2) of Directive 95/46/EC provides as follows:

> Without prejudice to paragraph 1, a Member State may authorize a transfer or a set of transfers of personal data to a third country which does not ensure an adequate level of protection within the meaning of Article 25(2), where the controller adduces adequate safeguards with respect to the protection of the privacy and fundamental rights and freedoms of individuals and as regards the exercise of the corresponding rights; such safeguards may in particular result from appropriate contractual clauses.

As approval is at a Member State level, not all data protection authorities have taken the same view of BCRs, with the result that they are recognised in some EU jurisdictions, but not in others. The GDPR rationalises the position, expressly recognising BCRs, and setting out the criteria upon which they must be approved by the competent supervisory authority.

The GDPR stipulates that the competent supervisory authority must approve BCRs if they fulfil the following requirements:

- they are legally binding and apply to and are enforced by every member concerned of the group of undertakings, or group of enterprises engaged in a joint economic activity (including employees);
- they expressly confer enforceable rights on the data subjects whose data are processed; and
- they fulfil the requirements below (Article 47(1)).

The GDPR requires that BCRs specify at least the following:

- the structure and contact details of the group of undertakings, or group of enterprises engaged in a joint economic activity and each of its members;
- the data transfers or set of transfers, including the categories of personal data, the type of processing and its purposes, the type of data subject and the identification of the third country or countries in question;
- their legally-binding nature, both internally and externally; and
- the application of the general data protection principles, in particular:

  (a) purpose limitation;
  (b) data minimisation;
  (c) limited storage periods;
  (d) data quality;
  (e) data protection by design and by default;
  (f) legal basis for processing;
  (g) processing of special categories of personal data;
  (h) measures to ensure data security; and
  (i) the requirements in respect of onward transfers to bodies not bound by the binding corporate rules;

- the rights of data subjects in regard to processing and the means to exercise those rights, including:

  (a) the right not to be subject to decisions based solely on automated processing, including profiling;
  (b) the right to lodge a complaint with the competent supervisory authority and before the competent courts of the Member States; and
  (c) the right to obtain redress and, where appropriate, compensation for the breach of the binding corporate rules;

- the acceptance by the controller or processor established in the territory of a Member State of liability for any breaches of the BCRs by any member concerned not established in the EU. Notwithstanding that the controller or processor shall be exempt from that liability, in whole or in part, only if it proves that the member is not responsible for the event giving rise to the damage;
- how the information on the binding corporate rules is provided to data subjects, in particular:

  (a) the application of the data protection principles;
  (b) the rights of data subjects;
  (c) the acceptance by the controller or processor of liability for breaches of the BCRs by members outside the EU; and
  (d) the transparency information to be provided to data subjects pursuant to Articles 13 and 14 of the GDPR;

- the tasks of the DPO if designated or any other person or entity responsible for monitoring compliance with the BCRs within the group of undertakings or group of enterprises engaged in the same joint activity, as well as monitoring training and complaint handling;
- the complaint procedures;

■ the mechanisms within the group of undertakings or enterprises engaged in the same joint economic activity for ensuring the verification of compliance with the BCRs, subject to the following requirements:

(a) such mechanisms should include data protection audits and methods for ensuring corrective actions to protect the rights of the data subject; and

(b) the results of such verification should be communicated to: the DPO or other person or entity responsible for monitoring compliance with the BCRs; the board of the controlling undertaking of a group of undertakings or of the group of enterprises engaged in a joint economic activity; and should be available upon request to the competent supervisory authority;

■ the mechanisms for reporting and recording changes to the rules and reporting those changes to the supervisory authority;

■ the co-operation mechanism with the supervisory authority to ensure compliance by any member of the group of undertakings, or group of enterprises engaged in a joint economic activity, in particular by making available to the supervisory authority the results of the verification measures for ensuring compliance with the BCRs (described above);

■ the mechanisms for reporting to the competent supervisory authority any legal requirements to which a member of the group of undertakings, or group of enterprises engaged in a joint economic activity in a third country is subject, which are likely to have a substantial adverse effect on the guarantees provided by the BCRs; and

■ the appropriate data protection training to personnel having permanent or regular access to personal data (Article 47(2)).

The GDPR specifies that the European Commission may specify the format and procedures for the exchange of information between data controllers, data processors and supervisory authorities pursuant to Article 47 (Article 47(3)).

5.4   DEROGATIONS FOR SPECIFIC SITUATIONS

In the absence of an adequacy decision or one of the appropriate safeguards, the GDPR allows the transfer of personal data in a number of specific situations. If one of the specified situations exists, a data controller or processor may rely upon one of the derogations under the GDPR, which has the effect of lifting the general prohibition on data transfers.

The GDPR allows the transfer of personal data to a third country or international organisation in the following circumstances:

■ the data subject has explicitly consented to the proposed transfer, after having been informed of the possible risks of such transfers, due to the absence of an adequacy decision and appropriate safeguards. This ground cannot apply to activities carried out by public authorities in the exercise of their public powers (Article 49(3));

- the transfer is necessary for the performance of a contract between the data subject and the data controller or the implementation of pre-contractual steps at the request of the data subject (this ground cannot apply to activities carried out by public authorities in the exercise of their public powers);
- the transfer is necessary for the conclusion or performance of a contract concluded in the interest of the data subject between the controller and another person (this ground cannot apply to activities carried out by public authorities in the exercise of their public powers);
- the transfer is necessary for important reasons in the public interest, which must be recognised in EU or Member State law (Recital 4), for example where the data transfer is between competition authorities, tax or customs administrations, between financial supervisory authorities, social security services, or in relation to public health issues such as contagious diseases or doping in sport (Recital 112);
- the transfer is necessary for the establishment, exercise or defence of legal claims;
- the transfer is necessary in order to protect the vital interests of the data subject or other person, where the data subject is physically or legally incapable of giving consent. For example, a transfer to an international humanitarian organisation of personal data of a data subject who is physically or legally incapable of giving consent, with a view to accomplishing a task incumbent under the Geneva Conventions or to complying with international humanitarian law applicable in armed conflicts, could be considered to be necessary for an important reason of public interest, or because it is in the vital interest of the data subject (Recital 112);
- the transfer is made from a register which according to EU or Member State law is intended to provide information to the public and which is open to consultation either by the public or in general or by any person who can demonstrate a legitimate interest. Such a transfer cannot involve the entirety of the personal data or entire categories of personal data contained in the register (Article 49(1)).

Finally, the GDPR provides a basis for transferring personal data where none of the other grounds are applicable. This residual ground allows non-repetitive transfers concerning a limited number of data subjects to be permitted if it is necessary for the data controller's compelling legitimate interests, provided the rights and freedoms of the data subject are not overridden and the controller has assessed all the circumstances of the transfer, in particular:

- the nature of the personal data;
- the purpose and duration of the proposed processing;
- the country of origin, third country and the final destination;

and, on the basis of such assessment has provided appropriate safeguards to ensure the protection of personal data (Article 49(1) and Recital 114).

This residual ground may only be relied upon where none of the other grounds established under the GDPR apply. Where a controller or processor uses the residual ground as a basis for a data transfer, it must inform the supervisory authority and affected data subjects (Article 49(1) and Recital 113). Controllers and processors must also document the assessment and safeguards implemented (Article 49(6)).

The GDPR envisages a 'joined up', pan-European approach, and specifically requires the European Commission and supervisory authorities to take steps to develop international co-operation mechanisms to facilitate the effective enforcement of data protection legislation. They must also provide international mutual assistance in the enforcement of data protection legislation, including through notification, complaint referral, assistance with investigations and the exchange of information, subject to appropriate safeguards to ensure the protection of personal data. The GDPR also requires the Commission and the supervisory authorities to engage relevant stakeholders in discussion and activities aimed at furthering international co-operation for the enforcement of data protection legislation. Finally, the Commission and supervisory authorities are encouraged to promote the exchange and documentation of data protection legislation and practice, including jurisdictional conflicts with third countries (Article 50).

6 INDEPENDENT SUPERVISORY AUTHORITIES

6.1 GENERAL

A designated supervisory authority, empowered to perform its tasks and exercise its powers with complete independence is a fundamental prerequisite for an effective data protection system (Recital 117). As explained in **Chapter 5**, the existence of an independent data protection authority that is able to ensure and enforce compliance with data protection law will be taken into account in ascertaining whether or not a third country adduces adequate protection in respect of personal data (Article 45(2) and Recital 104, examined at **5.1**). To enshrine this principle, the GDPR imposes specific obligations upon Member States *vis-à-vis* the establishment and maintenance of independent supervisory authorities. The provisions of the GDPR relating to supervisory authorities are significantly more prescriptive than those of the Directive (Directive, Article 28), in part at least to enable the 'one stop shop' mechanism and to promote a consistent approach between supervisory authorities throughout the EU.

The GDPR allows Member States to establish more than one supervisory authority to reflect their constitutional, organisational and administrative structure (Recital 117). Where a Member State does establish more than one supervisory authority, it must implement appropriate legal mechanisms for ensuring the effective participation of those authorities in the consistency mechanism (explained in **Chapter 7**). In particular, each Member State must designate the supervisory authority which functions as a single contact point for the effective participation in the consistency mechanism, to ensure consistent co-operation with other data protection authorities, the Board and the European Commission (Recital 119).

The GDPR requires each Member State to appoint at least one independent public authority to monitor the application of its provisions in order to protect individuals' fundamental rights and freedoms, and to facilitate the free flow of personal data within the EU (Article 51(1)). The supervisory authority must contribute to the consistent application of the GDPR throughout the EU, and, in order to do so, must co-operate with the other supervisory authorities of the Member States as well as the European Commission (Article 51(2)). Each Member State must notify the European Commission of the relevant legal provisions it has adopted in order to bring the GDPR requirements *vis-à-vis* supervisory authorities into effect by 25 May 2018 (Article 51(4)).

Each Member State must ensure that its supervisory authority (or authorities, if more than one has been established) is provided with sufficient financial, technical and human resources, as well as premises and infrastructure, to be able to perform its tasks. Supervisory authorities must be allocated a separate, public annual budget, which may be part of the overall state or national budget (Recital 120 and Article 52(4)). The GDPR envisages co-operation between the European Commission and European supervisory authorities and the competent authorities in jurisdictions outside Europe, to facilitate and provide international mutual assistance (Recital 116).

Supervisory authorities are expressly required to perform their tasks and exercise their functions with complete independence (Article 52(1)). To this end, members of a supervisory authority must, in performing their tasks and exercising their powers under the GDPR, remain free from direct or indirect external influence, and must not seek or take instructions from any person (Article 52(2)). To ensure independence, members of the supervisory authority must be appointed by a transparent procedure, established in law, either by the parliament, government or the head of state (Article 53(1) and Recital 121). Members must have the qualifications, experience and skills, in particular in the area of data protection, to be able to perform their duties and exercise their powers (Article 53(2)). Supervisory authorities' members' duties expire at the end of their term of office (in accordance with Member State law) (Article 53(3)) and a member may only be dismissed in cases of serious misconduct, or if he or she no longer fulfils the conditions required for the performance of his or her duties (Article 53(4)). Appointed members must act independently, with integrity, and must not engage in any activities which would result in a conflict of interests (Article 52(3) and Recital 121).

The supervisory authority must be free to choose its own staff, who, once employed, must be subject to the exclusive direction of the member (or members) of that supervisory authority (Article 52(5) and Recital 121). However, the ability to operate independently does not mean that supervisory authorities cannot be subject to control or monitoring mechanisms regarding their financial expenditure, or to judicial review (Recital 118). Indeed, the GDPR specifies that Member States must ensure supervisory authorities are subject to appropriate financial controls, though these must not affect the supervisory authority's independence (Article 52(6)).

The GDPR requires that each Member State must enact legislation to provide for the following:

- the establishment of each supervisory authority;
- the qualifications and eligibility conditions required to be appointed as a member of each supervisory authority;
- the rules and procedures for the appointment of the member(s) of each supervisory authority;
- the duration of the term of the member(s) of each supervisory authority of no less than four years, except for the first appointment after 24 May 2016, part of

which may take place for a shorter period where it is necessary to protect the independence of the supervisory authority by means of a staggered appointment procedure;

- whether the member(s) may be reappointed, and if so, for how many terms; and
- the conditions governing the obligations of the member(s) and staff of each supervisory authority, and any prohibitions on actions, occupations and benefits that are incompatible with such obligations during and after the term of office and rules governing the cessation of employment (Article 54(1)).

The member(s) and staff of each supervisory authority are, in accordance with EU or Member State law, subject to an obligation of professional secrecy, both during and after their term of office, with regard to any confidential information which comes to their knowledge in the course of performing their tasks or exercising their powers. This obligation is intended to apply to reported infringements of the GDPR (Article 54(2)).

6.2   COMPETENCE, TASKS AND POWERS

Each supervisory authority must be competent to perform its tasks and exercise its powers in the territory of the Member State in which it is established (Article 55(1)). In particular, this should cover processing in the territory of the supervisory authority's Member State by:

- controllers and processors established within the territory of the Member State;
- processing of personal data by public authorities or private bodies acting in the public interest within the territory of the Member State;
- processing that affects data subjects within the territory of the Member State; and
- processing carried out by a controller or processor established outside the territory of the Member State, when targeting data subjects residing within the Member State.

The supervisory authority's tasks should include:

- handling complaints lodged by data subjects;
- conducting investigations on the application of the GDPR; and
- promoting public awareness of data protection risks, rules, safeguards and rights (Recital 122).

Where processing in question is based on the legal ground that the processing of personal data is necessary for compliance with a legal obligation to which the data controller is subject (Article 6(1)(c)), or the ground that the processing is necessary for the performance of a task carried out in the public interest or in the exercise of official authority vested in the data controller (Article 6(1)(e)), the supervisory authority of the Member State concerned is competent to act as the lead supervisory authority, and the lead supervisory mechanism (explained below) does not apply

(Article 55(2)). Further, supervisory authorities are not competent to supervise the processing operations of courts acting in their judicial capacity (Article 55(3)).

6.3   THE 'ONE STOP SHOP' MECHANISM AND LEAD SUPERVISORY AUTHORITIES

A shortcoming of the Directive is the requirement that international organisations with offices in more than one Member State must submit to the supervisory authority in each jurisdiction in which they have an establishment. In practice, this means notifying each competent supervisory authority (in the absence of an applicable exemption), following its guidance and, in the case of an incident involving personal data, potentially being subject to that authority's investigative and enforcement powers. Each Member State's data protection legislation implements the Directive slightly differently, and the approach taken by supervisory authorities varies between jurisdictions, with the result that a multinational organisation potentially faces a patchwork of differing compliance requirements. This widely recognised compliance challenge is an inefficient use of organisations' time and resources, and is detrimental to business. The GDPR addresses the challenges brought by the inconsistent implementation of the Directive by way of the 'one stop shop' mechanism, which allows multinational organisations to report to one supervisory authority. This feature of the legislation was widely publicised by the European Commission as a pro-business innovation that would streamline compliance and allow organisations significant cost savings, particularly when coupled with the GDPR's abolition of the notification requirement. It is also perceived as a key area where organisations are likely to require guidance, and as such is the subject of an opinion[1] issued by the Article 29 Working Party.

The GDPR designates the supervisory authority of the main establishment or single establishment of the controller or processor as the competent lead supervisory authority (Article 56(1)). Identifying a lead supervisory authority will only be relevant where the controller or processor is carrying out 'cross-border processing' (WP 244, Section I). Cross-border processing takes place where a controller or processor is established in more than one Member State, or where a controller or processor is only established in one Member State, but its processing activities substantially affect (or are likely to substantially affect) data subjects in more than one Member State (Article 4(23)). The GDPR does not define the term 'substantially affects'; however, WP 244 states that supervisory authorities will decide on a case-by-case basis, taking into account factors such as whether the processing:

- causes, or is likely to cause, damage, loss or distress to individuals;
- has or is likely to have, an actual effect in terms of limiting rights or denying an opportunity;
- affects, or is likely to affect individuals' health, well-being or peace of mind;

---

[1]   Article 29 Data Protection Working Party Guidelines for identifying a controller or processor's lead supervisory authority (WP 244), adopted on 13 December 2016.

- affects, or is likely to affect individuals' financial or economic status or circumstances;
- leaves individuals open to discrimination or unfair treatment;
- involves the analysis of the special categories of personal data or other intrusive data, particularly the personal data of children;
- causes or is likely to cause individuals to change their behaviour in a significant way;
- has unlikely, unanticipated or unwanted consequences for individuals;
- creates embarrassment or other negative outcomes, including reputational damage; or
- involves the processing of a wide range of personal data.[2]

In simple terms, the 'lead supervisory authority' is the authority with the primary responsibility for dealing with a cross-border data processing activity, and will be the supervisory authority of the Member State where the 'main establishment', or single establishment of a controller or processor is located. In the context of a multinational organisation, the 'main establishment' is the decisive factor in ascertaining the lead supervisory authority. A potential weakness of the GDPR, discussed by commentators as the draft legislation evolved, was the risk of multinational operators 'forum shopping' by artificially nominating an entity as its main establishment to benefit from a perceived 'lighter touch' approach from some EU data protection authorities. However, the GDPR establishes specific rules for identifying the 'main establishment'.

Under the GDPR, there are slightly different rules for data controllers and data processors for identifying the main establishment. In the case of controllers, the main establishment is generally the place of its central administration in the EU. However, where decisions on the purposes and means of processing personal data are taken in another establishment, and that establishment has the power to have such decisions implemented, that decision making entity will be deemed the main establishment.

In the case of a processor with establishments in multiple Member States, the place of its central administration will be its main establishment. In the absence of a processor having such an administrative centre in a Member State, the establishment where the main processing activities take place will be deemed the main establishment (Article 4(16), a brief explanation of which appears in **Chapter 1**). In cases involving a controller and a processor, the competent authority will be the supervisory authority for the controller, while the authority for the processor will be a 'supervisory authority concerned' (as explained below) (Recital 36 and WP 244, Section II(A)(2)).

---

[2]   WP 244, Section I(A). Note that the 'substantial effects' test is, according to WP 244, intended to ensure that supervisory authorities are only required to formally co-operate through the consistency mechanism where an authority intends to adopt a measure that will produce legal effects in relation to processing activities which substantially affect data subjects in several Member States.

WP 244 observes that the main establishment is relevant in relation to various compliance duties under the GDPR, including registering a DPO, notifying a risky processing activity or notifying a data security breach. The opinion recognises that there may be a degree of granularity concerning a multinational organisation's processing activities. WP 244 illustrates this with the example of a bank with corporate headquarters established in Frankfurt from which its banking activities are organised, and an insurance department located in Vienna, which directs its insurance data processing activities. The Article 29 Working Party opines that in such a case, the bank's Frankfurt office would be the main establishment for the banking business, and the Hessen supervisory authority in Germany would be the lead supervisory authority for the banking business, while the Austrian authority would be the lead supervisory authority for the insurance business (WP 244, Section II(A)1).

The rules on identifying the main establishment in the context of multinational organisations with centralised decision making headquarters are relatively straightforward to apply. However, multinational groups of companies with independent decision making powers may present more of a challenge. The GDPR determines a multinational organisation's main establishment objectively by reference to the real exercise of management activities through stable arrangements (discussed in **Chapter 1**). In other words, it is a question of fact rather than what an organisation may claim in order to benefit from a favourable jurisdiction. Notably, the main establishment is not determined by where the actual data processing takes place, nor where the technological means for processing are located (Recital 36, and WP 244, Section II(A)(1)(i)). The onus falls upon the data controller to identify its main establishment, and hence lead supervisory authority; however, this may subsequently be challenged by a supervisory authority that forms the view that it should be competent (WP 244, Section II(A)(1)(i)).

Where the identity of the location of a controller's main establishment is not clear, the factors that may be taken into account include the following:

- Where are decisions about the purposes and means of the processing given 'final sign off'?
- Where are decisions about business activities that involve processing personal data made?
- Where does the power to have decisions implemented effectively lie?
- Where is the director (or directors) with overall management responsibility for the cross border processing located?
- Where is the controller or processor registered as a company, if in a single territory?

This is not an exhaustive list, and other factors to be taken into account may include the controller or the processing activity in question. A supervisory authority that is in doubt as to whether the establishment identified by the controller genuinely is the main establishment may require additional information from the controller to support its assertion (WP 244, Section II(A)(1)(i)).

(Note: 'supervisory authority concerned' is defined as:

> a supervisory authority which is concerned by the processing of personal data because:
>
> (a) the controller or processor is established on the territory of the Member State of that supervisory authority;
> (b) data subjects residing in the Member State of that supervisory authority are substantially affected or likely to be substantially affected by the processing; or
> (c) a complaint has been lodged with that supervisory authority;

in Article 4(22).)

WP 244 recognises that borderline and complex situations may exist where it is difficult to identify the main establishment or determine where decisions are taken, and that the GDPR does not offer a solution. In such borderline cases, the Article 29 Working Party suggests that the controller should designate the acting main establishment. Where a controller designates an establishment that does not exercise real management as the main establishment, this may require active enquiry by the supervisory authorities concerned and ultimately the Board (WP 244, Section II(A)(1)(ii)).

A supervisory authority other than the lead supervisory authority, referred to in the GDPR as the 'supervisory authority concerned', may handle a complaint lodged with it, or a possible infringement of the GDPR, if that complaint or infringement arises in relation to a controller or processor in its Member State, or affects data subjects in its Member State (for example in the case of an employment matter) (Article 56(2) and Recital 127). A supervisory authority concerned that receives a complaint concerning subject matter exclusively within its territory should seek to resolve the matter amicably, and, if unsuccessful, may exercise its range of powers (Recital 131).

Where a supervisory authority concerned receives a complaint or becomes aware of a possible infringement, it must inform the lead supervisory authority without delay, and the lead supervisory authority must decide whether or not to handle the case (in accordance with the co-operation procedure explained in **Chapter 7**) within a period of three weeks after having been informed (Article 56(3)). WP 244 illustrates how this might work in practice with the example of a marketing company with a main establishment in Paris that launches a product that only affects data subjects residing in Portugal. In such a case, WP 244 suggests the French and Portuguese supervisory authorities might agree that it is appropriate for the Portuguese authority to take the lead in dealing with the matter (WP 244, Section II(A)(iii)).

The GDPR stipulates that if the lead supervisory authority decides to handle the case, the supervisory authority concerned may submit a draft decision to the lead authority, which the lead authority must take into account when preparing its draft decision (Article 56(4)). The lead supervisory authority should closely co-operate with any supervisory authority concerned receiving a complaint, and should take into account the view of that authority (Recital 130). WP 244 observes that co-operation and goodwill between supervisory authorities is essential for the success of the GDPR's co-operation and consistency processes (WP 244, Section II(A)(iii)). If the lead supervisory authority decides not to handle the case, the supervisory authority concerned which informed the lead authority shall do so (Article 56(5)).

Note that the rules around lead supervisory authorities (or the 'one-stop-shop' mechanism) do not apply to public authorities or private bodies acting in the public interest, which are subject only to the competence of the authority of the Member State in which they are established (Recital 128). Local processing activities do not fall within the GDPR's co-operation and consistency provisions (WP 244, Section II(A)(iv)), nor do controllers without an establishment in the EU. Representatives of controllers without an establishment in the EU would need to deal with the supervisory authority in every Member State they are established in, acting through their local representative (WP 244, Section II(A)(v)).

6.4 SUPERVISORY AUTHORITIES' TASKS

Each supervisory authority is responsible for the following tasks on its territory:

- monitoring and enforcing the application of the GDPR;
- promoting public awareness of the risks, rules, safeguards and rights in relation to processing, paying particular attention to activities addressed specifically to children;
- advising the national parliament, government and other institutions and bodies on legislative and administrative measures relating to the protection of individuals' rights and freedoms with regard to processing;
- promoting the awareness of controllers and processors of their obligations under the GDPR;
- upon request, providing information to data subjects concerning the exercise of their rights under the GDPR and co-operating with other supervisory authorities to that end where necessary;
- handling complaints lodged by a data subject, body, organisation or association, conducting an appropriate investigation and informing the complainant of the progress and outcome of such investigation within a reasonable period, particularly if further investigation or co-operation with other supervisory authorities is necessary;
- co-operating with other supervisory authorities, including sharing information and providing mutual assistance where necessary, with a view to ensuring the consistent application and enforcement of the GDPR;
- conducting investigations on the application of the GDPR, including on the basis of information received from other supervisory authorities or public authorities;
- monitoring relevant developments that have an impact on the protection of personal data, in particular the development of information and communication technology and commercial practices;

- adopting standard contractual clauses for the appointment of data processors by data controllers, and for the transfer of personal data out of the EEA;
- establishing and maintaining a list of the kinds of data processing activities that require a data protection impact assessment;
- advising on high-risk processing operations;
- encouraging the drawing up of codes of conduct, providing opinions and approving such codes that provide sufficient safeguards in accordance with the requirements of the GDPR;
- encouraging the establishment of data protection certification mechanisms, seals and marks, and approving those that meet the requirements of the GDPR;
- carrying out the periodic review of approved certifications;
- drafting and publishing the criteria for accrediting a body for monitoring codes of conduct and certification bodies;
- authorising contractual clauses and provisions and BCRs;
- contributing to the activities of the Board (explained in **Chapter 7**);
- keeping internal records of infringements of the GDPR and any corrective measures taken; and
- fulfilling any other tasks related to the protection of personal data (Article 57(1)).

Supervisory authorities are expected to facilitate the submission of complaints by measures such as a complaints submission form, which may be completed electronically (Article 57(2)). Performance of the supervisory authority's tasks shall be free of charge for data subjects and DPOs where applicable (Article 57(3)), except in the case of manifestly unfounded or excessive requests (in particular, repetitive requests), for which the authority may charge a reasonable fee based on its administrative costs. In such a case, the supervisory authority bears the burden of demonstrating the manifestly unfounded or excessive character of the request (Article 57(4)).

6.5   SUPERVISORY AUTHORITIES' POWERS

The GDPR confers upon supervisory authorities a range of investigative, corrective and advisory powers, as well as powers of authorisation (Article 58), expanding significantly on those granted under the Directive (Article 28). These powers are as follows:

1. Investigative powers to order a controller or processor (or their respective representatives, where applicable) to provide any information necessary for the supervisory authority to perform its tasks. The supervisory authority may carry out investigations in the form of data protection audits, review any data protection certifications that may have been issued under the GDPR, and notify data controllers or processors of an alleged infringement of the GDPR. In doing so, controllers and processors must provide access to all personal data and all information necessary for the performance of the supervisory authority's tasks, and grant the authority access to any of the controller or processor's premises

including to any data processing equipment in accordance with any procedural requirements of the Member State's law (Article 58(1)).

2. Corrective powers to issue warnings to controllers and processors that their intended processing operations are likely to infringe the provisions of the GDPR, and issue reprimands where processing operations result in an actual infringement. Supervisory authorities may order a controller or processor to comply with a data subject's request to exercise his or her rights. Authorities may order a data controller or processor to bring processing operations into compliance with the provisions of the GDPR, in a specified manner and within a specified period where appropriate. Supervisory authorities may impose a temporary or definitive limitation on processing, including a ban, and may order the suspension of data transfers to third countries and international organisations. The authority may order the rectification or erasure of personal data or restriction of processing, pursuant to data subjects' rights to rectification, erasure and restriction of processing granted by the GDPR. In such a case the supervisory authority may notify any third parties to which the personal data may have been disclosed. The authority may also withdraw a certification, or order the certifying body to do so, or not to issue a certification if the requirements have not been met or are no longer met. In addition to the above powers, the supervisory authority may also issue an administrative fine (Article 58(2)).

3. Authorisation powers, and powers to advise controllers in accordance with the consultation procedure (explained at **4.11**) and to issue opinions to the national parliament or government or other institutions and bodies, and to the public. Supervisory authorities may authorise high-risk processing carried out in the public interest where prior authorisation is required by Member State law. They may issue opinions, approve draft codes of conduct, accredit certification bodies, issue certifications and approve certification criteria. The supervisory authority may adopt standard contractual clauses for appointing data processors and standard contractual clauses for data transfers to third countries, and approve BCRs (Article 58(3)).

The exercise of supervisory authorities' powers must be subject to appropriate safeguards, including effective judicial remedy and due process, as set out in Member State law (Article 58(4)). Member State law must enable the supervisory authority to bring infringements of the provisions of the GDPR to the attention of the judicial authorities, and where necessary commence legal proceedings to enforce the provisions of the GDPR (Article 58(5)). Member states may, by law, grant supervisory authorities additional powers to those described above (Article 58(6)).

Each supervisory authority must complete an annual report on its activities, which may include the types of infringement notified, and the measures it has taken in response. The annual activity report must be transmitted to the national parliament, government and any other authorities designated by Member State law, and must be made available to the public, the European Commission and the Board.

7 CO-OPERATION AND CONSISTENCY

The GDPR envisages a harmonised approach by supervisory authorities within the EU, which it formalises with a number of provisions that seek to promote co-operation and mutual assistance, and encourage joint operations. These provisions establish detailed procedures, with prescribed time limits, and will be relevant in the case of cross-border processing activities.

7.1 CO-OPERATION BETWEEN THE LEAD SUPERVISORY AUTHORITY AND SUPERVISORY AUTHORITIES CONCERNED

The 'one stop shop' mechanism envisages one lead supervisory authority with which the main establishment of an organisation involved in cross-border processing would deal (as explained in the previous chapter). In practice, there may be circumstances in which other supervisory authorities concerned may be involved. The GDPR includes detailed provisions that prescribe how supervisory authorities must work together, in the case of cross-border processing. The underlying aim is to encourage supervisory authorities to assist one another in performing their tasks and to provide mutual assistance in order to ensure the consistent application of the GDPR throughout the EU (Recital 133).

The GDPR requires the lead supervisory authority and other supervisory authorities concerned to co-operate with one another, exchanging all relevant information where necessary in order to reach consensus (Article 60(1)). Relevant information should be exchanged by electronic means, using a standardised format (Article 60(12)). Arrangements for the exchange of information, particularly in relation to specified forms, may be specified by implementing acts (Article 67). The lead supervisory authority may at any time request that the other supervisory authorities concerned provide mutual assistance (as explained below). Supervisory authorities may also conduct joint operations (again, as explained below) particularly in the context of investigations or monitoring the implementation of measures concerning a controller or processor established in another Member State (Article 60(2) and Recital 134).

Lead supervisory authorities must communicate relevant information on a matter to the other supervisory authorities concerned without delay. The lead authority should submit a draft decision to the authorities concerned, again without delay, inviting the opinion of other authorities and taking due account of any such views submitted (Article 60(3)). Other supervisory authorities concerned are then given a period of four weeks to submit a relevant and reasoned objection to the draft decision. Where the lead authority and other authorities concerned are unable to reach agreement, they must apply the consistency mechanism (explained below) (Article 60(4)). However, where the lead supervisory authority agrees with the relevant and reasoned objection made by a supervisory authority concerned, the lead authority must submit a revised draft decision to the supervisory authorities concerned within a four-week period, requesting their views (Article 60(5)). Where the supervisory authorities concerned do not object to a draft decision submitted by the lead supervisory authority, the supervisory authorities will be deemed to be in agreement, and will be bound by the decision (Article 60(6)).

When a decision has been agreed in accordance with the process described above, the lead supervisory authority must adopt the decision and notify it to the main establishment of the controller or processor, or single establishment (as the case may be). The lead authority must inform the supervisory authorities concerned and the Board, providing a summary of the relevant facts and grounds. The supervisory authority with which a complaint has been lodged must also inform the complainant of the decision (Article 60(7)). Where a complaint is dismissed or rejected, the supervisory authority that received the complaint must adopt the decision to dismiss or reject, and inform the complainant and the affected data controller (Article 60(8)). Where the lead supervisory authority and the supervisory authorities concerned dismiss or reject parts of a complaint, but agree to act on others, they must adopt a separate decision for each part of the matter. In such a case, the lead authority must inform the main establishment (or single establishment, as the case may be) of the controller or processor of the part of its decision that concerns actions vis-à-vis the controller or processor, while the supervisory authority for the complainant must inform the processor of the part (or parts) of the complaint that have been dismissed or rejected (Article 60(9)).

Where a controller or processor has been notified of a decision concerning its processing activities in accordance with the process explained above, it must take the necessary measures required to comply with the decision and notify the lead supervisory authority. The lead supervisory authority must then inform the other supervisory authorities concerned (Article 60(10)). In exceptional circumstances, a supervisory authority concerned may consider that urgent action is necessary, in order to protect the interests of data subjects. In such a case, the urgency procedure (explained below) will apply (Article 60(11)).

7.2   MUTUAL ASSISTANCE

The GDPR actively promotes co-operation between supervisory authorities, and to this end includes provisions that enable authorities to provide one another with mutual assistance. Supervisory authorities are required to provide each other with relevant information and mutual assistance, in order to implement and apply the provisions of the GDPR in a consistent manner. Authorities are required to put in place measures to aid effective co-operation. In particular, mutual assistance is intended to cover information requests and supervisory measures such as requests to carry out prior authorisations and consultations, inspections and investigations (Article 61(1)). Supervisory authorities must reply to requests from other supervisory authorities promptly, and within one month. Requests may include the transmission of relevant information on the conduct of an investigation (Article 61(2)). A request for assistance must contain all the necessary information, including the purpose of and reasons for the request, and any information exchanged must only be used for the purpose for which it was requested (Article 61(3)).

A supervisory authority cannot refuse to comply with a request unless it is not competent on the subject matter of the request or the measures it is asked to execute, or complying with the request would infringe the GDPR, or other EU or Member State law (Article 61(4)). A supervisory authority that has received a request for assistance or information must inform the requesting authority of the results or progress (as the case may be) or the reasons for refusing to comply (Article 61(5)). Requested information should be supplied by electronic means in a standardised format (Article 61(6)). A supervisory authority cannot charge a fee for responding to a request, though authorities may agree on rules to indemnify one another in relation to specific expenditure incurred in exceptional circumstances (Article 61(7)). Where a supervisory authority does not provide the information that has been requested within one month of receiving the request, the authority that made the request may adopt a provisional measure in the territory of its Member State. In such a case, the criteria specified in the urgency procedure (explained below) will be deemed to be met, and the supervisory authority may request an urgent binding decision (Article 61(8)). The European Commission may, by way of implementing acts, specify the format and procedures for mutual assistance (explained in this section) and the exchange of information by electronic means between supervisory authorities and the Board (Article 61(9)).

7.3   JOINT OPERATIONS

In addition to the co-operation and mutual assistance procedures, a coordinated approach by supervisory authorities is further facilitated by way of the joint operations provisions. The joint operations procedures facilitate joint operations by supervisory authorities, in particular joint investigations and enforcement measures, in which staff or members of other Member States' supervisory authorities are involved (Article 62(1)).

Where a controller or processor has establishments in several Member States, or where a significant number of data subjects from more than one Member State are likely to be affected by processing activities, a supervisory authority from each of those Member States may participate in joint operations. The competent supervisory authority of the controller or processor's main or single establishment shall invite supervisory authorities from the relevant Member States to participate in the joint operations, and respond to any request from a supervisory authority that wishes to participate (Article 62(2)). Where a supervisory authority does not comply with its obligations within one month, the other supervisory authorities may adopt a provisional measure, and the criteria necessary for seeking an opinion of an urgent binding decision from the Board will be presumed to have been met (Article 62(7)).

Supervisory authorities may, in accordance with local law and the seconding authority's authorisation, confer powers, including investigative powers, upon the staff or members of the seconding authority involved in joint operations. Alternatively, the host authority may, to the extent permitted by its local law, allow the seconding authority's members or staff to exercise their powers, under the guidance and in the presence of members of the host supervisory authority (Article 62(3)). Where the staff of a seconding authority operate in another Member State, the host authority remains liable for any damage caused by the seconding authority during their operations, in accordance with local Member State law (Article 62(4)). In such a case, the host supervisory authority should make good any damage caused and seek reimbursement from the seconding authority (Article 62(5)). Subject to this specific exception, and without prejudice to the exercise of its rights against third parties, Member States should refrain from seeking reimbursement from other Member States arising from joint operations between supervisory authorities (Article 62(6)).

7.4   CONSISTENCY

The GDPR includes a consistency mechanism, which is intended to ensure the consistent application of its provisions, through co-operation between the supervisory authorities and one another, and where relevant, between the supervisory authorities and the European Commission (Article 63).

The Board will issue an opinion where a supervisory authority intends to adopt one of the measures listed below. The competent supervisory authority must communicate the draft decision to the Board where it:

- aims to adopt a list of the processing operations that are subject to the requirement of a data protection impact assessment;
- intends to adopt, amend or extend a code of conduct that relates to processing activities in several Member States;
- aims to approve the criteria for accrediting a body for monitoring compliance with approved codes of conduct;
- aims to determine standard data protection clauses adopted by a supervisory authority and approved by the European Commission, for transferring personal data to third countries, or standard contractual clauses for the appointment of a data processor by a data controller, or the appointment by a processor of a sub-processor;

- aims to authorise contractual clauses that provide appropriate safeguards for the transfer of personal data to third countries; or
- aims to approve BCRs (Article 64(1)).

Where a matter is of general application, or has an effect in more than one Member State, any supervisory authority, the Chair of the Board (explained below) or the European Commission may request that the Board examines the matter with a view to issuing an opinion. In particular, this should be appropriate where a competent authority does not comply with the obligations for mutual assistance, or for joint operations (Article 64(2)).

In either of the circumstances explained above, the Board must adopt an opinion on the matter submitted to it, unless it has already issued an opinion on the same matter, within eight weeks. The Board's opinion requires a simple majority, and the eight-week period may be extended by a further six weeks in the case of a complex matter. Any member that has not objected to a draft opinion within a reasonable period (as indicated by the Chair of the Board) will be deemed to be in agreement with the draft decision (Article 64(3) and Recital 136). Supervisory authorities and the European Commission must communicate to the Board by electronic means without undue delay, using a standardised format, any relevant information, including a summary of the facts, the draft decision, the grounds that make the enactment of such a measure necessary and the views of the other supervisory authorities concerned (Article 64(4)).

The Chair of the Board must inform the members of the Board and the European Commission of any relevant information that has been communicated to it using a standardised format. Where necessary, the Secretariat of the Board (explained below) must provide translations of the relevant information. The Chair must then inform the Commission of its opinion and make its opinion public (Article 64(5)). During the eight-week period the Board has in which to formulate its opinion, the competent supervisory authority may not adopt its draft decision (Article 64(6)). The supervisory authority requesting the opinion must take the utmost account of the Board's opinion, and within two weeks of receiving the opinion, communicate to the Chair of the Board whether it will maintain or amend its draft decision and provide a copy of its amended draft (if any) in a standardised format (Article 64(7)). If a supervisory authority concerned informs the Chair of the Board, within the two-week period, that it does not intend to follow the Board's opinion, in whole or in part and providing the relevant grounds, the dispute resolution provisions will apply, and the parties must follow the procedure explained below (Article 64(8)).

The GDPR includes specific provisions that set out a procedure for resolution by the Board of disputes between supervisory authorities (Article 65). The dispute resolution provisions apply where supervisory authorities cannot reach agreement on a relevant and reasoned objection, where there is disagreement regarding which of the supervisory authorities concerned is competent for the main establishment of a controller or processor, or where a supervisory authority has not requested the Board's opinion in any of the circumstances listed earlier in this section, or where a supervisory authority has not followed the opinion issued by the Board (in which case, any of the supervisory authorities concerned or the European Commission may communicate the matter to the Board) (Article 65(1)).

Where the dispute resolution provisions apply, the Board must adopt a binding decision, within one month of receiving the referral. Agreement requires a two-thirds majority, and the period for issuing an opinion may be extended by a further month where the subject matter is complex. The Board must then address the reasoned decision to the lead supervisory authority and the supervisory authorities concerned, each of which will be bound by it (Article 65(2) and Recital 136). If the Board is unable to adopt a decision within two weeks following the expiry of the two-month period, it may adopt a decision by a simple majority vote, and if the members of the board are split, the decision will be adopted on the basis of the casting vote of the Chair of the Board (Article 65(3)). Supervisory authorities may not adopt a decision during the prescribed periods explained above (Article 65(4)).

Once the Board has reached a final decision in accordance with the above procedure, the Chair of the Board must notify the supervisory authorities concerned without undue delay. The decision of the Board must be posted on the Board's website after the supervisory authority has notified the decision to the controller or processor and data subject (as explained in the following part of this paragraph) (Article 65(5)). The lead supervisory authority, or the supervisory authority with which the complaint has been lodged (as the case may be), must adopt the decision without undue delay and, in any event, no longer than one month after the Board has notified its decision. That supervisory authority must then inform the Board of the date when its final decision was notified to the controller or processor, and to the data subject. The final decision of the supervisory authority must then be adopted in accordance with the procedure explained above. Such decision must refer to the decision of the Board, and must specify that the decision of the Board will be published on the Board's website (Article 65(6)).

Notwithstanding the process explained above, the GDPR recognises that, in some circumstances, there will be an urgent need to act in order to protect the rights and freedoms of data subjects. In such cases, particularly where there is a danger that the enforcement of a right of a data subject could be impeded, a supervisory authority may adopt provisional measures for a specified period of up to a maximum of three months. Where it does so, the supervisory authority must communicate those measures and the reasons for adopting them to the supervisory authorities concerned, to the Board and to the European Commission (Article 66(1) and Recital 137). Where the supervisory authority considers that final measures need to be urgently adopted, it may request an urgent opinion or urgent binding decision from the Board, giving its reasons for the request (Article 66(2)). Any supervisory authority may make such a request of the Board where the competent supervisory authority has not taken appropriate steps and there is an urgent need to act in order to protect the rights and freedoms of data subjects. The request must give reasons, including an explanation of the need for urgency (Article 66(3)). An urgent opinion or an urgent binding decision, as described above, must be adopted within two weeks by the Board by way of a simple majority (Article 66(4)).

7.5   THE EUROPEAN DATA PROTECTION BOARD

The Article 29 Working Party was established under the Directive as an independent, advisory body, made up of representatives from each of the European supervisory authorities (Directive, Article 29). It was established to examine Member States' implementation of the Directive, in order to promote consistency across the EU. The Working Party's tasks include providing an opinion to the European Commission on the level of protection in the EU and in third countries, as well as advising on proposed amendments to the Directive (and any additional or specific data protection measures). It is also expected to give an opinion on codes of conduct drawn up at an EU level (Directive, Article 30). The GDPR establishes the Board as an independent body and a legal person to replace the Article 29 Working Party (Recital 139).

The Board is represented by the Chair of the Board, and consists of the head of the supervisory authority of each Member State and the European Data Protection Supervisor (EDPS), or their respective representatives. Where a Member State has more than one supervisory authority, a joint representative should be appointed. The European Commission may participate, but does not have voting rights. The EDPS has specific voting rights. The Chair of the Board must communicate the activities of the Board to the European Commission. The Board's function is to contribute to the consistent application of the provisions of the GDPR (Article 68). It must act independently and cannot seek or take instructions in relation to the performance of its tasks or the exercise of its powers (Article 69).

The purpose of the Board is to ensure the consistent application of the GDPR. In particular, it is responsible for monitoring the application of the GDPR and advising the European Commission on any issue related to the protection of personal data in the EU (including any proposed amendment of the GDPR). The Board is expected to examine on its own initiative on the request of one of its members, or on the request of the European Commission, any question on the application of the GDPR, and it should issue guidelines, recommendations and best practices. It should also review the practical application of such guidelines, recommendations and best practices. The Board is required to encourage the drawing up of codes of conduct and the establishment of data protection certification mechanisms and data protection seals, and carry out the accreditation and review of certification bodies and accredited controllers or processors established in third countries. It should provide the European Commission with opinions on certification requirements, standardised icons, and adequacy assessments for third countries, territories or specified sectors within a third country. The Board is to issue opinions on draft decisions of supervisory authorities pursuant to the consistency mechanism, and issue binding decisions as required by the GDPR. It should promote co-operation and the exchange of information and best practices between supervisory authorities, promote training programmes and facilitate personnel exchanges between authorities, including those of third countries, or with international organisations. The Board is expected to promote the exchange of knowledge and documentation on data protection legislation and practice with data protection authorities worldwide, issue opinions on codes of conduct drawn up at EU level, and maintain a publicly accessible electronic register of decisions taken by supervisory authorities and courts on issues handled in the consistency mechanism (Article 70(1)).

Where the European Commission requests advice from the Board, it may indicate a timetable, taking into account the urgency of the matter (Article 70(2)). The Board must forward its opinions, guidelines, recommendations and best practices to the European Commission, and make them public (Article 70(3)). Where appropriate, the Board should consult interested parties and give them the opportunity to submit comments within a reasonable period, and (subject to any requirement of confidentiality it may deem necessary) make the results of such consultation public (Article 70(4)). Like the Article 29 Working Party before it (Directive, Article 30(6)), the Board must draw up an annual report on data protection in the EU and, where relevant, data protection in third countries and international organisations. The annual report should be made public, and transmitted to the European Parliament, the European Council and the European Commission (Article 71(1)). It should include a review of the practical application of any guidelines, recommendations and best practices issued by the Board (Article 71(2)).

In the absence of any express provisions to the contrary, Board decisions require a simple majority of its members (Article 72(1)). The Board should adopt its own rules of procedure by a two-thirds majority of its members, and organise its own operational arrangements (Article 72(2)). The Board must elect a chair and two deputy chairs from its members, by a simple majority (Article 73(1)). The Chair of the Board and deputy chairs are elected for a five-year term of office, which may be renewed once (Article 73(2)). This contrasts with the rules concerning the chairman of the Article 29 Working Party, who was elected for a renewable two-year term, though the Directive is silent on how many times the term may be renewed (Directive, Article 29(4)). The Chair of the Board is responsible for convening meetings of the Board and preparing an agenda, notifying the lead supervisory authority and supervisory authorities concerned of decisions adopted by the Board, and ensuring the timely performance of the Board's tasks, in particular in relation to the application of the consistency mechanism (Article 74(1)). The allocation of tasks between the Chair of the Board and deputy chairs should be laid down in the Board's rules of procedure (Article 74(2)).

The Board is to be assisted by a secretariat, provided by the EDPS (Article 75(1) and Recital 140), in contrast with the Article 29 Working Party, which was provided with a secretariat by the European Commission (Directive, Article 29(5)). The secretariat must perform its tasks under the instructions of the Chair of the Board (Article 75(2) and Recital 140), and any EDPS staff carrying out tasks conferred on the Board under the GDPR must be subject to separate reporting lines from those EDPS staff carrying out tasks conferred on the EDPS (Article 75(3)). These terms may be set out in a Memorandum of Understanding between the Board and the EDPS (Article 75(4)). The secretariat's purpose is to provide analytical, administrative and logistical support to the Board (Article 75(5)). In particular, the secretariat is responsible for the day-to-day business of the Board, communications between Board members, the Chair of the Board and the European Commission, communications with other institutions and the public, electronic internal and external communications, translations, preparation and follow up around Board meetings and the preparation, drafting and publication of opinions, decisions on disputes between supervisory authorities and other texts adopted by the Board (Article 75(6)). The Board may, in accordance with its rules of procedure, deem certain discussions as confidential as may be necessary (Article 76(1)). Access to documents submitted to members of the Board, experts and representatives of third parties is governed by Regulation (EC) No. 1049/2001 of the European Parliament and the Council of 30 May 2001 regarding public access to European Parliament, Council and Commission documents (Article 76(2)).

8 REMEDIES, LIABILITY AND PENALTIES

8.1 REMEDIES

A fundamental aim of the GDPR is to enhance the rights of data subjects. As such, it grants every data subject the right to lodge a complaint with a supervisory authority if he or she believes that personal data concerning him or her has been processed in breach of the GDPR. In particular, a data subject may lodge a complaint with the supervisory authority of the Member State of his or her habitual residence, place of work, or place of the alleged infringement, at the data subject's choice. A supervisory authority that receives a complaint from a data subject must conduct an appropriate investigation within a reasonable timeframe and inform the data subject of the progress and outcome of the complaint. The GDPR suggests that supervisory authorities should facilitate the submission of complaints with measures such as electronic complaint submission forms, though such measures should not exclude other means of communication (Article 77 and Recital 141).

The GDPR grants individuals and organisations the right to an effective judicial remedy against a decision by a supervisory authority concerning them (Article 78(1)). Data subjects are granted the right to an effective judicial remedy where the competent supervisory authority does not handle a complaint, or does not inform the data subject of the outcome or progress of such a complaint (Article 78(2) and Recital 141). Proceedings against a supervisory authority must be brought in the courts of the Member State in which the authority is established (Article 78(3)). Where proceedings are brought in relation to a decision by a supervisory authority which was preceded by an opinion or decision of the Board, the supervisory authority must forward that opinion or decision to the Court (Article 78(4)).

While it does not appear as an express provision in the Articles, the Recitals state that any legal person has the right to bring an action before the CJEU for the annulment of a Board decision (Recital 143), as provided for by Article 263 TFEU, as well as a judicial remedy before the competent national court against a legally-binding decision of the supervisory authority of that territory. Article 263 TFEU grants the CJEU jurisdiction to review the legality of acts of the EU institutions, including the European Commission, that are intended to produce legal effects vis-à-vis third parties. Proceedings under Article 263 TFEU must be initiated within two months of the publication of the measure in issue.

Article 263 TFEU (formerly Article 230 TEC) provides:

> The Court of Justice of the European Union shall review the legality of legislative acts, of acts of the Council, of the Commission and of the European Central Bank, other than recommendations and opinions, and of acts of the European Parliament and of the European Council intended to produce legal effects vis-à-vis third parties. It shall also review the legality of acts of bodies, offices or agencies of the Union intended to produce legal effects vis-à-vis third parties.
>
> It shall for this purpose have jurisdiction in actions brought by a Member State, the European Parliament, the Council or the Commission on grounds of lack of competence, infringement of an essential procedural requirement, infringement of the Treaties or of any rule of law relating to their application, or misuse of powers.
>
> The Court shall have jurisdiction under the same conditions in actions brought by the Court of Auditors, by the European Central Bank and by the Committee of the Regions for the purpose of protecting their prerogatives.
>
> Any natural or legal person may, under the conditions laid down in the first and second paragraphs, institute proceedings against an act addressed to that person or which is of direct and individual concern to them, and against a regulatory act which is of direct concern to them and does not entail implementing measures.
>
> Acts setting up bodies, offices and agencies of the Union may lay down specific conditions and arrangements concerning actions brought by natural or legal persons against acts of these bodies, offices or agencies intended to produce legal effects in relation to them.
>
> The proceedings provided for in this Article shall be instituted within two months of the publication of the measure, or of its notification to the plaintiff, or, in the absence thereof, of the day on which it came to the knowledge of the latter, as the case may be.

Article 267 TFEU specifies that national courts which act as a final resort (in other words, courts against whose decisions there is no judicial remedy), are obliged to make a request to the CJEU for a preliminary ruling, unless the CJEU has already ruled on the matter or the interpretation of the EU rule of law in question is obvious.

Article 267 TFEU (formerly Article 234 TEC) provides:

> The Court of Justice of the European Union shall have jurisdiction to give preliminary rulings concerning:
>
> (a) the interpretation of the Treaties;
> (b) the validity and interpretation of acts of the institutions, bodies, offices or agencies of the Union;
>
> Where such a question is raised before any court or tribunal of a Member State, that court or tribunal may, if it considers that a decision on the question is necessary to enable it to give judgment, request the Court to give a ruling thereon.
>
> Where any such question is raised in a case pending before a court or tribunal of a Member State against whose decisions there is no judicial remedy under national law, that court or tribunal shall bring the matter before the Court.
>
> If such a question is raised in a case pending before a court or tribunal of a Member State with regard to a person in custody, the Court of Justice of the European Union shall act with the minimum of delay.

In contrast, national courts which do not rule in final resort are not obliged to exercise the request for a preliminary ruling, even if one of the parties requests it. As an example of this mechanism in action, the CJEU ruling of 2015 which invalidated the US Safe Harbour scheme arose from a request for a preliminary ruling by the Irish Data Protection Commissioner.[1]

The GDPR grants each data subject the right to an effective judicial remedy where he or she considers his or her rights have been infringed as a result of the processing of his or her personal data in contravention of the GDPR. Proceedings against a controller or processor should be brought before the court of the Member State in which the controller is established, or where the data subject is habitually resident, unless the controller or processor is a public authority of a Member State acting in the exercise of its powers, in which case proceedings should be brought before the courts of that Member State (Article 79 and Recital 145).

Data subjects may lodge their own complaints, or may do so through a designated representative, which lodges the types of complaint explained above on behalf of data subjects. These representatives must be bodies, organisations or associations that operate on a not-for-profit basis, are properly constituted under Member State law, have statutory objectives which are in the public interest, and are active in the field of data protection. A data subject has the right to mandate that the representative exercises the data subject's rights (as described above in this section) including the right to receive compensation. Member States may provide that representatives may lodge complaints independently of a data subject's mandate, if the representative considers that the rights of a data subject have been infringed. However, in such a case, the representative body, organisation or association may not claim compensation on a data subject's behalf independently of the data subject's mandate (Article 80 and Recital 142).

The possibility exists that separate proceedings concerning the same subject matter could be brought in different Member States, creating a risk of irreconcilable judgments. In keeping with its aim to achieve consistent application throughout the EU, the GDPR includes provisions to address this risk, where proceedings concerning the same subject matter are brought before more than one court. The GDPR provides that, where a competent court of a Member State holds information on proceedings concerning the same subject matter arising from processing by the same controller or processor that are pending in another Member State, it must contact the court in the other Member State to confirm the existence of such proceedings. Where proceedings concern the same subject matter arising from processing by the same controller or processor, any competent court in a Member State other than the first may suspend its proceedings. Where proceedings are pending at first instance, any court other than the first may, on the application of one of the parties, decline jurisdiction (Article 81 and Recital 144).

8.2   RIGHT TO COMPENSATION AND LIABILITY

The GDPR establishes a right to compensation for damage suffered as a direct result of processing that infringes its provisions, including delegated and implementing

---

[1]   *Maximillian Schrems* v. *Data Protection Commissioner* Case 362/14 (joined party: Digital Rights Ireland Ltd) (6 October 2015)

acts (Recital 146). A person who has suffered material damage (such as financial loss) or non-material damage (such as distress, embarrassment or humiliation) as a result of infringing processing has a right to claim compensation (Article 82(1)). Any controller that causes damage as a result of processing activities that infringe the GDPR will be liable. Processors can only be liable to the extent that their processing activities infringe those provisions of the GDPR that are specifically directed at processors, or to the extent that the processor has acted outside the scope of the controller's lawful instructions (Article 82(2)).

A controller or processor will not be liable if it is able to prove that it is not in any way responsible for the event giving rise to the damage (Article 82(3)). Where more than one controller or processor, or both a controller and a processor, are involved in the same processing, and are responsible for any damage caused, each controller and processor bears liability for the entire damage, in order to ensure that the data subject is fully compensated (Article 82(4)). Following this rule, where one controller or processor pays full compensation to the data subject in respect of damages caused by multiple controllers and/or processors, the paying controller or processor may claim back a part of the compensation from the other controller(s) and/or processor(s) corresponding to their part of the damage (Article 82(5)). Court proceedings for compensation should be brought before the court competent in the Member State where the infringing controller or processor is established, or that of the habitual residence of the data subject (Article 82(6)).

8.3   PENALTIES

The substantial penalties available to supervisory authorities for breaches of the GDPR have been the subject of widespread discussion. These penalties were included in the draft legislation as a deliberate measure by the European Commission to escalate the significance of data protection to a corporate board level concern. Given the widespread publicity the GDPR has generated even before its provisions take effect, this aim has been at least partially effective.

The GDPR requires that penalties imposed for breaches of the GDPR should be proportionate to the gravity of the infringement, taking into account all the circumstances (Recital 148). Supervisory authorities must ensure that each individual penalty it issues is effective, proportionate and dissuasive (Article 83(1)). The requirement that fines must have a dissuasive effect suggests that fines that are sufficiently large to make news headlines may be issued in an effort to deter infringement generally. A supervisory authority may issue a fine instead of, or in addition to the exercise of its other powers (Article 83(2)) such as the power to issue a warning or reprimand, to order compliance with a data subject's request and to limit or ban processing on a temporary or permanent basis.[2] When deciding whether to issue a fine and deciding on the amount, supervisory authorities must take into account the following factors:

---

[2]   Supervisory authorities' corrective powers are set out in GDPR, Article 58(2).

- the nature, gravity and duration of the infringement, taking into account the nature, scope or purpose of the processing, the number of data subjects affected and the level of damage suffered by them;
- whether the infringement was intentional or negligent;
- any steps taken by the controller or processor to mitigate the damage suffered by data subjects;
- the degree of responsibility of the controller or processor, taking into account the technical and organisational measures adopted by them;
- any relevant previous infringements by the controller or processor concerned;
- any degree of co-operation by the controller or processor with the authority in order to remedy the infringement and mitigate the adverse effect of the breach;
- the manner in which the infringement became known to the supervisory authority, in particular the extent to which the controller or processor notified the infringement;
- what measures have previously been ordered against the controller or processor concerned (such as warnings, reprimands, orders, and limitations or bans on processing) in relation to the same subject matter and the extent to which it has complied with those measures;
- adherence to any approved codes of conduct or approved certification mechanisms; and
- any other aggravating or mitigating factors in the circumstances, such as financial benefits gained or lost, or losses avoided directly or indirectly, from the infringement (Article 83(2)).

The provisions governing penalties include a two-tier structure, with the most serious infringements potentially subject to fines of up to €20,000,000, or, in the case of an undertaking, up to 4 per cent of worldwide annual turnover. Lesser infringements are potentially subject to fines of up to €10,000,000 or, in the case of an undertaking, up to 2 per cent of worldwide annual turnover. The GDPR specifies that the maximum fine is whichever is greater of the percentage figure or the sums quoted in Euro, so for a large undertaking the maximum permissible fine could potentially be significantly more than €20,000,000. However, where a controller or processor intentionally or negligently infringes the provisions by way of the same or linked processing activities, the GDPR provides that the total amount of the fine may not exceed the maximum sums stated for the gravest infringement (Article 83(3)).

Supervisory authorities may issue fines of up to €10,000,000 or, in the case of an undertaking, up to 2 per cent of worldwide annual turnover, for the following types of infringement:

A failure to:

- obtain valid consent from a child;

- comply with the provisions applicable to processing which does not require identification;[3]
- incorporate the data protection by design and default principles, i.e. designing systems to be 'privacy friendly', for example, implementing a CRM system to protect customers' privacy;
- properly apportion risk in a data-sharing situation (i.e. where two organisations use the same data, they must properly manage the risk between one another, for example in a joint venture or customer data-sharing arrangement between two group companies);
- designate a representative where required;
- comply with the requirements concerning the appointment of data processors;
- maintain proper records of data processing, and co-operate with the supervisory authority in response to any request for information;
- implement appropriate security measures;
- notify the data protection authority (within 72 hours) or affected data subject(s) of a data protection breach;
- conduct a data protection impact assessment, i.e. assess the potential impact upon individuals' privacy of a new activity (such as a new system, business line or corporate acquisition or disposal) and address any associated risks identified; or
- properly appoint a DPO (Article 83(4)(a)).

In addition to the above, certification bodies that fail to meet their obligations in relation to data protection certification mechanisms, seals and marks can be fined up to a maximum of 2 per cent of worldwide annual turnover (Article 83(4)(b)), as may bodies that have been accredited to monitor compliance with codes of conduct (Article 83(4)(c)).

Supervisory authorities may issue fines of up to €20,000,000 or, in the case of an undertaking, 4 per cent of worldwide annual turnover (whichever is the greater) for the following types of infringement:

A failure by a controller or processor to:

- comply with the data protection principles, namely lawfulness, fairness and transparency, purpose limitation, data minimisation, accuracy, storage limitation, integrity and confidentiality, and accountability;
- fulfil the requirements imposed by the GDPR in relation to obtaining valid consent;
- fulfil the requirements imposed by the GDPR in relation to processing sensitive personal data;
- fulfil its obligations in relation to data subjects' rights under the GDPR, namely the right to transparency, the right to access to personal data, the right to

---

[3]   Article 83(4)(a) refers to a failure to comply with the obligations under Article 11 (Processing which does not require identification) as a potential ground for a fine. This does not appear to make sense, which gives rise to the possibility that the reference to Article 11 was erroneous, and the correct reference should have been to Article 10 (Processing of personal data related to criminal convictions and offences).

rectification and erasure, the right to restrict processing (and to communicate to third parties to which the personal data has been disclosed the data subject's exercise of his or her right); the right to data portability, and data subjects' rights around automated decision taking including profiling;

- transfer personal data to a third country in accordance with the rules on data transfers;
- comply with its obligations under Member State law adopted to implement the provisions to specific processing situations; or
- non-compliance with an order by a supervisory authority to limit processing, suspend data flows, comply with a data subject's request to exercise his or her rights, bring processing operations into compliance with the GDPR, communicate a personal data breach to the affected data subject, or rectify or erase personal data or a failure to provide access to information requested by the supervisory authority (Article 83(5)).

Member States may establish rules on whether and the extent to which fines may be imposed upon public authorities and bodies established in their territory (Article 83(7)). The exercise of supervisory authorities' powers is subject to appropriate procedural safeguards under Member State and EU law, including an effective judicial remedy and due process (Article 83(8)).

Each supervisory authority should have the power to impose administrative fines for breaches of the GDPR, in contrast with the existing permission under the Directive where not all data protection authorities from EU Member States are empowered to issue fines (Recital 150). Where the legal system of a Member State does not provide for administrative fines, such as in Denmark or Estonia (Recital 151), the GDPR should be applied so that the fine is initiated by the competent supervisory authority, and imposed by the competent national courts. In such a case, this should have the equivalent effective, proportionate and dissuasive effect as though it had been administered by the supervisory authority (Article 83(9)).

The GDPR requires Member States to implement rules on the penalties applicable to infringements, particularly those which are not subject to administrative fines. Member States must notify the European Commission of any such rules by 25 May 2018 and of any subsequent amendments without delay (Article 84). Member States have a discretion to establish rules on criminal penalties for infringements; however, they should not breach the principle of *ne bis in idem*, (or 'not twice in the same thing', more commonly known as the double jeopardy rule), which is the legal doctrine that legal proceedings cannot be brought twice for the same cause of action (Recital 149).

9 PROVISIONS RELATING TO SPECIFIC PROCESSING SITUATIONS

The GDPR recognises a number of unrelated situations which give rise to processing activities that require specific provisions. The first of the 'special cases' is in relation to processing personal data for the purposes of freedom of expression and freedom of information. The GDPR requires that Member States' laws should reconcile the rules governing freedom of expression and information, including journalistic, academic, artistic or literary expression with the rights around the protection of personal data granted by the GDPR. Processing personal data for journalism, academic, artistic or literary purposes should be subject to specific derogations or exemptions from certain obligations (specified in GDPR, Article 85(2)), and Member States must notify the European Commission of the relevant provision (Article 85(3)). Where such exemptions or derogations differ from one Member State to another, the law of the Member State to which the controller is subject should apply (Article 85(1) and Recital 153).

Public access to official documents that contain personal data is another special processing situation. The GDPR recognises that public access to official documents may be in the public interest, which may in turn necessitate the disclosure of any personal data that may be present in such official documents. Where personal data is present in official documents held by a public authority, public body or a private body for the performance of a task carried out in the public interest, such personal data may be disclosed by that authority or body. Any such disclosures must be made in accordance with EU or Member State laws applicable to the public authority or body, or private body performing a public function, which reconcile the right of public access to official documents with the right to protection of personal data (Article 86 and Recital 154).

Member States may determine specific provisions for processing individuals' national identification numbers, provided that such provisions include appropriate safeguards to protect data subjects' rights and freedoms (Article 87). Member States may also make specific provision for processing in an employment context, by way of legislation or collective agreements. Such rules must include appropriate measures to safeguard data subjects' rights and freedoms. Member States must notify the European Commission of any such provisions adopted, and of any subsequent amendments (Article 88 and Recital 155).

The GDPR recognises that coupling information obtained from registries in the course of research may create valuable new knowledge, for example in relation to medical conditions such as cardiovascular disease, depression and cancer, which may serve the public interest. Personal data may be processed for scientific research purposes, provided that it is subject to appropriate safeguards (Recital 157). It applies to processing personal data for archival purposes (Recital 158), and scientific research purposes, which should be interpreted broadly so as to include technological development and demonstration, fundamental research, applied research and privately funded research (Recital 159). The GDPR also applies to the processing of personal data for statistical purposes, though 'statistical purposes' implies aggregate rather than personal data (Recital 162).

Processing personal data for archiving purposes in the public interest, scientific or historical research purposes, or statistical purposes should be subject to appropriate safeguards to protect data subjects' rights and freedoms, as provided for under the GDPR. Such safeguards must ensure appropriate technical and organisational measures are in place to protect data subjects, in particular, data minimisation. Measures may also include an assessment as to whether pseudonymisation may be appropriate (Article 89(1) and Recital 156). Where personal data are processed for scientific or historical research purposes or for statistical purposes, Member States may specify derogations to the right to access information, to rectification, to restriction of processing, and the right to object to processing, conferred upon data subjects under the GDPR. Such a derogation must include appropriate safeguards and is only applicable to the extent that such rights render impossible or impair the achievement of the specific purpose (Article 89(2)). Where personal data are processed for archiving purposes in the public interest, Member State law may provide for derogations from data subjects' right to access information, to rectification, to restriction of processing, the right to have any third parties to whom the data have been disclosed notified of a data subject's exercise of his or her right to rectification or restriction of processing, the right to data portability and the right to object to processing. Again, any such derogations must incorporate appropriate safeguards and may only operate to the extent that the data subjects' right would prevent or impair the achievement of the specific purpose (Article 89(3)).

In relation to supervisory authorities' powers to conduct compulsory audits, Member States may adopt specific rules to protect professional or other secrecy obligations in the context of audits upon controllers' or processors' premises. Where a Member State does so, it must inform the European Commission of the rule or any subsequent amendment by 25 May 2018 (Article 90 and Recital 164). Churches and religious associations or communities in Member States that apply comprehensive data protection rules, for example under their constitutional laws, may continue to apply such rules provided that they are brought into line with the GDPR when its provisions take effect (Article 91 and Recital 165).

10 DELEGATED ACTS AND IMPLEMENTING ACTS

EU institutions adopt various legal acts to accomplish their tasks. To this end, Article 290 of the TFEU allows the EU legislator (generally the European Parliament and the European Council) to delegate to the European Commission the power to adopt acts, including EU regulations. However, the delegation of the power to adopt acts is subject to strict limits, and the objectives, content, scope and duration of the delegation of power must be defined in the legislative act.[1]

The GDPR confers the power to adopt delegated acts upon the European Commission (Article 92(1)), for an indeterminate period commencing on 24 May 2016 (Article 92(2)). This delegation of power may be revoked at any time by the European Parliament or the European Council, which would take effect the day following publication of the revocation in the *Official Journal of the European Union* or such later date as may be specified. Such a revocation would not affect the validity of any delegated acts already in force (Article 92(3)).

The European Commission must notify the European Council and the European Parliament simultaneously as soon as it adopts any delegated act (Article 92(4)). A delegated act can then only enter into force if there is no objection from either the European Parliament or the European Council within three months of notification of the act, or if the Parliament and Council confirm that they have no objection prior to the end of that period. The period may be extended by three months by the European Parliament or the Council (Article 92(5)).

Regulation (EU) No 182/2011 of the European Parliament and the Council establishes the rules and general principles concerning mechanisms for control by EU countries of the Commission's exercise of implementing powers. This control is performed by means of the so called 'comitology' procedure, whereby the European Commission is assisted by committees consisting of Member States' representatives and is chaired by a representative of the European Commission (Article 93). As part of the comitology procedure, comitology committees give an opinion on implementing acts proposed by the European Commission, and follow two types of procedures; examination and advisory. The GDPR specifies that the examination procedure should be used for various specific topics including the adoption of

---

[1]   GDPR, Recital 166 and EU legal acts explanation on EUR-Lex (**http://eur-lex.europa.eu/ legal-content/EN/TXT/?uri=uriserv%3Aai0032** (last updated 8 September 2015)).

standard contractual clauses for data transfers and the appointment of data processors, codes of conduct, technical standards and mechanisms for certification, and the level of adequate protection provided by a third country, territory or sector within that third country or an international organisation (Recital 168). The European Commission should, if there is an urgent need to do so, adopt immediately applicable implementing acts where a third country, territory or sector within a third country or international organisation does not ensure an adequate level of protection (Recital 169). The GDPR requires that implementing powers should be conferred upon the European Commission to ensure uniform conditions for its implementation. The European Commission should consider specific measures for micro, small and medium-sized enterprises (Recital 167).

To ensure an equivalent level of protection to individuals and to enable the free flow of personal data throughout, the EU may adopt measures in accordance with Article 5 of the Treaty on European Union (TEU) (Recital 170). For ease of reference, Article 5 TEU provides as follows:

1. The limits of Union competences are governed by the principle of conferral. The use of Union competences is governed by the principles of subsidiarity and proportionality.
2. Under the principle of conferral, the Union shall act only within the limits of the competences conferred upon it by the Member States in the Treaties to attain the objectives set out therein. Competences not conferred upon the Union in the Treaties remain with the Member States.
3. Under the principle of subsidiarity, in areas which do not fall within its exclusive competence, the Union shall act only if and insofar as the objectives of the proposed action cannot be sufficiently achieved by the Member States, either at central level or at regional and local level, but can rather, by reason of the scale or effects of the proposed action, be better achieved at Union level.

    The institutions of the Union shall apply the principle of subsidiarity as laid down in the Protocol on the application of the principles of subsidiarity and proportionality. National Parliaments ensure compliance with the principle of subsidiarity in accordance with the procedure set out in that Protocol.
4. Under the principle of proportionality, the content and form of Union action shall not exceed what is necessary to achieve the objectives of the Treaties.

    The institutions of the Union shall apply the principle of proportionality as laid down in the Protocol on the application of the principles of subsidiarity and proportionality.

11 FINAL PROVISIONS

The GDPR was published in the *Official Journal of the European Union* on 4 May 2016 ([2016] OJ L119/1) and entered into force 20 days later, on 25 May 2016 (Article 99(1)). However, its provisions do not apply until 25 May 2018 (Article 99(2)), at which time it repeals the Directive (Article 94(1)). This two year 'sunrise period' was intended to enable organisations to bring their processing operations into compliance with the new law. Accordingly, controllers and processors must ensure that any processing already underway is brought into conformity with the provisions of the GDPR by 25 May 2018; in other words, there is no further 'grace period'. Nonetheless, where processing is based on consent pursuant to the Directive, data subjects' consent need not be obtained again if it is already in line with the consent requirements of the GDPR, in order to allow controllers and processors to continue processing when the new provisions come into force (Recital 171).

Any European Commission decisions that have been adopted and any authorisations by supervisory authorities based on the Directive will remain in force until amended, replaced or repealed (Recital 171). Where any Member State has concluded an international agreement for the transfer of personal data to third countries or international organisations prior to 24 May 2016, and that agreement is in compliance with EU law in force at the time of the agreement, such agreement will remain in force until amended, repealed or revoked (Article 96).

With effect from 25 May 2018, any references to the repealed Directive are to be construed as references to the GDPR, and any references to the Article 29 Working Party are to be construed as references to the Board (Article 94(2)). The GDPR is not intended to impose additional obligations on any natural or legal persons arising from Directive 2002/58/EC[1] (GDPR, Article 95). However, once the GDPR has been adopted, Directive 2002/58/EC should be amended in order to clarify the relationship between the two legislative instruments (Recital 173).

---

[1]   Directive 2002/58/EC of the European Parliament and of the Council of 12 July 2002 concerning the processing of personal data and the protection of privacy in the electronic communications sector (Directive on privacy and electronic communications).

At the time of writing, review of Directive 2002/58/EC is well underway.[2]

On 25 May 2020, and every four years thereafter, the European Commission must submit a report on the evaluation of the GDPR to the European Parliament and Council, which is to be made public. In particular, the European Commission must evaluate the application and functioning of the provisions on data transfers and the co-operation and consistency mechanisms. In the course of drafting its report the European Commission may request information from Member States and supervisory authorities. The European Commission must take into account any findings by the European Parliament, Council and any other relevant bodies or sources, and may submit proposals to amend the provisions of the GDPR as may become necessary in the light of technological developments.

---

[2] See, for example, Executive Summary of the Ex-post REFIT evaluation of the ePrivacy Directive 2002/58/EC, Accompanying the document Proposal for a Regulation of the European Parliament and the Council on the protection of privacy and confidentiality in relation to electronic communications and repealing Directive 2002/58/EC (Regulation on Privacy and Electronic Communications) dated 10 January 2017.

Appendix A
EU GENERAL DATA PROTECTION REGULATION (REGULATION 2016/679)

REGULATION (EU) 2016/679: REGULATION ON THE PROTECTION OF NATURAL PERSONS WITH REGARD TO THE PROCESSING OF PERSONAL DATA AND ON THE FREE MOVEMENT OF SUCH DATA, AND REPEALING DIRECTIVE 95/46/EC (GENERAL DATA PROTECTION REGULATION)

THE EUROPEAN PARLIAMENT AND THE COUNCIL OF THE EUROPEAN UNION,

Having regard to the Treaty on the Functioning of the European Union, and in particular Article 16 thereof,

Having regard to the proposal from the European Commission,

After transmission of the draft legislative act to the national parliaments,

Having regard to the opinion of the European Economic and Social Committee,[1]

Having regard to the opinion of the Committee of the Regions,[2]

Acting in accordance with the ordinary legislative procedure,[3]

Whereas:

(1) The protection of natural persons in relation to the processing of personal data is a fundamental right. Article 8(1) of the Charter of Fundamental Rights of the European Union (the 'Charter') and Article 16(1) of the Treaty on the Functioning of the European Union (TFEU) provide that everyone has the right to the protection of personal data concerning him or her.

(2) The principles of, and rules on the protection of natural persons with regard to the processing of their personal data should, whatever their nationality or residence, respect their fundamental rights and freedoms, in particular their right to the protection of personal data. This Regulation is intended to contribute to the accomplishment of an area of freedom, security and justice and of an economic union, to economic and social progress, to the strengthening and the convergence of the economies within the internal market, and to the well-being of natural persons.

(3) Directive 95/46/EC of the European Parliament and of the Council[4] seeks to harmonise the protection of fundamental rights and freedoms of natural persons in respect of processing activities and to ensure the free flow of personal data between Member States.

(4) The processing of personal data should be designed to serve mankind. The right to the

---

[1] OJ C 229, 31.7.2012, p.90.
[2] OJ C 391, 18.12.2012, p.127.
[3] Position of the European Parliament of 12 March 2014 (not yet published in the Official Journal) and position of the Council at first reading of 8 April 2016 (not yet published in the Official Journal). Position of the European Parliament of 14 April 2016.
[4] Directive 95/46/EC of the European Parliament and of the Council of 24 October 1995 on the protection of individuals with regard to the processing of personal data and on the free movement of such data (OJ L 281, 23.11.1995, p.31).

protection of personal data is not an absolute right; it must be considered in relation to its function in society and be balanced against other fundamental rights, in accordance with the principle of proportionality. This Regulation respects all fundamental rights and observes the freedoms and principles recognised in the Charter as enshrined in the Treaties, in particular the respect for private and family life, home and communications, the protection of personal data, freedom of thought, conscience and religion, freedom of expression and information, freedom to conduct a business, the right to an effective remedy and to a fair trial, and cultural, religious and linguistic diversity.

(5) The economic and social integration resulting from the functioning of the internal market has led to a substantial increase in cross-border flows of personal data. The exchange of personal data between public and private actors, including natural persons, associations and undertakings across the Union has increased. National authorities in the Member States are being called upon by Union law to cooperate and exchange personal data so as to be able to perform their duties or carry out tasks on behalf of an authority in another Member State.

(6) Rapid technological developments and globalisation have brought new challenges for the protection of personal data. The scale of the collection and sharing of personal data has increased significantly. Technology allows both private companies and public authorities to make use of personal data on an unprecedented scale in order to pursue their activities. Natural persons increasingly make personal information available publicly and globally. Technology has transformed both the economy and social life, and should further facilitate the free flow of personal data within the Union and the transfer to third countries and international organisations, while ensuring a high level of the protection of personal data.

(7) Those developments require a strong and more coherent data protection framework in the Union, backed by strong enforcement, given the importance of creating the trust that will allow the digital economy to develop across the internal market. Natural persons should have control of their own personal data. Legal and practical certainty for natural persons, economic operators and public authorities should be enhanced.

(8) Where this Regulation provides for specifications or restrictions of its rules by Member State law, Member States may, as far as necessary for coherence and for making the national provisions comprehensible to the persons to whom they apply, incorporate elements of this Regulation into their national law.

(9) The objectives and principles of Directive 95/46/EC remain sound, but it has not prevented fragmentation in the implementation of data protection across the Union, legal uncertainty or a widespread public perception that there are significant risks to the protection of natural persons, in particular with regard to online activity. Differences in the level of protection of the rights and freedoms of natural persons, in particular the right to the protection of personal data, with regard to the processing of personal data in the Member States may prevent the free flow of personal data throughout the Union. Those differences may therefore constitute an obstacle to the pursuit of economic activities at the level of the Union, distort competition and impede authorities in the discharge of their responsibilities under Union law. Such a difference in levels of protection is due to the existence of differences in the implementation and application of Directive 95/46/EC.

(10) In order to ensure a consistent and high level of protection of natural persons and to remove the obstacles to flows of personal data within the Union, the level of protection of the rights and freedoms of natural persons with regard to the processing of such data should be equivalent in all Member States. Consistent and homogenous application of the rules for the protection of the fundamental rights and freedoms of natural persons with regard to the processing of personal data should be ensured throughout the Union. Regarding the processing of personal data for compliance with a legal obligation, for the performance of a task carried out in the public interest or in the exercise of official authority vested in the controller, Member States should be allowed to maintain or introduce national provisions to further specify the application of the rules of this

Regulation. In conjunction with the general and horizontal law on data protection implementing Directive 95/46/EC, Member States have several sector-specific laws in areas that need more specific provisions. This Regulation also provides a margin of manoeuvre for Member States to specify its rules, including for the processing of special categories of personal data ('sensitive data'). To that extent, this Regulation does not exclude Member State law that sets out the circumstances for specific processing situations, including determining more precisely the conditions under which the processing of personal data is lawful.

(11) Effective protection of personal data throughout the Union requires the strengthening and setting out in detail of the rights of data subjects and the obligations of those who process and determine the processing of personal data, as well as equivalent powers for monitoring and ensuring compliance with the rules for the protection of personal data and equivalent sanctions for infringements in the Member States.

(12) Article 16(2) TFEU mandates the European Parliament and the Council to lay down the rules relating to the protection of natural persons with regard to the processing of personal data and the rules relating to the free movement of personal data.

(13) In order to ensure a consistent level of protection for natural persons throughout the Union and to prevent divergences hampering the free movement of personal data within the internal market, a Regulation is necessary to provide legal certainty and transparency for economic operators, including micro, small and medium-sized enterprises, and to provide natural persons in all Member States with the same level of legally enforceable rights and obligations and responsibilities for controllers and processors, to ensure consistent monitoring of the processing of personal data, and equivalent sanctions in all Member States as well as effective cooperation between the supervisory authorities of different Member States. The proper functioning of the internal market requires that the free movement of personal data within the Union is not restricted or prohibited for reasons connected with the protection of natural persons with regard to the processing of personal data. To take account of the specific situation of micro, small and medium-sized enterprises, this Regulation includes a derogation for organisations with fewer than 250 employees with regard to record-keeping. In addition, the Union institutions and bodies, and Member States and their supervisory authorities, are encouraged to take account of the specific needs of micro, small and medium-sized enterprises in the application of this Regulation. The notion of micro, small and medium-sized enterprises should draw from Article 2 of the Annex to Commission Recommendation 2003/361/EC.[5]

(14) The protection afforded by this Regulation should apply to natural persons, whatever their nationality or place of residence, in relation to the processing of their personal data. This Regulation does not cover the processing of personal data which concerns legal persons and in particular undertakings established as legal persons, including the name and the form of the legal person and the contact details of the legal person.

(15 In order to prevent creating a serious risk of circumvention, the protection of natural persons should be technologically neutral and should not depend on the techniques used. The protection of natural persons should apply to the processing of personal data by automated means, as well as to manual processing, if the personal data are contained or are intended to be contained in a filing system. Files or sets of files, as well as their cover pages, which are not structured according to specific criteria should not fall within the scope of this Regulation.

(16) This Regulation does not apply to issues of protection of fundamental rights and freedoms or the free flow of personal data related to activities which fall outside the scope of Union law, such as activities concerning national security. This Regulation does not apply to the processing of personal data by the Member States when carrying out activities in relation to the common foreign and security policy of the Union.

---

[5] Commission Recommendation of 6 May 2003 concerning the definition of micro, small and medium-sized enterprises (C(2003) 1422) (OJ L 124, 20.5.2003, p.36).

(17) Regulation (EC) No 45/2001 of the European Parliament and of the Council[6] applies to the processing of personal data by the Union institutions, bodies, offices and agencies. Regulation (EC) No 45/2001 and other Union legal acts applicable to such processing of personal data should be adapted to the principles and rules established in this Regulation and applied in the light of this Regulation. In order to provide a strong and coherent data protection framework in the Union, the necessary adaptations of Regulation (EC) No 45/2001 should follow after the adoption of this Regulation, in order to allow application at the same time as this Regulation.

(18) This Regulation does not apply to the processing of personal data by a natural person in the course of a purely personal or household activity and thus with no connection to a professional or commercial activity. Personal or household activities could include correspondence and the holding of addresses, or social networking and online activity undertaken within the context of such activities. However, this Regulation applies to controllers or processors which provide the means for processing personal data for such personal or household activities.

(19) The protection of natural persons with regard to the processing of personal data by competent authorities for the purposes of the prevention, investigation, detection or prosecution of criminal offences or the execution of criminal penalties, including the safeguarding against and the prevention of threats to public security and the free movement of such data, is the subject of a specific Union legal act. This Regulation should not, therefore, apply to processing activities for those purposes. However, personal data processed by public authorities under this Regulation should, when used for those purposes, be governed by a more specific Union legal act, namely Directive (EU) 2016/680 of the European Parliament and of the Council.[7] Member States may entrust competent authorities within the meaning of Directive (EU) 2016/680 with tasks which are not necessarily carried out for the purposes of the prevention, investigation, detection or prosecution of criminal offences or the execution of criminal penalties, including the safeguarding against and prevention of threats to public security, so that the processing of personal data for those other purposes, in so far as it is within the scope of Union law, falls within the scope of this Regulation.

With regard to the processing of personal data by those competent authorities for purposes falling within scope of this Regulation, Member States should be able to maintain or introduce more specific provisions to adapt the application of the rules of this Regulation. Such provisions may determine more precisely specific requirements for the processing of personal data by those competent authorities for those other purposes, taking into account the constitutional, organisational and administrative structure of the respective Member State. When the processing of personal data by private bodies falls within the scope of this Regulation, this Regulation should provide for the possibility for Member States under specific conditions to restrict by law certain obligations and rights when such a restriction constitutes a necessary and proportionate measure in a democratic society to safeguard specific important interests including public security and the prevention, investigation, detection or prosecution of criminal offences or the execution of criminal penalties, including the safeguarding against and the prevention of threats to public security. This is relevant for instance in the framework of anti-money laundering or the activities of forensic laboratories.

---

[6]   Regulation (EC) No 45/2001 of the European Parliament and of the Council of 18 December 2000 on the protection of individuals with regard to the processing of personal data by the Community institutions and bodies and on the free movement of such data (OJ L 8, 12.1.2001, p.1).

[7]   Directive (EU) 2016/680 of the European Parliament and of the Council of 27 April 2016 on the protection of natural persons with regard to the processing of personal data by competent authorities for the purposes of prevention, investigation, detection or prosecution of criminal offences or the execution of criminal penalties, and the free movement of such data and repealing Council Framework Decision 2008/977/JHA (see page 89 of this Official Journal).

(20) While this Regulation applies, inter alia, to the activities of courts and other judicial authorities, Union or Member State law could specify the processing operations and processing procedures in relation to the processing of personal data by courts and other judicial authorities. The competence of the supervisory authorities should not cover the processing of personal data when courts are acting in their judicial capacity, in order to safeguard the independence of the judiciary in the performance of its judicial tasks, including decision- making. It should be possible to entrust supervision of such data processing operations to specific bodies within the judicial system of the Member State, which should, in particular ensure compliance with the rules of this Regulation, enhance awareness among members of the judiciary of their obligations under this Regulation and handle complaints in relation to such data processing operations.

(21) This Regulation is without prejudice to the application of Directive 2000/31/EC of the European Parliament and of the Council,[8] in particular of the liability rules of intermediary service providers in Articles 12 to 15 of that Directive. That Directive seeks to contribute to the proper functioning of the internal market by ensuring the free movement of information society services between Member States.

(22) Any processing of personal data in the context of the activities of an establishment of a controller or a processor in the Union should be carried out in accordance with this Regulation, regardless of whether the processing itself takes place within the Union. Establishment implies the effective and real exercise of activity through stable arrangements. The legal form of such arrangements, whether through a branch or a subsidiary with a legal personality, is not the determining factor in that respect.

(23) In order to ensure that natural persons are not deprived of the protection to which they are entitled under this Regulation, the processing of personal data of data subjects who are in the Union by a controller or a processor not established in the Union should be subject to this Regulation where the processing activities are related to offering goods or services to such data subjects irrespective of whether connected to a payment. In order to determine whether such a controller or processor is offering goods or services to data subjects who are in the Union, it should be ascertained whether it is apparent that the controller or processor envisages offering services to data subjects in one or more Member States in the Union. Whereas the mere accessibility of the controller's, processor's or an intermediary's website in the Union, of an email address or of other contact details, or the use of a language generally used in the third country where the controller is established, is insufficient to ascertain such intention, factors such as the use of a language or a currency generally used in one or more Member States with the possibility of ordering goods and services in that other language, or the mentioning of customers or users who are in the Union, may make it apparent that the controller envisages offering goods or services to data subjects in the Union.

(24) The processing of personal data of data subjects who are in the Union by a controller or processor not established in the Union should also be subject to this Regulation when it is related to the monitoring of the behaviour of such data subjects in so far as their behaviour takes place within the Union. In order to determine whether a processing activity can be considered to monitor the behaviour of data subjects, it should be ascertained whether natural persons are tracked on the internet including potential subsequent use of personal data processing techniques which consist of profiling a natural person, particularly in order to take decisions concerning her or him or for analysing or predicting her or his personal preferences, behaviours and attitudes.

(25) Where Member State law applies by virtue of public international law, this Regulation should also apply to a controller not established in the Union, such as in a Member State's diplomatic mission or consular post.

(26) The principles of data protection should apply to any information concerning an

---

8   Directive 2000/31/EC of the European Parliament and of the Council of 8 June 2000 on certain legal aspects of information society services, in particular electronic commerce, in the Internal Market ('Directive on electronic commerce') (OJ L 178, 17.7.2000, p.1).

identified or identifiable natural person. Personal data which have undergone pseu-donymisation, which could be attributed to a natural person by the use of additional information should be considered to be information on an identifiable natural person. To determine whether a natural person is identifiable, account should be taken of all the means reasonably likely to be used, such as singling out, either by the controller or by another person to identify the natural person directly or indirectly. To ascertain whether means are reasonably likely to be used to identify the natural person, account should be taken of all objective factors, such as the costs of and the amount of time required for identification, taking into consideration the available technology at the time of the processing and technological developments. The principles of data protec-tion should therefore not apply to anonymous information, namely information which does not relate to an identified or identifiable natural person or to personal data rendered anonymous in such a manner that the data subject is not or no longer identifiable. This Regulation does not therefore concern the processing of such anony-mous information, including for statistical or research purposes.

(27) This Regulation does not apply to the personal data of deceased persons. Member States may provide for rules regarding the processing of personal data of deceased persons.

(28) The application of pseudonymisation to personal data can reduce the risks to the data subjects concerned and help controllers and processors to meet their data-protection obligations. The explicit introduction of 'pseudonymisation' in this Regulation is not intended to preclude any other measures of data protection.

(29) In order to create incentives to apply pseudonymisation when processing personal data, measures of pseudonymisation should, whilst allowing general analysis, be possible within the same controller when that controller has taken technical and organisational measures necessary to ensure, for the processing concerned, that this Regulation is implemented, and that additional information for attributing the personal data to a specific data subject is kept separately. The controller processing the personal data should indicate the authorised persons within the same controller.

(30) Natural persons may be associated with online identifiers provided by their devices, applications, tools and protocols, such as internet protocol addresses, cookie identifiers or other identifiers such as radio frequency identification tags. This may leave traces which, in particular when combined with unique identifiers and other information received by the servers, may be used to create profiles of the natural persons and identify them.

(31) Public authorities to which personal data are disclosed in accordance with a legal obligation for the exercise of their official mission, such as tax and customs authorities, financial investigation units, independent administrative authorities, or financial mar-ket authorities responsible for the regulation and supervision of securities markets should not be regarded as recipients if they receive personal data which are necessary to carry out a particular inquiry in the general interest, in accordance with Union or Member State law. The requests for disclosure sent by the public authorities should always be in writing, reasoned and occasional and should not concern the entirety of a filing system or lead to the interconnection of filing systems. The processing of personal data by those public authorities should comply with the applicable data-protection rules according to the purposes of the processing.

(32) Consent should be given by a clear affirmative act establishing a freely given, specific, informed and unambiguous indication of the data subject's agreement to the processing of personal data relating to him or her, such as by a written statement, including by electronic means, or an oral statement. This could include ticking a box when visiting an internet website, choosing technical settings for information society services or another statement or conduct which clearly indicates in this context the data subject's acceptance of the proposed processing of his or her personal data. Silence, pre-ticked boxes or inactivity should not therefore constitute consent. Consent should cover all processing activities carried out for the same purpose or purposes. When the processing has multiple purposes, consent should be given for all of them. If the data subject's

consent is to be given following a request by electronic means, the request must be clear, concise and not unnecessarily disruptive to the use of the service for which it is provided.

(33) It is often not possible to fully identify the purpose of personal data processing for scientific research purposes at the time of data collection. Therefore, data subjects should be allowed to give their consent to certain areas of scientific research when in keeping with recognised ethical standards for scientific research. Data subjects should have the opportunity to give their consent only to certain areas of research or parts of research projects to the extent allowed by the intended purpose.

(34) Genetic data should be defined as personal data relating to the inherited or acquired genetic characteristics of a natural person which result from the analysis of a biological sample from the natural person in question, in particular chromosomal, deoxyribonucleic acid (DNA) or ribonucleic acid (RNA) analysis, or from the analysis of another element enabling equivalent information to be obtained.

(35) Personal data concerning health should include all data pertaining to the health status of a data subject which reveal information relating to the past, current or future physical or mental health status of the data subject. This includes information about the natural person collected in the course of the registration for, or the provision of, health care services as referred to in Directive 2011/24/EU of the European Parliament and of the Council[9] to that natural person; a number, symbol or particular assigned to a natural person to uniquely identify the natural person for health purposes; information derived from the testing or examination of a body part or bodily substance, including from genetic data and biological samples; and any information on, for example, a disease, disability, disease risk, medical history, clinical treatment or the physiological or biomedical state of the data subject independent of its source, for example from a physician or other health professional, a hospital, a medical device or an in vitro diagnostic test.

(36) The main establishment of a controller in the Union should be the place of its central administration in the Union, unless the decisions on the purposes and means of the processing of personal data are taken in another establishment of the controller in the Union, in which case that other establishment should be considered to be the main establishment. The main establishment of a controller in the Union should be determined according to objective criteria and should imply the effective and real exercise of management activities determining the main decisions as to the purposes and means of processing through stable arrangements. That criterion should not depend on whether the processing of personal data is carried out at that location. The presence and use of technical means and technologies for processing personal data or processing activities do not, in themselves, constitute a main establishment and are therefore not determining criteria for a main establishment. The main establishment of the processor should be the place of its central administration in the Union or, if it has no central administration in the Union, the place where the main processing activities take place in the Union. In cases involving both the controller and the processor, the competent lead supervisory authority should remain the supervisory authority of the Member State where the controller has its main establishment, but the supervisory authority of the processor should be considered to be a supervisory authority concerned and that supervisory authority should participate in the cooperation procedure provided for by this Regulation. In any case, the supervisory authorities of the Member State or Member States where the processor has one or more establishments should not be considered to be supervisory authorities concerned where the draft decision concerns only the controller. Where the processing is carried out by a group of undertakings, the main establishment of the controlling undertaking should be considered to be the main establishment

---

9   Directive 2011/24/EU of the European Parliament and of the Council of 9 March 2011 on the application of patients' rights in cross-border healthcare (OJ L 88, 4.4.2011, p.45).

of the group of undertakings, except where the purposes and means of processing are determined by another undertaking.

(37) A group of undertakings should cover a controlling undertaking and its controlled undertakings, whereby the controlling undertaking should be the undertaking which can exert a dominant influence over the other undertakings by virtue, for example, of ownership, financial participation or the rules which govern it or the power to have personal data protection rules implemented. An undertaking which controls the processing of personal data in undertakings affiliated to it should be regarded, together with those undertakings, as a group of undertakings.

(38) Children merit specific protection with regard to their personal data, as they may be less aware of the risks, consequences and safeguards concerned and their rights in relation to the processing of personal data. Such specific protection should, in particular, apply to the use of personal data of children for the purposes of marketing or creating personality or user profiles and the collection of personal data with regard to children when using services offered directly to a child. The consent of the holder of parental responsibility should not be necessary in the context of preventive or counselling services offered directly to a child.

(39) Any processing of personal data should be lawful and fair. It should be transparent to natural persons that personal data concerning them are collected, used, consulted or otherwise processed and to what extent the personal data are or will be processed. The principle of transparency requires that any information and communication relating to the processing of those personal data be easily accessible and easy to understand, and that clear and plain language be used. That principle concerns, in particular, information to the data subjects on the identity of the controller and the purposes of the processing and further information to ensure fair and transparent processing in respect of the natural persons concerned and their right to obtain confirmation and communication of personal data concerning them which are being processed. Natural persons should be made aware of risks, rules, safeguards and rights in relation to the processing of personal data and how to exercise their rights in relation to such processing. In particular, the specific purposes for which personal data are processed should be explicit and legitimate and determined at the time of the collection of the personal data. The personal data should be adequate, relevant and limited to what is necessary for the purposes for which they are processed. This requires, in particular, ensuring that the period for which the personal data are stored is limited to a strict minimum. Personal data should be processed only if the purpose of the processing could not reasonably be fulfilled by other means. In order to ensure that the personal data are not kept longer than necessary, time limits should be established by the controller for erasure or for a periodic review. Every reasonable step should be taken to ensure that personal data which are inaccurate are rectified or deleted. Personal data should be processed in a manner that ensures appropriate security and confidentiality of the personal data, including for preventing unauthorised access to or use of personal data and the equipment used for the processing.

(40) In order for processing to be lawful, personal data should be processed on the basis of the consent of the data subject concerned or some other legitimate basis, laid down by law, either in this Regulation or in other Union or Member State law as referred to in this Regulation, including the necessity for compliance with the legal obligation to which the controller is subject or the necessity for the performance of a contract to which the data subject is party or in order to take steps at the request of the data subject prior to entering into a contract.

(41) Where this Regulation refers to a legal basis or a legislative measure, this does not necessarily require a legislative act adopted by a parliament, without prejudice to requirements pursuant to the constitutional order of the Member State concerned. However, such a legal basis or legislative measure should be clear and precise and its application should be foreseeable to persons subject to it, in accordance with the

case-law of the Court of Justice of the European Union (the 'Court of Justice') and the European Court of Human Rights.

(42) Where processing is based on the data subject's consent, the controller should be able to demonstrate that the data subject has given consent to the processing operation. In particular in the context of a written declaration on another matter, safeguards should ensure that the data subject is aware of the fact that and the extent to which consent is given. In accordance with Council Directive 93/13/EEC[10] a declaration of consent pre-formulated by the controller should be provided in an intelligible and easily accessible form, using clear and plain language and it should not contain unfair terms. For consent to be informed, the data subject should be aware at least of the identity of the controller and the purposes of the processing for which the personal data are intended. Consent should not be regarded as freely given if the data subject has no genuine or free choice or is unable to refuse or withdraw consent without detriment.

(43) In order to ensure that consent is freely given, consent should not provide a valid legal ground for the processing of personal data in a specific case where there is a clear imbalance between the data subject and the controller, in particular where the controller is a public authority and it is therefore unlikely that consent was freely given in all the circumstances of that specific situation. Consent is presumed not to be freely given if it does not allow separate consent to be given to different personal data processing operations despite it being appropriate in the individual case, or if the performance of a contract, including the provision of a service, is dependent on the consent despite such consent not being necessary for such performance.

(44) Processing should be lawful where it is necessary in the context of a contract or the intention to enter into a contract.

(45) Where processing is carried out in accordance with a legal obligation to which the controller is subject or where processing is necessary for the performance of a task carried out in the public interest or in the exercise of official authority, the processing should have a basis in Union or Member State law. This Regulation does not require a specific law for each individual processing. A law as a basis for several processing operations based on a legal obligation to which the controller is subject or where processing is necessary for the performance of a task carried out in the public interest or in the exercise of an official authority may be sufficient. It should also be for Union or Member State law to determine the purpose of processing. Furthermore, that law could specify the general conditions of this Regulation governing the lawfulness of personal data processing, establish specifications for determining the controller, the type of personal data which are subject to the processing, the data subjects concerned, the entities to which the personal data may be disclosed, the purpose limitations, the storage period and other measures to ensure lawful and fair processing. It should also be for Union or Member State law to determine whether the controller performing a task carried out in the public interest or in the exercise of official authority should be a public authority or another natural or legal person governed by public law, or, where it is in the public interest to do so, including for health purposes such as public health and social protection and the management of health care services, by private law, such as a professional association.

(46) The processing of personal data should also be regarded to be lawful where it is necessary to protect an interest which is essential for the life of the data subject or that of another natural person. Processing of personal data based on the vital interest of another natural person should in principle take place only where the processing cannot be manifestly based on another legal basis. Some types of processing may serve both important grounds of public interest and the vital interests of the data subject as for

---

[10]   Council Directive 93/13/EEC of 5 April 1993 on unfair terms in consumer contracts (OJ L 95, 21.4.1993, p.29).

instance when processing is necessary for humanitarian purposes, including for monitoring epidemics and their spread or in situations of humanitarian emergencies, in particular in situations of natural and man-made disasters.

(47) The legitimate interests of a controller, including those of a controller to which the personal data may be disclosed, or of a third party, may provide a legal basis for processing, provided that the interests or the fundamental rights and freedoms of the data subject are not overriding, taking into consideration the reasonable expectations of data subjects based on their relationship with the controller. Such legitimate interest could exist for example where there is a relevant and appropriate relationship between the data subject and the controller in situations such as where the data subject is a client or in the service of the controller. At any rate the existence of a legitimate interest would need careful assessment including whether a data subject can reasonably expect at the time and in the context of the collection of the personal data that processing for that purpose may take place. The interests and fundamental rights of the data subject could in particular override the interest of the data controller where personal data are processed in circumstances where data subjects do not reasonably expect further processing. Given that it is for the legislator to provide by law for the legal basis for public authorities to process personal data, that legal basis should not apply to the processing by public authorities in the performance of their tasks. The processing of personal data strictly necessary for the purposes of preventing fraud also constitutes a legitimate interest of the data controller concerned. The processing of personal data for direct marketing purposes may be regarded as carried out for a legitimate interest.

(48) Controllers that are part of a group of undertakings or institutions affiliated to a central body may have a legitimate interest in transmitting personal data within the group of undertakings for internal administrative purposes, including the processing of clients' or employees' personal data. The general principles for the transfer of personal data, within a group of undertakings, to an undertaking located in a third country remain unaffected.

(49) The processing of personal data to the extent strictly necessary and proportionate for the purposes of ensuring network and information security, i.e. the ability of a network or an information system to resist, at a given level of confidence, accidental events or unlawful or malicious actions that compromise the availability, authenticity, integrity and confidentiality of stored or transmitted personal data, and the security of the related services offered by, or accessible via, those networks and systems, by public authorities, by computer emergency response teams (CERTs), computer security incident response teams (CSIRTs), by providers of electronic communications networks and services and by providers of security technologies and services, constitutes a legitimate interest of the data controller concerned. This could, for example, include preventing unauthorised access to electronic communications networks and malicious code distribution and stopping 'denial of service' attacks and damage to computer and electronic communication systems.

(50) The processing of personal data for purposes other than those for which the personal data were initially collected should be allowed only where the processing is compatible with the purposes for which the personal data were initially collected. In such a case, no legal basis separate from that which allowed the collection of the personal data is required. If the processing is necessary for the performance of a task carried out in the public interest or in the exercise of official authority vested in the controller, Union or Member State law may determine and specify the tasks and purposes for which the further processing should be regarded as compatible and lawful. Further processing for archiving purposes in the public interest, scientific or historical research purposes or statistical purposes should be considered to be compatible lawful processing operations. The legal basis provided by Union or Member State law for the processing of personal data may also provide a legal basis for further processing. In order to ascertain whether a purpose of further processing is compatible with the purpose for which the personal data are initially collected, the controller, after having met all the requirements

for the lawfulness of the original processing, should take into account, inter alia: any link between those purposes and the purposes of the intended further processing; the context in which the personal data have been collected, in particular the reasonable expectations of data subjects based on their relationship with the controller as to their further use; the nature of the personal data; the consequences of the intended further processing for data subjects; and the existence of appropriate safeguards in both the original and intended further processing operations.

Where the data subject has given consent or the processing is based on Union or Member State law which constitutes a necessary and proportionate measure in a democratic society to safeguard, in particular, important objectives of general public interest, the controller should be allowed to further process the personal data irrespective of the compatibility of the purposes. In any case, the application of the principles set out in this Regulation and in particular the information of the data subject on those other purposes and on his or her rights including the right to object, should be ensured. Indicating possible criminal acts or threats to public security by the controller and transmitting the relevant personal data in individual cases or in several cases relating to the same criminal act or threats to public security to a competent authority should be regarded as being in the legitimate interest pursued by the controller. However, such transmission in the legitimate interest of the controller or further processing of personal data should be prohibited if the processing is not compatible with a legal, professional or other binding obligation of secrecy.

(51) Personal data which are, by their nature, particularly sensitive in relation to fundamental rights and freedoms merit specific protection as the context of their processing could create significant risks to the fundamental rights and freedoms. Those personal data should include personal data revealing racial or ethnic origin, whereby the use of the term 'racial origin' in this Regulation does not imply an acceptance by the Union of theories which attempt to determine the existence of separate human races. The processing of photographs should not systematically be considered to be processing of special categories of personal data as they are covered by the definition of biometric data only when processed through a specific technical means allowing the unique identification or authentication of a natural person. Such personal data should not be processed, unless processing is allowed in specific cases set out in this Regulation, taking into account that Member States law may lay down specific provisions on data protection in order to adapt the application of the rules of this Regulation for compliance with a legal obligation or for the performance of a task carried out in the public interest or in the exercise of official authority vested in the controller. In addition to the specific requirements for such processing, the general principles and other rules of this Regulation should apply, in particular as regards the conditions for lawful processing. Derogations from the general prohibition for processing such special categories of personal data should be explicitly provided, inter alia, where the data subject gives his or her explicit consent or in respect of specific needs in particular where the processing is carried out in the course of legitimate activities by certain associations or foundations the purpose of which is to permit the exercise of fundamental freedoms.

(52) Derogating from the prohibition on processing special categories of personal data should also be allowed when provided for in Union or Member State law and subject to suitable safeguards, so as to protect personal data and other fundamental rights, where it is in the public interest to do so, in particular processing personal data in the field of employment law, social protection law including pensions and for health security, monitoring and alert purposes, the prevention or control of communicable diseases and other serious threats to health. Such a derogation may be made for health purposes, including public health and the management of health-care services, especially in order to ensure the quality and cost-effectiveness of the procedures used for settling claims for benefits and services in the health insurance system, or for archiving purposes in the public interest, scientific or historical research purposes or statistical purposes. A

derogation should also allow the processing of such personal data where necessary for the establishment, exercise or defence of legal claims, whether in court proceedings or in an administrative or out-of-court procedure.

(53) Special categories of personal data which merit higher protection should be processed for health-related purposes only where necessary to achieve those purposes for the benefit of natural persons and society as a whole, in particular in the context of the management of health or social care services and systems, including processing by the management and central national health authorities of such data for the purpose of quality control, management information and the general national and local supervision of the health or social care system, and ensuring continuity of health or social care and cross-border healthcare or health security, monitoring and alert purposes, or for archiving purposes in the public interest, scientific or historical research purposes or statistical purposes, based on Union or Member State law which has to meet an objective of public interest, as well as for studies conducted in the public interest in the area of public health. Therefore, this Regulation should provide for harmonised conditions for the processing of special categories of personal data concerning health, in respect of specific needs, in particular where the processing of such data is carried out for certain health-related purposes by persons subject to a legal obligation of professional secrecy. Union or Member State law should provide for specific and suitable measures so as to protect the fundamental rights and the personal data of natural persons. Member States should be allowed to maintain or introduce further conditions, including limitations, with regard to the processing of genetic data, biometric data or data concerning health. However, this should not hamper the free flow of personal data within the Union when those conditions apply to cross-border processing of such data.

(54) The processing of special categories of personal data may be necessary for reasons of public interest in the areas of public health without consent of the data subject. Such processing should be subject to suitable and specific measures so as to protect the rights and freedoms of natural persons. In that context, 'public health' should be interpreted as defined in Regulation (EC) No 1338/2008 of the European Parliament and of the Council,[11] namely all elements related to health, namely health status, including morbidity and disability, the determinants having an effect on that health status, health care needs, resources allocated to health care, the provision of, and universal access to, health care as well as health care expenditure and financing, and the causes of mortality. Such processing of data concerning health for reasons of public interest should not result in personal data being processed for other purposes by third parties such as employers or insurance and banking companies.

(55) Moreover, the processing of personal data by official authorities for the purpose of achieving the aims, laid down by constitutional law or by international public law, of officially recognised religious associations, is carried out on grounds of public interest.

(56) Where in the course of electoral activities, the operation of the democratic system in a Member State requires that political parties compile personal data on people's political opinions, the processing of such data may be permitted for reasons of public interest, provided that appropriate safeguards are established.

(57) If the personal data processed by a controller do not permit the controller to identify a natural person, the data controller should not be obliged to acquire additional information in order to identify the data subject for the sole purpose of complying with any provision of this Regulation. However, the controller should not refuse to take additional information provided by the data subject in order to support the exercise of his or her rights. Identification should include the digital identification of a data subject, for example through authentication mechanism such as the same credentials, used by the data subject to log-in to the on-line service offered by the data controller.

---

[11] Regulation (EC) No 1338/2008 of the European Parliament and of the Council of 16 December 2008 on Community statistics on public health and health and safety at work (OJ L 354, 31.12.2008, p.70).

(58) The principle of transparency requires that any information addressed to the public or to the data subject be concise, easily accessible and easy to understand, and that clear and plain language and, additionally, where appropriate, visualisation be used. Such information could be provided in electronic form, for example, when addressed to the public, through a website. This is of particular relevance in situations where the proliferation of actors and the technological complexity of practice make it difficult for the data subject to know and understand whether, by whom and for what purpose personal data relating to him or her are being collected, such as in the case of online advertising. Given that children merit specific protection, any information and communication, where processing is addressed to a child, should be in such a clear and plain language that the child can easily understand.

(59) Modalities should be provided for facilitating the exercise of the data subject's rights under this Regulation, including mechanisms to request and, if applicable, obtain, free of charge, in particular, access to and rectification or erasure of personal data and the exercise of the right to object. The controller should also provide means for requests to be made electronically, especially where personal data are processed by electronic means. The controller should be obliged to respond to requests from the data subject without undue delay and at the latest within one month and to give reasons where the controller does not intend to comply with any such requests.

(60) The principles of fair and transparent processing require that the data subject be informed of the existence of the processing operation and its purposes. The controller should provide the data subject with any further information necessary to ensure fair and transparent processing taking into account the specific circumstances and context in which the personal data are processed. Furthermore, the data subject should be informed of the existence of profiling and the consequences of such profiling. Where the personal data are collected from the data subject, the data subject should also be informed whether he or she is obliged to provide the personal data and of the consequences, where he or she does not provide such data. That information may be provided in combination with standardised icons in order to give in an easily visible, intelligible and clearly legible manner, a meaningful overview of the intended processing. Where the icons are presented electronically, they should be machine-readable.

(61) The information in relation to the processing of personal data relating to the data subject should be given to him or her at the time of collection from the data subject, or, where the personal data are obtained from another source, within a reasonable period, depending on the circumstances of the case. Where personal data can be legitimately disclosed to another recipient, the data subject should be informed when the personal data are first disclosed to the recipient. Where the controller intends to process the personal data for a purpose other than that for which they were collected, the controller should provide the data subject prior to that further processing with information on that other purpose and other necessary information. Where the origin of the personal data cannot be provided to the data subject because various sources have been used, general information should be provided.

(62) However, it is not necessary to impose the obligation to provide information where the data subject already possesses the information, where the recording or disclosure of the personal data is expressly laid down by law or where the provision of information to the data subject proves to be impossible or would involve a disproportionate effort. The latter could in particular be the case where processing is carried out for archiving purposes in the public interest, scientific or historical research purposes or statistical purposes. In that regard, the number of data subjects, the age of the data and any appropriate safeguards adopted should be taken into consideration.

(63) A data subject should have the right of access to personal data which have been collected concerning him or her, and to exercise that right easily and at reasonable intervals, in order to be aware of, and verify, the lawfulness of the processing. This includes the right for data subjects to have access to data concerning their health, for example the data in their medical records containing information such as diagnoses, examination results,

assessments by treating physicians and any treatment or interventions provided. Every data subject should therefore have the right to know and obtain communication in particular with regard to the purposes for which the personal data are processed, where possible the period for which the personal data are processed, the recipients of the personal data, the logic involved in any automatic personal data processing and, at least when based on profiling, the consequences of such processing. Where possible, the controller should be able to provide remote access to a secure system which would provide the data subject with direct access to his or her personal data. That right should not adversely affect the rights or freedoms of others, including trade secrets or intellectual property and in particular the copyright protecting the software. However, the result of those considerations should not be a refusal to provide all information to the data subject. Where the controller processes a large quantity of information concerning the data subject, the controller should be able to request that, before the information is delivered, the data subject specify the information or processing activities to which the request relates.

(64) The controller should use all reasonable measures to verify the identity of a data subject who requests access, in particular in the context of online services and online identifiers. A controller should not retain personal data for the sole purpose of being able to react to potential requests.

(65) A data subject should have the right to have personal data concerning him or her rectified and a 'right to be forgotten' where the retention of such data infringes this Regulation or Union or Member State law to which the controller is subject. In particular, a data subject should have the right to have his or her personal data erased and no longer processed where the personal data are no longer necessary in relation to the purposes for which they are collected or otherwise processed, where a data subject has withdrawn his or her consent or objects to the processing of personal data concerning him or her, or where the processing of his or her personal data does not otherwise comply with this Regulation. That right is relevant in particular where the data subject has given his or her consent as a child and is not fully aware of the risks involved by the processing, and later wants to remove such personal data, especially on the internet. The data subject should be able to exercise that right notwithstanding the fact that he or she is no longer a child. However, the further retention of the personal data should be lawful where it is necessary, for exercising the right of freedom of expression and information, for compliance with a legal obligation, for the performance of a task carried out in the public interest or in the exercise of official authority vested in the controller, on the grounds of public interest in the area of public health, for archiving purposes in the public interest, scientific or historical research purposes or statistical purposes, or for the establishment, exercise or defence of legal claims.

(66) To strengthen the right to be forgotten in the online environment, the right to erasure should also be extended in such a way that a controller who has made the personal data public should be obliged to inform the controllers which are processing such personal data to erase any links to, or copies or replications of those personal data. In doing so, that controller should take reasonable steps, taking into account available technology and the means available to the controller, including technical measures, to inform the controllers which are processing the personal data of the data subject's request.

(67) Methods by which to restrict the processing of personal data could include, inter alia, temporarily moving the selected data to another processing system, making the selected personal data unavailable to users, or temporarily removing published data from a website. In automated filing systems, the restriction of processing should in principle be ensured by technical means in such a manner that the personal data are not subject to further processing operations and cannot be changed. The fact that the processing of personal data is restricted should be clearly indicated in the system.

(68) To further strengthen the control over his or her own data, where the processing of personal data is carried out by automated means, the data subject should also be allowed to receive personal data concerning him or her which he or she has provided to a

controller in a structured, commonly used, machine-readable and interoperable format, and to transmit it to another controller. Data controllers should be encouraged to develop interoperable formats that enable data portability. That right should apply where the data subject provided the personal data on the basis of his or her consent or the processing is necessary for the performance of a contract. It should not apply where processing is based on a legal ground other than consent or contract. By its very nature, that right should not be exercised against controllers processing personal data in the exercise of their public duties. It should therefore not apply where the processing of the personal data is necessary for compliance with a legal obligation to which the controller is subject or for the performance of a task carried out in the public interest or in the exercise of an official authority vested in the controller. The data subject's right to transmit or receive personal data concerning him or her should not create an obligation for the controllers to adopt or maintain processing systems which are technically compatible. Where, in a certain set of personal data, more than one data subject is concerned, the right to receive the personal data should be without prejudice to the rights and freedoms of other data subjects in accordance with this Regulation. Furthermore, that right should not prejudice the right of the data subject to obtain the erasure of personal data and the limitations of that right as set out in this Regulation and should, in particular, not imply the erasure of personal data concerning the data subject which have been provided by him or her for the performance of a contract to the extent that and for as long as the personal data are necessary for the performance of that contract. Where technically feasible, the data subject should have the right to have the personal data transmitted directly from one controller to another.

(69) Where personal data might lawfully be processed because processing is necessary for the performance of a task carried out in the public interest or in the exercise of official authority vested in the controller, or on grounds of the legitimate interests of a controller or a third party, a data subject should, nevertheless, be entitled to object to the processing of any personal data relating to his or her particular situation. It should be for the controller to demonstrate that its compelling legitimate interest overrides the interests or the fundamental rights and freedoms of the data subject.

(70) Where personal data are processed for the purposes of direct marketing, the data subject should have the right to object to such processing, including profiling to the extent that it is related to such direct marketing, whether with regard to initial or further processing, at any time and free of charge. That right should be explicitly brought to the attention of the data subject and presented clearly and separately from any other information.

(71) The data subject should have the right not to be subject to a decision, which may include a measure, evaluating personal aspects relating to him or her which is based solely on automated processing and which produces legal effects concerning him or her or similarly significantly affects him or her, such as automatic refusal of an online credit application or e-recruiting practices without any human intervention. Such processing includes 'profiling' that consists of any form of automated processing of personal data evaluating the personal aspects relating to a natural person, in particular to analyse or predict aspects concerning the data subject's performance at work, economic situation, health, personal preferences or interests, reliability or behaviour, location or movements, where it produces legal effects concerning him or her or similarly significantly affects him or her. However, decision-making based on such processing, including profiling, should be allowed where expressly authorised by Union or Member State law to which the controller is subject, including for fraud and tax-evasion monitoring and prevention purposes conducted in accordance with the regulations, standards and recommendations of Union institutions or national oversight bodies and to ensure the security and reliability of a service provided by the controller, or necessary for the entering or performance of a contract between the data subject and a controller, or when the data subject has given his or her explicit consent. In any case, such processing should be subject to suitable safeguards, which should include specific information to

the data subject and the right to obtain human intervention, to express his or her point of view, to obtain an explanation of the decision reached after such assessment and to challenge the decision. Such measure should not concern a child.

In order to ensure fair and transparent processing in respect of the data subject, taking into account the specific circumstances and context in which the personal data are processed, the controller should use appropriate mathematical or statistical procedures for the profiling, implement technical and organisational measures appropriate to ensure, in particular, that factors which result in inaccuracies in personal data are corrected and the risk of errors is minimised, secure personal data in a manner that takes account of the potential risks involved for the interests and rights of the data subject and that prevents, inter alia, discriminatory effects on natural persons on the basis of racial or ethnic origin, political opinion, religion or beliefs, trade union membership, genetic or health status or sexual orientation, or that result in measures having such an effect. Automated decision-making and profiling based on special categories of personal data should be allowed only under specific conditions.

(72) Profiling is subject to the rules of this Regulation governing the processing of personal data, such as the legal grounds for processing or data protection principles. The European Data Protection Board established by this Regulation (the 'Board') should be able to issue guidance in that context.

(73) Restrictions concerning specific principles and the rights of information, access to and rectification or erasure of personal data, the right to data portability, the right to object, decisions based on profiling, as well as the communication of a personal data breach to a data subject and certain related obligations of the controllers may be imposed by Union or Member State law, as far as necessary and proportionate in a democratic society to safeguard public security, including the protection of human life especially in response to natural or manmade disasters, the prevention, investigation and prosecution of criminal offences or the execution of criminal penalties, including the safeguarding against and the prevention of threats to public security, or of breaches of ethics for regulated professions, other important objectives of general public interest of the Union or of a Member State, in particular an important economic or financial interest of the Union or of a Member State, the keeping of public registers kept for reasons of general public interest, further processing of archived personal data to provide specific information related to the political behaviour under former totalitarian state regimes or the protection of the data subject or the rights and freedoms of others, including social protection, public health and humanitarian purposes. Those restrictions should be in accordance with the requirements set out in the Charter and in the European Convention for the Protection of Human Rights and Fundamental Freedoms.

(74) The responsibility and liability of the controller for any processing of personal data carried out by the controller or on the controller's behalf should be established. In particular, the controller should be obliged to implement appropriate and effective measures and be able to demonstrate the compliance of processing activities with this Regulation, including the effectiveness of the measures. Those measures should take into account the nature, scope, context and purposes of the processing and the risk to the rights and freedoms of natural persons.

(75) The risk to the rights and freedoms of natural persons, of varying likelihood and severity, may result from personal data processing which could lead to physical, material or non-material damage, in particular: where the processing may give rise to discrimination, identity theft or fraud, financial loss, damage to the reputation, loss of confidentiality of personal data protected by professional secrecy, unauthorised reversal of pseudonymisation, or any other significant economic or social disadvantage; where data subjects might be deprived of their rights and freedoms or prevented from exercising control over their personal data; where personal data are processed which reveal racial or ethnic origin, political opinions, religion or philosophical beliefs, trade union membership, and the processing of genetic data, data concerning health or data

concerning sex life or criminal convictions and offences or related security measures; where personal aspects are evaluated, in particular analysing or predicting aspects concerning performance at work, economic situation, health, personal preferences or interests, reliability or behaviour, location or movements, in order to create or use personal profiles; where personal data of vulnerable natural persons, in particular of children, are processed; or where processing involves a large amount of personal data and affects a large number of data subjects.

(76) The likelihood and severity of the risk to the rights and freedoms of the data subject should be determined by reference to the nature, scope, context and purposes of the processing. Risk should be evaluated on the basis of an objective assessment, by which it is established whether data processing operations involve a risk or a high risk.

(77) Guidance on the implementation of appropriate measures and on the demonstration of compliance by the controller or the processor, especially as regards the identification of the risk related to the processing, their assessment in terms of origin, nature, likelihood and severity, and the identification of best practices to mitigate the risk, could be provided in particular by means of approved codes of conduct, approved certifications, guidelines provided by the Board or indications provided by a data protection officer. The Board may also issue guidelines on processing operations that are considered to be unlikely to result in a high risk to the rights and freedoms of natural persons and indicate what measures may be sufficient in such cases to address such risk.

(78) The protection of the rights and freedoms of natural persons with regard to the processing of personal data require that appropriate technical and organisational measures be taken to ensure that the requirements of this Regulation are met. In order to be able to demonstrate compliance with this Regulation, the controller should adopt internal policies and implement measures which meet in particular the principles of data protection by design and data protection by default. Such measures could consist, inter alia, of minimising the processing of personal data, pseudonymising personal data as soon as possible, transparency with regard to the functions and processing of personal data, enabling the data subject to monitor the data processing, enabling the controller to create and improve security features. When developing, designing, select- ing and using applications, services and products that are based on the processing of personal data or process personal data to fulfil their task, producers of the products, services and applications should be encouraged to take into account the right to data protection when developing and designing such products, services and applications and, with due regard to the state of the art, to make sure that controllers and processors are able to fulfil their data protection obligations. The principles of data protection by design and by default should also be taken into consideration in the context of public tenders.

(79) The protection of the rights and freedoms of data subjects as well as the responsibility and liability of controllers and processors, also in relation to the monitoring by and measures of supervisory authorities, requires a clear allocation of the responsibilities under this Regulation, including where a controller determines the purposes and means of the processing jointly with other controllers or where a processing operation is carried out on behalf of a controller.

(80) Where a controller or a processor not established in the Union is processing personal data of data subjects who are in the Union whose processing activities are related to the offering of goods or services, irrespective of whether a payment of the data subject is required, to such data subjects in the Union, or to the monitoring of their behaviour as far as their behaviour takes place within the Union, the controller or the processor should designate a representative, unless the processing is occasional, does not include processing, on a large scale, of special categories of personal data or the processing of personal data relating to criminal convictions and offences, and is unlikely to result in a risk to the rights and freedoms of natural persons, taking into account the nature, context, scope and purposes of the processing or if the controller is a public authority or body. The representative should act on behalf of the controller or the processor and may

be addressed by any supervisory authority. The representative should be explicitly designated by a written mandate of the controller or of the processor to act on its behalf with regard to its obligations under this Regulation. The designation of such a representative does not affect the responsibility or liability of the controller or of the processor under this Regulation. Such a representative should perform its tasks according to the mandate received from the controller or processor, including cooperating with the competent supervisory authorities with regard to any action taken to ensure compliance with this Regulation. The designated representative should be subject to enforcement proceedings in the event of non-compliance by the controller or processor.

(81) To ensure compliance with the requirements of this Regulation in respect of the processing to be carried out by the processor on behalf of the controller, when entrusting a processor with processing activities, the controller should use only processors providing sufficient guarantees, in particular in terms of expert knowledge, reliability and resources, to implement technical and organisational measures which will meet the requirements of this Regulation, including for the security of processing. The adherence of the processor to an approved code of conduct or an approved certification mechanism may be used as an element to demonstrate compliance with the obligations of the controller. The carrying-out of processing by a processor should be governed by a contract or other legal act under Union or Member State law, binding the processor to the controller, setting out the subject- matter and duration of the processing, the nature and purposes of the processing, the type of personal data and categories of data subjects, taking into account the specific tasks and responsibilities of the processor in the context of the processing to be carried out and the risk to the rights and freedoms of the data subject. The controller and processor may choose to use an individual contract or standard contractual clauses which are adopted either directly by the Commission or by a supervisory authority in accordance with the consistency mechanism and then adopted by the Commission. After the completion of the processing on behalf of the controller, the processor should, at the choice of the controller, return or delete the personal data, unless there is a requirement to store the personal data under Union or Member State law to which the processor is subject.

(82) In order to demonstrate compliance with this Regulation, the controller or processor should maintain records of processing activities under its responsibility. Each controller and processor should be obliged to cooperate with the supervisory authority and make those records, on request, available to it, so that it might serve for monitoring those processing operations.

(83) In order to maintain˙security and to prevent processing in infringement of this Regulation, the controller or processor should evaluate the risks inherent in the processing and implement measures to mitigate those risks, such as encryption. Those measures should ensure an appropriate level of security, including confidentiality, taking into account the state of the art and the costs of implementation in relation to the risks and the nature of the personal data to be protected. In assessing data security risk, consideration should be given to the risks that are presented by personal data processing, such as accidental or unlawful destruction, loss, alteration, unauthorised disclosure of, or access to, personal data transmitted, stored or otherwise processed which may in particular lead to physical, material or non-material damage.

(84) In order to enhance compliance with this Regulation where processing operations are likely to result in a high risk to the rights and freedoms of natural persons, the controller should be responsible for the carrying-out of a data protection impact assessment to evaluate, in particular, the origin, nature, particularity and severity of that risk. The outcome of the assessment should be taken into account when determining the appropriate measures to be taken in order to demonstrate that the processing of personal data complies with this Regulation. Where a data-protection impact assessment indicates that processing operations involve a high risk which the controller

cannot mitigate by appropriate measures in terms of available technology and costs of implementation, a consultation of the supervisory authority should take place prior to the processing.

(85) A personal data breach may, if not addressed in an appropriate and timely manner, result in physical, material or non-material damage to natural persons such as loss of control over their personal data or limitation of their rights, discrimination, identity theft or fraud, financial loss, unauthorised reversal of pseudonymisation, damage to reputation, loss of confidentiality of personal data protected by professional secrecy or any other significant economic or social disadvantage to the natural person concerned. Therefore, as soon as the controller becomes aware that a personal data breach has occurred, the controller should notify the personal data breach to the supervisory authority without undue delay and, where feasible, not later than 72 hours after having become aware of it, unless the controller is able to demonstrate, in accordance with the accountability principle, that the personal data breach is unlikely to result in a risk to the rights and freedoms of natural persons. Where such notification cannot be achieved within 72 hours, the reasons for the delay should accompany the notification and information may be provided in phases without undue further delay.

(86) The controller should communicate to the data subject a personal data breach, without undue delay, where that personal data breach is likely to result in a high risk to the rights and freedoms of the natural person in order to allow him or her to take the necessary precautions. The communication should describe the nature of the personal data breach as well as recommendations for the natural person concerned to mitigate potential adverse effects. Such communications to data subjects should be made as soon as reasonably feasible and in close cooperation with the supervisory authority, respecting guidance provided by it or by other relevant authorities such as law-enforcement authorities. For example, the need to mitigate an immediate risk of damage would call for prompt communication with data subjects whereas the need to implement appropriate measures against continuing or similar personal data breaches may justify more time for communication.

(87) It should be ascertained whether all appropriate technological protection and organisational measures have been implemented to establish immediately whether a personal data breach has taken place and to inform promptly the supervisory authority and the data subject. The fact that the notification was made without undue delay should be established taking into account in particular the nature and gravity of the personal data breach and its consequences and adverse effects for the data subject. Such notification may result in an intervention of the supervisory authority in accordance with its tasks and powers laid down in this Regulation.

(88) In setting detailed rules concerning the format and procedures applicable to the notification of personal data breaches, due consideration should be given to the circumstances of that breach, including whether or not personal data had been protected by appropriate technical protection measures, effectively limiting the likelihood of identity fraud or other forms of misuse. Moreover, such rules and procedures should take into account the legitimate interests of law-enforcement authorities where early disclosure could unnecessarily hamper the investigation of the circumstances of a personal data breach.

(89) Directive 95/46/EC provided for a general obligation to notify the processing of personal data to the supervisory authorities. While that obligation produces administrative and financial burdens, it did not in all cases contribute to improving the protection of personal data. Such indiscriminate general notification obligations should therefore be abolished, and replaced by effective procedures and mechanisms which focus instead on those types of processing operations which are likely to result in a high risk to the rights and freedoms of natural persons by virtue of their nature, scope, context and purposes. Such types of processing operations may be those which in, particular, involve using new technologies, or are of a new kind and where no data

protection impact assessment has been carried out before by the controller, or where they become necessary in the light of the time that has elapsed since the initial processing.

(90) In such cases, a data protection impact assessment should be carried out by the controller prior to the processing in order to assess the particular likelihood and severity of the high risk, taking into account the nature, scope, context and purposes of the processing and the sources of the risk. That impact assessment should include, in particular, the measures, safeguards and mechanisms envisaged for mitigating that risk, ensuring the protection of personal data and demonstrating compliance with this Regulation.

(91) This should in particular apply to large-scale processing operations which aim to process a considerable amount of personal data at regional, national or supranational level and which could affect a large number of data subjects and which are likely to result in a high risk, for example, on account of their sensitivity, where in accordance with the achieved state of technological knowledge a new technology is used on a large scale as well as to other processing operations which result in a high risk to the rights and freedoms of data subjects, in particular where those operations render it more difficult for data subjects to exercise their rights. A data protection impact assessment should also be made where personal data are processed for taking decisions regarding specific natural persons following any systematic and extensive evaluation of personal aspects relating to natural persons based on profiling those data or following the processing of special categories of personal data, biometric data, or data on criminal convictions and offences or related security measures. A data protection impact assessment is equally required for monitoring publicly accessible areas on a large scale, especially when using optic-electronic devices or for any other operations where the competent supervisory authority considers that the processing is likely to result in a high risk to the rights and freedoms of data subjects, in particular because they prevent data subjects from exercising a right or using a service or a contract, or because they are carried out systematically on a large scale. The processing of personal data should not be considered to be on a large scale if the processing concerns personal data from patients or clients by an individual physician, other health care professional or lawyer. In such cases, a data protection impact assessment should not be mandatory.

(92) There are circumstances under which it may be reasonable and economical for the subject of a data protection impact assessment to be broader than a single project, for example where public authorities or bodies intend to establish a common application or processing platform or where several controllers plan to introduce a common application or processing environment across an industry sector or segment or for a widely used horizontal activity.

(93) In the context of the adoption of the Member State law on which the performance of the tasks of the public authority or public body is based and which regulates the specific processing operation or set of operations in question, Member States may deem it necessary to carry out such assessment prior to the processing activities.

(94) Where a data protection impact assessment indicates that the processing would, in the absence of safeguards, security measures and mechanisms to mitigate the risk, result in a high risk to the rights and freedoms of natural persons and the controller is of the opinion that the risk cannot be mitigated by reasonable means in terms of available technologies and costs of implementation, the supervisory authority should be consulted prior to the start of processing activities. Such high risk is likely to result from certain types of processing and the extent and frequency of processing, which may result also in a realisation of damage or interference with the rights and freedoms of the natural person. The supervisory authority should respond to the request for consultation within a specified period. However, the absence of a reaction of the supervisory authority within that period should be without prejudice to any intervention of the supervisory authority in accordance with its tasks and powers laid down in this Regulation, including the power to prohibit processing operations. As part of that

consultation process, the outcome of a data protection impact assessment carried out with regard to the processing at issue may be submitted to the supervisory authority, in particular the measures envisaged to mitigate the risk to the rights and freedoms of natural persons.

(95) The processor should assist the controller, where necessary and upon request, in ensuring compliance with the obligations deriving from the carrying out of data protection impact assessments and from prior consultation of the supervisory authority.

(96) A consultation of the supervisory authority should also take place in the course of the preparation of a legislative or regulatory measure which provides for the processing of personal data, in order to ensure compliance of the intended processing with this Regulation and in particular to mitigate the risk involved for the data subject.

(97) Where the processing is carried out by a public authority, except for courts or independent judicial authorities when acting in their judicial capacity, where, in the private sector, processing is carried out by a controller whose core activities consist of processing operations that require regular and systematic monitoring of the data subjects on a large scale, or where the core activities of the controller or the processor consist of processing on a large scale of special categories of personal data and data relating to criminal convictions and offences, a person with expert knowledge of data protection law and practices should assist the controller or processor to monitor internal compliance with this Regulation. In the private sector, the core activities of a controller relate to its primary activities and do not relate to the processing of personal data as ancillary activities. The necessary level of expert knowledge should be determined in particular according to the data processing operations carried out and the protection required for the personal data processed by the controller or the processor. Such data protection officers, whether or not they are an employee of the controller, should be in a position to perform their duties and tasks in an independent manner.

(98) Associations or other bodies representing categories of controllers or processors should be encouraged to draw up codes of conduct, within the limits of this Regulation, so as to facilitate the effective application of this Regulation, taking account of the specific characteristics of the processing carried out in certain sectors and the specific needs of micro, small and medium enterprises. In particular, such codes of conduct could calibrate the obligations of controllers and processors, taking into account the risk likely to result from the processing for the rights and freedoms of natural persons.

(99) When drawing up a code of conduct, or when amending or extending such a code, associations and other bodies representing categories of controllers or processors should consult relevant stakeholders, including data subjects where feasible, and have regard to submissions received and views expressed in response to such consultations.

(100) In order to enhance transparency and compliance with this Regulation, the establishment of certification mechanisms and data protection seals and marks should be encouraged, allowing data subjects to quickly assess the level of data protection of relevant products and services.

(101) Flows of personal data to and from countries outside the Union and international organisations are necessary for the expansion of international trade and international cooperation. The increase in such flows has raised new challenges and concerns with regard to the protection of personal data. However, when personal data are transferred from the Union to controllers, processors or other recipients in third countries or to international organisations, the level of protection of natural persons ensured in the Union by this Regulation should not be undermined, including in cases of onward transfers of personal data from the third country or international organisation to controllers, processors in the same or another third country or international organisation. In any event, transfers to third countries and international organisations may only be carried out in full compliance with this Regulation. A transfer could take place only if, subject to the other provisions of this Regulation, the conditions laid down in

the provisions of this Regulation relating to the transfer of personal data to third countries or international organisations are complied with by the controller or processor.

(102) This Regulation is without prejudice to international agreements concluded between the Union and third countries regulating the transfer of personal data including appropriate safeguards for the data subjects. Member States may conclude international agreements which involve the transfer of personal data to third countries or international organisations, as far as such agreements do not affect this Regulation or any other provisions of Union law and include an appropriate level of protection for the fundamental rights of the data subjects.

(103) The Commission may decide with effect for the entire Union that a third country, a territory or specified sector within a third country, or an international organisation, offers an adequate level of data protection, thus providing legal certainty and uniformity throughout the Union as regards the third country or international organisation which is considered to provide such level of protection. In such cases, transfers of personal data to that third country or international organisation may take place without the need to obtain any further authorisation. The Commission may also decide, having given notice and a full statement setting out the reasons to the third country or international organisation, to revoke such a decision.

(104) In line with the fundamental values on which the Union is founded, in particular the protection of human rights, the Commission should, in its assessment of the third country, or of a territory or specified sector within a third country, take into account how a particular third country respects the rule of law, access to justice as well as international human rights norms and standards and its general and sectoral law, including legislation concerning public security, defence and national security as well as public order and criminal law. The adoption of an adequacy decision with regard to a territory or a specified sector in a third country should take into account clear and objective criteria, such as specific processing activities and the scope of applicable legal standards and legislation in force in the third country. The third country should offer guarantees ensuring an adequate level of protection essentially equivalent to that ensured within the Union, in particular where personal data are processed in one or several specific sectors. In particular, the third country should ensure effective independent data protection supervision and should provide for cooperation mechanisms with the Member States' data protection authorities, and the data subjects should be provided with effective and enforceable rights and effective administrative and judicial redress.

(105) Apart from the international commitments the third country or international organisation has entered into, the Commission should take account of obligations arising from the third country's or international organisation's participation in multilateral or regional systems in particular in relation to the protection of personal data, as well as the implementation of such obligations. In particular, the third country's accession to the Council of Europe Convention of 28 January 1981 for the Protection of Individuals with regard to the Automatic Processing of Personal Data and its Additional Protocol should be taken into account. The Commission should consult the Board when assessing the level of protection in third countries or international organisations.

(106) The Commission should monitor the functioning of decisions on the level of protection in a third country, a territory or specified sector within a third country, or an international organisation, and monitor the functioning of decisions adopted on the basis of Article 25(6) or Article 26(4) of Directive 95/46/EC. In its adequacy decisions, the Commission should provide for a periodic review mechanism of their functioning. That periodic review should be conducted in consultation with the third country or international organisation in question and take into account all relevant developments in the third country or international organisation. For the purposes of monitoring and of carrying out the periodic reviews, the Commission should take into consideration the views and findings of the European Parliament and of the Council as well as of

other relevant bodies and sources. The Commission should evaluate, within a reasonable time, the functioning of the latter decisions and report any relevant findings to the Committee within the meaning of Regulation (EU) No 182/2011 of the European Parliament and of the Council[12] as established under this Regulation, to the European Parliament and to the Council.

(107) The Commission may recognise that a third country, a territory or a specified sector within a third country, or an international organisation no longer ensures an adequate level of data protection. Consequently the transfer of personal data to that third country or international organisation should be prohibited, unless the requirements in this Regulation relating to transfers subject to appropriate safeguards, including binding corporate rules, and derogations for specific situations are fulfilled. In that case, provision should be made for consultations between the Commission and such third countries or international organisations. The Commission should, in a timely manner, inform the third country or international organisation of the reasons and enter into consultations with it in order to remedy the situation.

(108) In the absence of an adequacy decision, the controller or processor should take measures to compensate for the lack of data protection in a third country by way of appropriate safeguards for the data subject. Such appropriate safeguards may consist of making use of binding corporate rules, standard data protection clauses adopted by the Commission, standard data protection clauses adopted by a supervisory authority or contractual clauses authorised by a supervisory authority. Those safeguards should ensure compliance with data protection requirements and the rights of the data subjects appropriate to processing within the Union, including the availability of enforceable data subject rights and of effective legal remedies, including to obtain effective administrative or judicial redress and to claim compensation, in the Union or in a third country. They should relate in particular to compliance with the general principles relating to personal data processing, the principles of data protection by design and by default. Transfers may also be carried out by public authorities or bodies with public authorities or bodies in third countries or with international organisations with corresponding duties or functions, including on the basis of provisions to be inserted into administrative arrangements, such as a memorandum of understanding, providing for enforceable and effective rights for data subjects. Authorisation by the competent supervisory authority should be obtained when the safeguards are provided for in administrative arrangements that are not legally binding.

(109) The possibility for the controller or processor to use standard data-protection clauses adopted by the Commission or by a supervisory authority should prevent controllers or processors neither from including the standard data-protection clauses in a wider contract, such as a contract between the processor and another processor, nor from adding other clauses or additional safeguards provided that they do not contradict, directly or indirectly, the standard contractual clauses adopted by the Commission or by a supervisory authority or prejudice the fundamental rights or freedoms of the data subjects. Controllers and processors should be encouraged to provide additional safeguards via contractual commitments that supplement standard protection clauses.

(110) A group of undertakings, or a group of enterprises engaged in a joint economic activity, should be able to make use of approved binding corporate rules for its international transfers from the Union to organisations within the same group of undertakings, or group of enterprises engaged in a joint economic activity, provided that such corporate rules include all essential principles and enforceable rights to ensure appropriate safeguards for transfers or categories of transfers of personal data.

(111) Provisions should be made for the possibility for transfers in certain circumstances where the data subject has given his or her explicit consent, where the transfer is

---

[12] Regulation (EU) No 182/2011 of the European Parliament and of the Council of 16 February 2011 laying down the rules and general principles concerning mechanisms for control by Member States of the Commission's exercise of implementing powers (OJ L 55, 28.2.2011, p.13).

occasional and necessary in relation to a contract or a legal claim, regardless of whether in a judicial procedure or whether in an administrative or any out-of-court procedure, including procedures before regulatory bodies. Provision should also be made for the possibility for transfers where important grounds of public interest laid down by Union or Member State law so require or where the transfer is made from a register established by law and intended for consultation by the public or persons having a legitimate interest. In the latter case, such a transfer should not involve the entirety of the personal data or entire categories of the data contained in the register and, when the register is intended for consultation by persons having a legitimate interest, the transfer should be made only at the request of those persons or, if they are to be the recipients, taking into full account the interests and fundamental rights of the data subject.

(112) Those derogations should in particular apply to data transfers required and necessary for important reasons of public interest, for example in cases of international data exchange between competition authorities, tax or customs administrations, between financial supervisory authorities, between services competent for social security matters, or for public health, for example in the case of contact tracing for contagious diseases or in order to reduce and/or eliminate doping in sport. A transfer of personal data should also be regarded as lawful where it is necessary to protect an interest which is essential for the data subject's or another person's vital interests, including physical integrity or life, if the data subject is incapable of giving consent. In the absence of an adequacy decision, Union or Member State law may, for important reasons of public interest, expressly set limits to the transfer of specific categories of data to a third country or an international organisation. Member States should notify such provisions to the Commission. Any transfer to an international humanitarian organisation of personal data of a data subject who is physically or legally incapable of giving consent, with a view to accomplishing a task incumbent under the Geneva Conventions or to complying with international humanitarian law applicable in armed conflicts, could be considered to be necessary for an important reason of public interest or because it is in the vital interest of the data subject.

(113) Transfers which can be qualified as not repetitive and that only concern a limited number of data subjects, could also be possible for the purposes of the compelling legitimate interests pursued by the controller, when those interests are not overridden by the interests or rights and freedoms of the data subject and when the controller has assessed all the circumstances surrounding the data transfer. The controller should give particular consideration to the nature of the personal data, the purpose and duration of the proposed processing operation or operations, as well as the situation in the country of origin, the third country and the country of final destination, and should provide suitable safeguards to protect fundamental rights and freedoms of natural persons with regard to the processing of their personal data. Such transfers should be possible only in residual cases where none of the other grounds for transfer are applicable. For scientific or historical research purposes or statistical purposes, the legitimate expectations of society for an increase of knowledge should be taken into consideration. The controller should inform the supervisory authority and the data subject about the transfer.

(114) In any case, where the Commission has taken no decision on the adequate level of data protection in a third country, the controller or processor should make use of solutions that provide data subjects with enforceable and effective rights as regards the processing of their data in the Union once those data have been transferred so that that they will continue to benefit from fundamental rights and safeguards.

(115) Some third countries adopt laws, regulations and other legal acts which purport to directly regulate the processing activities of natural and legal persons under the jurisdiction of the Member States. This may include judgments of courts or tribunals or decisions of administrative authorities in third countries requiring a controller or processor to transfer or disclose personal data, and which are not based on an

international agreement, such as a mutual legal assistance treaty, in force between the requesting third country and the Union or a Member State. The extraterritorial application of those laws, regulations and other legal acts may be in breach of international law and may impede the attainment of the protection of natural persons ensured in the Union by this Regulation. Transfers should only be allowed where the conditions of this Regulation for a transfer to third countries are met. This may be the case, inter alia, where disclosure is necessary for an important ground of public interest recognised in Union or Member State law to which the controller is subject.

(116) When personal data moves across borders outside the Union it may put at increased risk the ability of natural persons to exercise data protection rights in particular to protect themselves from the unlawful use or disclosure of that information. At the same time, supervisory authorities may find that they are unable to pursue complaints or conduct investigations relating to the activities outside their borders. Their efforts to work together in the cross-border context may also be hampered by insufficient preventative or remedial powers, inconsistent legal regimes, and practical obstacles like resource constraints. Therefore, there is a need to promote closer cooperation among data protection supervisory authorities to help them exchange information and carry out investigations with their international counterparts. For the purposes of developing international cooperation mechanisms to facilitate and provide international mutual assistance for the enforcement of legislation for the protection of personal data, the Commission and the supervisory authorities should exchange information and cooperate in activities related to the exercise of their powers with competent authorities in third countries, based on reciprocity and in accordance with this Regulation.

(117) The establishment of supervisory authorities in Member States, empowered to perform their tasks and exercise their powers with complete independence, is an essential component of the protection of natural persons with regard to the processing of their personal data. Member States should be able to establish more than one supervisory authority, to reflect their constitutional, organisational and administrative structure.

(118) The independence of supervisory authorities should not mean that the supervisory authorities cannot be subject to control or monitoring mechanisms regarding their financial expenditure or to judicial review.

(119) Where a Member State establishes several supervisory authorities, it should establish by law mechanisms for ensuring the effective participation of those supervisory authorities in the consistency mechanism. That Member State should in particular designate the supervisory authority which functions as a single contact point for the effective participation of those authorities in the mechanism, to ensure swift and smooth cooperation with other supervisory authorities, the Board and the Commission.

(120) Each supervisory authority should be provided with the financial and human resources, premises and infrastructure necessary for the effective performance of their tasks, including those related to mutual assistance and cooperation with other supervisory authorities throughout the Union. Each supervisory authority should have a separate, public annual budget, which may be part of the overall state or national budget.

(121) The general conditions for the member or members of the supervisory authority should be laid down by law in each Member State and should in particular provide that those members are to be appointed, by means of a transparent procedure, either by the parliament, government or the head of State of the Member State on the basis of a proposal from the government, a member of the government, the parliament or a chamber of the parliament, or by an independent body entrusted under Member State law. In order to ensure the independence of the supervisory authority, the member or members should act with integrity, refrain from any action that is incompatible with their duties and should not, during their term of office, engage in any incompatible occupation, whether gainful or not. The supervisory authority should have its own

staff, chosen by the supervisory authority or an independent body established by Member State law, which should be subject to the exclusive direction of the member or members of the supervisory authority.

(122) Each supervisory authority should be competent on the territory of its own Member State to exercise the powers and to perform the tasks conferred on it in accordance with this Regulation. This should cover in particular the processing in the context of the activities of an establishment of the controller or processor on the territory of its own Member State, the processing of personal data carried out by public authorities or private bodies acting in the public interest, processing affecting data subjects on its territory or processing carried out by a controller or processor not established in the Union when targeting data subjects residing on its territory. This should include handling complaints lodged by a data subject, conducting investigations on the application of this Regulation and promoting public awareness of the risks, rules, safeguards and rights in relation to the processing of personal data.

(123) The supervisory authorities should monitor the application of the provisions pursuant to this Regulation and contribute to its consistent application throughout the Union, in order to protect natural persons in relation to the processing of their personal data and to facilitate the free flow of personal data within the internal market. For that purpose, the supervisory authorities should cooperate with each other and with the Commission, without the need for any agreement between Member States on the provision of mutual assistance or on such cooperation.

(124) Where the processing of personal data takes place in the context of the activities of an establishment of a controller or a processor in the Union and the controller or processor is established in more than one Member State, or where processing taking place in the context of the activities of a single establishment of a controller or processor in the Union substantially affects or is likely to substantially affect data subjects in more than one Member State, the supervisory authority for the main establishment of the controller or processor or for the single establishment of the controller or processor should act as lead authority. It should cooperate with the other authorities concerned, because the controller or processor has an establishment on the territory of their Member State, because data subjects residing on their territory are substantially affected, or because a complaint has been lodged with them. Also where a data subject not residing in that Member State has lodged a complaint, the supervisory authority with which such complaint has been lodged should also be a supervisory authority concerned. Within its tasks to issue guidelines on any question covering the application of this Regulation, the Board should be able to issue guidelines in particular on the criteria to be taken into account in order to ascertain whether the processing in question substantially affects data subjects in more than one Member State and on what constitutes a relevant and reasoned objection.

(125) The lead authority should be competent to adopt binding decisions regarding measures applying the powers conferred on it in accordance with this Regulation. In its capacity as lead authority, the supervisory authority should closely involve and coordinate the supervisory authorities concerned in the decision-making process. Where the decision is to reject the complaint by the data subject in whole or in part, that decision should be adopted by the supervisory authority with which the complaint has been lodged.

(126) The decision should be agreed jointly by the lead supervisory authority and the supervisory authorities concerned and should be directed towards the main or single establishment of the controller or processor and be binding on the controller and processor. The controller or processor should take the necessary measures to ensure compliance with this Regulation and the implementation of the decision notified by the lead supervisory authority to the main establishment of the controller or processor as regards the processing activities in the Union.

(127) Each supervisory authority not acting as the lead supervisory authority should be competent to handle local cases where the controller or processor is established in

more than one Member State, but the subject matter of the specific processing concerns only processing carried out in a single Member State and involves only data subjects in that single Member State, for example, where the subject matter concerns the processing of employees' personal data in the specific employment context of a Member State. In such cases, the supervisory authority should inform the lead supervisory authority without delay about the matter. After being informed, the lead supervisory authority should decide, whether it will handle the case pursuant to the provision on cooperation between the lead supervisory authority and other supervisory authorities concerned ('one-stop-shop mechanism'), or whether the supervisory authority which informed it should handle the case at local level. When deciding whether it will handle the case, the lead supervisory authority should take into account whether there is an establishment of the controller or processor in the Member State of the supervisory authority which informed it in order to ensure effective enforcement of a decision vis-à-vis the controller or processor. Where the lead supervisory authority decides to handle the case, the supervisory authority which informed it should have the possibility to submit a draft for a decision, of which the lead supervisory authority should take utmost account when preparing its draft decision in that one-stop-shop mechanism.

(128) The rules on the lead supervisory authority and the one-stop-shop mechanism should not apply where the processing is carried out by public authorities or private bodies in the public interest. In such cases the only supervisory authority competent to exercise the powers conferred to it in accordance with this Regulation should be the supervisory authority of the Member State where the public authority or private body is established.

(129) In order to ensure consistent monitoring and enforcement of this Regulation throughout the Union, the supervisory authorities should have in each Member State the same tasks and effective powers, including powers of investigation, corrective powers and sanctions, and authorisation and advisory powers, in particular in cases of complaints from natural persons, and without prejudice to the powers of prosecutorial authorities under Member State law, to bring infringements of this Regulation to the attention of the judicial authorities and engage in legal proceedings. Such powers should also include the power to impose a temporary or definitive limitation, including a ban, on processing. Member States may specify other tasks related to the protection of personal data under this Regulation. The powers of supervisory authorities should be exercised in accordance with appropriate procedural safeguards set out in Union and Member State law, impartially, fairly and within a reasonable time. In particular each measure should be appropriate, necessary and proportionate in view of ensuring compliance with this Regulation, taking into account the circumstances of each individual case, respect the right of every person to be heard before any individual measure which would affect him or her adversely is taken and avoid superfluous costs and excessive inconveniences for the persons concerned. Investigatory powers as regards access to premises should be exercised in accordance with specific requirements in Member State procedural law, such as the requirement to obtain a prior judicial authorisation. Each legally binding measure of the supervisory authority should be in writing, be clear and unambiguous, indicate the supervisory authority which has issued the measure, the date of issue of the measure, bear the signature of the head, or a member of the supervisory authority authorised by him or her, give the reasons for the measure, and refer to the right of an effective remedy. This should not preclude additional requirements pursuant to Member State procedural law. The adoption of a legally binding decision implies that it may give rise to judicial review in the Member State of the supervisory authority that adopted the decision.

(130) Where the supervisory authority with which the complaint has been lodged is not the lead supervisory authority, the lead supervisory authority should closely cooperate with the supervisory authority with which the complaint has been lodged in accordance with the provisions on cooperation and consistency laid down in this Regulation.

In such cases, the lead supervisory authority should, when taking measures intended to produce legal effects, including the imposition of administrative fines, take utmost account of the view of the supervisory authority with which the complaint has been lodged and which should remain competent to carry out any investigation on the territory of its own Member State in liaison with the competent supervisory authority.

(131) Where another supervisory authority should act as a lead supervisory authority for the processing activities of the controller or processor but the concrete subject matter of a complaint or the possible infringement concerns only processing activities of the controller or processor in the Member State where the complaint has been lodged or the possible infringement detected and the matter does not substantially affect or is not likely to substantially affect data subjects in other Member States, the supervisory authority receiving a complaint or detecting or being informed otherwise of situations that entail possible infringements of this Regulation should seek an amicable settlement with the controller and, if this proves unsuccessful, exercise its full range of powers. This should include: specific processing carried out in the territory of the Member State of the supervisory authority or with regard to data subjects on the territory of that Member State; processing that is carried out in the context of an offer of goods or services specifically aimed at data subjects in the territory of the Member State of the supervisory authority; or processing that has to be assessed taking into account relevant legal obligations under Member State law.

(132) Awareness-raising activities by supervisory authorities addressed to the public should include specific measures directed at controllers and processors, including micro, small and medium-sized enterprises, as well as natural persons in particular in the educational context.

(133) The supervisory authorities should assist each other in performing their tasks and provide mutual assistance, so as to ensure the consistent application and enforcement of this Regulation in the internal market. A supervisory authority requesting mutual assistance may adopt a provisional measure if it receives no response to a request for mutual assistance within one month of the receipt of that request by the other supervisory authority.

(134) Each supervisory authority should, where appropriate, participate in joint operations with other supervisory authorities. The requested supervisory authority should be obliged to respond to the request within a specified time period.

(135) In order to ensure the consistent application of this Regulation throughout the Union, a consistency mechanism for cooperation between the supervisory authorities should be established. That mechanism should in particular apply where a supervisory authority intends to adopt a measure intended to produce legal effects as regards processing operations which substantially affect a significant number of data subjects in several Member States. It should also apply where any supervisory authority concerned or the Commission requests that such matter should be handled in the consistency mechanism. That mechanism should be without prejudice to any measures that the Commission may take in the exercise of its powers under the Treaties.

(136) In applying the consistency mechanism, the Board should, within a determined period of time, issue an opinion, if a majority of its members so decides or if so requested by any supervisory authority concerned or the Commission. The Board should also be empowered to adopt legally binding decisions where there are disputes between supervisory authorities. For that purpose, it should issue, in principle by a two-thirds majority of its members, legally binding decisions in clearly specified cases where there are conflicting views among supervisory authorities, in particular in the cooperation mechanism between the lead supervisory authority and supervisory authorities concerned on the merits of the case, in particular whether there is an infringement of this Regulation.

(137) There may be an urgent need to act in order to protect the rights and freedoms of data subjects, in particular when the danger exists that the enforcement of a right of a data subject could be considerably impeded. A supervisory authority should therefore be

able to adopt duly justified provisional measures on its territory with a specified period of validity which should not exceed three months.

(138) The application of such mechanism should be a condition for the lawfulness of a measure intended to produce legal effects by a supervisory authority in those cases where its application is mandatory. In other cases of cross- border relevance, the cooperation mechanism between the lead supervisory authority and supervisory authorities concerned should be applied and mutual assistance and joint operations might be carried out between the supervisory authorities concerned on a bilateral or multilateral basis without triggering the consistency mechanism.

(139) In order to promote the consistent application of this Regulation, the Board should be set up as an independent body of the Union. To fulfil its objectives, the Board should have legal personality. The Board should be represented by its Chair. It should replace the Working Party on the Protection of Individuals with Regard to the Processing of Personal Data established by Directive 95/46/EC. It should consist of the head of a supervisory authority of each Member State and the European Data Protection Supervisor or their respective representatives. The Commission should participate in the Board's activities without voting rights and the European Data Protection Supervisor should have specific voting rights. The Board should contribute to the consistent application of this Regulation throughout the Union, including by advising the Commission, in particular on the level of protection in third countries or international organisations, and promoting cooperation of the supervisory authorities throughout the Union. The Board should act independently when performing its tasks.

(140) The Board should be assisted by a secretariat provided by the European Data Protection Supervisor. The staff of the European Data Protection Supervisor involved in carrying out the tasks conferred on the Board by this Regulation should perform its tasks exclusively under the instructions of, and report to, the Chair of the Board.

(141) Every data subject should have the right to lodge a complaint with a single supervisory authority, in particular in the Member State of his or her habitual residence, and the right to an effective judicial remedy in accordance with Article 47 of the Charter if the data subject considers that his or her rights under this Regulation are infringed or where the supervisory authority does not act on a complaint, partially or wholly rejects or dismisses a complaint or does not act where such action is necessary to protect the rights of the data subject. The investigation following a complaint should be carried out, subject to judicial review, to the extent that is appropriate in the specific case. The supervisory authority should inform the data subject of the progress and the outcome of the complaint within a reasonable period. If the case requires further investigation or coordination with another supervisory authority, intermediate information should be given to the data subject. In order to facilitate the submission of complaints, each supervisory authority should take measures such as providing a complaint submission form which can also be completed electronically, without excluding other means of communication.

(142) Where a data subject considers that his or her rights under this Regulation are infringed, he or she should have the right to mandate a not-for-profit body, organisation or association which is constituted in accordance with the law of a Member State, has statutory objectives which are in the public interest and is active in the field of the protection of personal data to lodge a complaint on his or her behalf with a supervisory authority, exercise the right to a judicial remedy on behalf of data subjects or, if provided for in Member State law, exercise the right to receive compensation on behalf of data subjects. A Member State may provide for such a body, organisation or association to have the right to lodge a complaint in that Member State, independently of a data subject's mandate, and the right to an effective judicial remedy where it has reasons to consider that the rights of a data subject have been infringed as a result of the processing of personal data which infringes this Regulation. That body, organisation or association may not be allowed to claim compensation on a data subject's behalf independently of the data subject's mandate.

(143) Any natural or legal person has the right to bring an action for annulment of decisions of the Board before the Court of Justice under the conditions provided for in Article 263 TFEU. As addressees of such decisions, the supervisory authorities concerned which wish to challenge them have to bring action within two months of being notified of them, in accordance with Article 263 TFEU. Where decisions of the Board are of direct and individual concern to a controller, processor or complainant, the latter may bring an action for annulment against those decisions within two months of their publication on the website of the Board, in accordance with Article 263 TFEU. Without prejudice to this right under Article 263 TFEU, each natural or legal person should have an effective judicial remedy before the competent national court against a decision of a supervisory authority which produces legal effects concerning that person. Such a decision concerns in particular the exercise of investigative, corrective and authorisation powers by the supervisory authority or the dismissal or rejection of complaints. However, the right to an effective judicial remedy does not encompass measures taken by supervisory authorities which are not legally binding, such as opinions issued by or advice provided by the supervisory authority. Proceedings against a supervisory authority should be brought before the courts of the Member State where the supervisory authority is established and should be conducted in accordance with that Member State's procedural law. Those courts should exercise full jurisdiction, which should include jurisdiction to examine all questions of fact and law relevant to the dispute before them.

Where a complaint has been rejected or dismissed by a supervisory authority, the complainant may bring proceedings before the courts in the same Member State. In the context of judicial remedies relating to the application of this Regulation, national courts which consider a decision on the question necessary to enable them to give judgment, may, or in the case provided for in Article 267 TFEU, must, request the Court of Justice to give a preliminary ruling on the interpretation of Union law, including this Regulation. Furthermore, where a decision of a supervisory authority implementing a decision of the Board is challenged before a national court and the validity of the decision of the Board is at issue, that national court does not have the power to declare the Board's decision invalid but must refer the question of validity to the Court of Justice in accordance with Article 267 TFEU as interpreted by the Court of Justice, where it considers the decision invalid. However, a national court may not refer a question on the validity of the decision of the Board at the request of a natural or legal person which had the opportunity to bring an action for annulment of that decision, in particular if it was directly and individually concerned by that decision, but had not done so within the period laid down in Article 263 TFEU.

(144) Where a court seized of proceedings against a decision by a supervisory authority has reason to believe that proceedings concerning the same processing, such as the same subject matter as regards processing by the same controller or processor, or the same cause of action, are brought before a competent court in another Member State, it should contact that court in order to confirm the existence of such related proceedings. If related proceedings are pending before a court in another Member State, any court other than the court first seized may stay its proceedings or may, on request of one of the parties, decline jurisdiction in favour of the court first seized if that court has jurisdiction over the proceedings in question and its law permits the consolidation of such related proceedings. Proceedings are deemed to be related where they are so closely connected that it is expedient to hear and determine them together in order to avoid the risk of irreconcilable judgments resulting from separate proceedings.

(145) For proceedings against a controller or processor, the plaintiff should have the choice to bring the action before the courts of the Member States where the controller or processor has an establishment or where the data subject resides, unless the controller is a public authority of a Member State acting in the exercise of its public powers.

(146) The controller or processor should compensate any damage which a person may suffer

as a result of processing that infringes this Regulation. The controller or processor should be exempt from liability if it proves that it is not in any way responsible for the damage. The concept of damage should be broadly interpreted in the light of the case-law of the Court of Justice in a manner which fully reflects the objectives of this Regulation. This is without prejudice to any claims for damage deriving from the violation of other rules in Union or Member State law. Processing that infringes this Regulation also includes processing that infringes delegated and implementing acts adopted in accordance with this Regulation and Member State law specifying rules of this Regulation. Data subjects should receive full and effective compensation for the damage they have suffered. Where controllers or processors are involved in the same processing, each controller or processor should be held liable for the entire damage. However, where they are joined to the same judicial proceedings, in accordance with Member State law, compensation may be apportioned according to the responsibility of each controller or processor for the damage caused by the processing, provided that full and effective compensation of the data subject who suffered the damage is ensured. Any controller or processor which has paid full compensation may subsequently institute recourse proceedings against other controllers or processors involved in the same processing.

(147) Where specific rules on jurisdiction are contained in this Regulation, in particular as regards proceedings seeking a judicial remedy including compensation, against a controller or processor, general jurisdiction rules such as those of Regulation (EU) No 1215/2012 of the European Parliament and of the Council[13] should not prejudice the application of such specific rules.

(148) In order to strengthen the enforcement of the rules of this Regulation, penalties including administrative fines should be imposed for any infringement of this Regulation, in addition to, or instead of appropriate measures imposed by the supervisory authority pursuant to this Regulation. In a case of a minor infringement or if the fine likely to be imposed would constitute a disproportionate burden to a natural person, a reprimand may be issued instead of a fine. Due regard should however be given to the nature, gravity and duration of the infringement, the intentional character of the infringement, actions taken to mitigate the damage suffered, degree of responsibility or any relevant previous infringements, the manner in which the infringement became known to the supervisory authority, compliance with measures ordered against the controller or processor, adherence to a code of conduct and any other aggravating or mitigating factor. The imposition of penalties including administrative fines should be subject to appropriate procedural safeguards in accordance with the general principles of Union law and the Charter, including effective judicial protection and due process.

(149) Member States should be able to lay down the rules on criminal penalties for infringements of this Regulation, including for infringements of national rules adopted pursuant to and within the limits of this Regulation. Those criminal penalties may also allow for the deprivation of the profits obtained through infringements of this Regulation. However, the imposition of criminal penalties for infringements of such national rules and of administrative penalties should not lead to a breach of the principle of *ne bis in idem*, as interpreted by the Court of Justice.

(150) In order to strengthen and harmonise administrative penalties for infringements of this Regulation, each supervisory authority should have the power to impose administrative fines. This Regulation should indicate infringements and the upper limit and criteria for setting the related administrative fines, which should be determined by the competent supervisory authority in each individual case, taking into account all relevant circumstances of the specific situation, with due regard in particular to the nature, gravity and duration of the infringement and of its consequences and the

---

[13] Regulation (EU) No 1215/2012 of the European Parliament and of the Council of 12 December 2012 on jurisdiction and the recognition and enforcement of judgments in civil and commercial matters (OJ L 351, 20.12.2012, p.1).

measures taken to ensure compliance with the obligations under this Regulation and to prevent or mitigate the consequences of the infringement. Where administrative fines are imposed on an undertaking, an undertaking should be understood to be an undertaking in accordance with Articles 101 and 102 TFEU for those purposes. Where administrative fines are imposed on persons that are not an undertaking, the supervisory authority should take account of the general level of income in the Member State as well as the economic situation of the person in considering the appropriate amount of the fine. The consistency mechanism may also be used to promote a consistent application of administrative fines. It should be for the Member States to determine whether and to which extent public authorities should be subject to administrative fines. Imposing an administrative fine or giving a warning does not affect the application of other powers of the supervisory authorities or of other penalties under this Regulation.

(151) The legal systems of Denmark and Estonia do not allow for administrative fines as set out in this Regulation. The rules on administrative fines may be applied in such a manner that in Denmark the fine is imposed by competent national courts as a criminal penalty and in Estonia the fine is imposed by the supervisory authority in the framework of a misdemeanour procedure, provided that such an application of the rules in those Member States has an equivalent effect to administrative fines imposed by supervisory authorities. Therefore the competent national courts should take into account the recommendation by the supervisory authority initiating the fine. In any event, the fines imposed should be effective, proportionate and dissuasive.

(152) Where this Regulation does not harmonise administrative penalties or where necessary in other cases, for example in cases of serious infringements of this Regulation, Member States should implement a system which provides for effective, proportionate and dissuasive penalties. The nature of such penalties, criminal or administrative, should be determined by Member State law.

(153) Member States law should reconcile the rules governing freedom of expression and information, including journalistic, academic, artistic and or literary expression with the right to the protection of personal data pursuant to this Regulation. The processing of personal data solely for journalistic purposes, or for the purposes of academic, artistic or literary expression should be subject to derogations or exemptions from certain provisions of this Regulation if necessary to reconcile the right to the protection of personal data with the right to freedom of expression and information, as enshrined in Article 11 of the Charter. This should apply in particular to the processing of personal data in the audiovisual field and in news archives and press libraries. Therefore, Member States should adopt legislative measures which lay down the exemptions and derogations necessary for the purpose of balancing those fundamental rights. Member States should adopt such exemptions and derogations on general principles, the rights of the data subject, the controller and the processor, the transfer of personal data to third countries or international organisations, the independent supervisory authorities, cooperation and consistency, and specific data-processing situations. Where such exemptions or derogations differ from one Member State to another, the law of the Member State to which the controller is subject should apply. In order to take account of the importance of the right to freedom of expression in every democratic society, it is necessary to interpret notions relating to that freedom, such as journalism, broadly.

(154) This Regulation allows the principle of public access to official documents to be taken into account when applying this Regulation. Public access to official documents may be considered to be in the public interest. Personal data in documents held by a public authority or a public body should be able to be publicly disclosed by that authority or body if the disclosure is provided for by Union or Member State law to which the public authority or public body is subject. Such laws should reconcile public access to official documents and the reuse of public sector information with the right to the protection of personal data and may therefore provide for the necessary reconciliation with the

right to the protection of personal data pursuant to this Regulation. The reference to public authorities and bodies should in that context include all authorities or other bodies covered by Member State law on public access to documents. Directive 2003/98/EC of the European Parliament and of the Council[14] leaves intact and in no way affects the level of protection of natural persons with regard to the processing of personal data under the provisions of Union and Member State law, and in particular does not alter the obligations and rights set out in this Regulation. In particular, that Directive should not apply to documents to which access is excluded or restricted by virtue of the access regimes on the grounds of protection of personal data, and parts of documents accessible by virtue of those regimes which contain personal data the re-use of which has been provided for by law as being incompatible with the law concerning the protection of natural persons with regard to the processing of personal data.

(155) Member State law or collective agreements, including 'works agreements', may provide for specific rules on the processing of employees' personal data in the employment context, in particular for the conditions under which personal data in the employment context may be processed on the basis of the consent of the employee, the purposes of the recruitment, the performance of the contract of employment, including discharge of obligations laid down by law or by collective agreements, management, planning and organisation of work, equality and diversity in the workplace, health and safety at work, and for the purposes of the exercise and enjoyment, on an individual or collective basis, of rights and benefits related to employment, and for the purpose of the termination of the employment relationship.

(156) The processing of personal data for archiving purposes in the public interest, scientific or historical research purposes or statistical purposes should be subject to appropriate safeguards for the rights and freedoms of the data subject pursuant to this Regulation. Those safeguards should ensure that technical and organisational measures are in place in order to ensure, in particular, the principle of data minimisation. The further processing of personal data for archiving purposes in the public interest, scientific or historical research purposes or statistical purposes is to be carried out when the controller has assessed the feasibility to fulfil those purposes by processing data which do not permit or no longer permit the identification of data subjects, provided that appropriate safeguards exist (such as, for instance, pseudonymisation of the data). Member States should provide for appropriate safeguards for the processing of personal data for archiving purposes in the public interest, scientific or historical research purposes or statistical purposes. Member States should be authorised to provide, under specific conditions and subject to appropriate safeguards for data subjects, specifications and derogations with regard to the information requirements and rights to rectification, to erasure, to be forgotten, to restriction of processing, to data portability, and to object when processing personal data for archiving purposes in the public interest, scientific or historical research purposes or statistical purposes. The conditions and safeguards in question may entail specific procedures for data subjects to exercise those rights if this is appropriate in the light of the purposes sought by the specific processing along with technical and organisational measures aimed at minimising the processing of personal data in pursuance of the proportionality and necessity principles. The processing of personal data for scientific purposes should also comply with other relevant legislation such as on clinical trials.

(157) By coupling information from registries, researchers can obtain new knowledge of great value with regard to widespread medical conditions such as cardiovascular disease, cancer and depression. On the basis of registries, research results can be enhanced, as they draw on a larger population. Within social science, research on the

---

[14] Directive 2003/98/EC of the European Parliament and of the Council of 17 November 2003 on the re-use of public sector information (OJ L 345, 31.12.2003, p.90).

basis of registries enables researchers to obtain essential knowledge about the long-term correlation of a number of social conditions such as unemployment and education with other life conditions. Research results obtained through registries provide solid, high-quality knowledge which can provide the basis for the formulation and implementation of knowledge-based policy, improve the quality of life for a number of people and improve the efficiency of social services. In order to facilitate scientific research, personal data can be processed for scientific research purposes, subject to appropriate conditions and safeguards set out in Union or Member State law.

(158) Where personal data are processed for archiving purposes, this Regulation should also apply to that processing, bearing in mind that this Regulation should not apply to deceased persons. Public authorities or public or private bodies that hold records of public interest should be services which, pursuant to Union or Member State law, have a legal obligation to acquire, preserve, appraise, arrange, describe, communicate, promote, disseminate and provide access to records of enduring value for general public interest. Member States should also be authorised to provide for the further processing of personal data for archiving purposes, for example with a view to providing specific information related to the political behaviour under former totalitarian state regimes, genocide, crimes against humanity, in particular the Holocaust, or war crimes.

(159) Where personal data are processed for scientific research purposes, this Regulation should also apply to that processing. For the purposes of this Regulation, the processing of personal data for scientific research purposes should be interpreted in a broad manner including for example technological development and demonstration, fundamental research, applied research and privately funded research. In addition, it should take into account the Union's objective under Article 179(1) TFEU of achieving a European Research Area. Scientific research purposes should also include studies conducted in the public interest in the area of public health. To meet the specificities of processing personal data for scientific research purposes, specific conditions should apply in particular as regards the publication or otherwise disclosure of personal data in the context of scientific research purposes. If the result of scientific research in particular in the health context gives reason for further measures in the interest of the data subject, the general rules of this Regulation should apply in view of those measures.

(160) Where personal data are processed for historical research purposes, this Regulation should also apply to that processing. This should also include historical research and research for genealogical purposes, bearing in mind that this Regulation should not apply to deceased persons.

(161) For the purpose of consenting to the participation in scientific research activities in clinical trials, the relevant provisions of Regulation (EU) No 536/2014 of the European Parliament and of the Council[15] should apply.

(162) Where personal data are processed for statistical purposes, this Regulation should apply to that processing. Union or Member State law should, within the limits of this Regulation, determine statistical content, control of access, specifications for the processing of personal data for statistical purposes and appropriate measures to safeguard the rights and freedoms of the data subject and for ensuring statistical confidentiality. Statistical purposes mean any operation of collection and the processing of personal data necessary for statistical surveys or for the production of statistical results. Those statistical results may further be used for different purposes, including a scientific research purpose. The statistical purpose implies that the result of processing for statistical purposes is not personal data, but aggregate data, and that this result

---

[15] Regulation (EU) No 536/2014 of the European Parliament and of the Council of 16 April 2014 on clinical trials on medicinal products for human use, and repealing Directive 2001/20/EC (OJ L 158, 27.5.2014, p.1).

or the personal data are not used in support of measures or decisions regarding any particular natural person.

(163) The confidential information which the Union and national statistical authorities collect for the production of official European and official national statistics should be protected. European statistics should be developed, produced and disseminated in accordance with the statistical principles as set out in Article 338(2) TFEU, while national statistics should also comply with Member State law. Regulation (EC) No 223/2009 of the European Parliament and of the Council[16] provides further specifications on statistical confidentiality for European statistics.

(164) As regards the powers of the supervisory authorities to obtain from the controller or processor access to personal data and access to their premises, Member States may adopt by law, within the limits of this Regulation, specific rules in order to safeguard the professional or other equivalent secrecy obligations, in so far as necessary to reconcile the right to the protection of personal data with an obligation of professional secrecy. This is without prejudice to existing Member State obligations to adopt rules on professional secrecy where required by Union law.

(165) This Regulation respects and does not prejudice the status under existing constitutional law of churches and religious associations or communities in the Member States, as recognised in Article 17 TFEU.

(166) In order to fulfil the objectives of this Regulation, namely to protect the fundamental rights and freedoms of natural persons and in particular their right to the protection of personal data and to ensure the free movement of personal data within the Union, the power to adopt acts in accordance with Article 290 TFEU should be delegated to the Commission. In particular, delegated acts should be adopted in respect of criteria and requirements for certification mechanisms, information to be presented by standardised icons and procedures for providing such icons. It is of particular importance that the Commission carry out appropriate consultations during its preparatory work, including at expert level. The Commission, when preparing and drawing-up delegated acts, should ensure a simultaneous, timely and appropriate transmission of relevant documents to the European Parliament and to the Council.

(167) In order to ensure uniform conditions for the implementation of this Regulation, implementing powers should be conferred on the Commission when provided for by this Regulation. Those powers should be exercised in accordance with Regulation (EU) No 182/2011. In that context, the Commission should consider specific measures for micro, small and medium-sized enterprises.

(168) The examination procedure should be used for the adoption of implementing acts on standard contractual clauses between controllers and processors and between processors; codes of conduct; technical standards and mechanisms for certification; the adequate level of protection afforded by a third country, a territory or a specified sector within that third country, or an international organisation; standard protection clauses; formats and procedures for the exchange of information by electronic means between controllers, processors and supervisory authorities for binding corporate rules; mutual assistance; and arrangements for the exchange of information by electronic means between supervisory authorities, and between supervisory authorities and the Board.

(169) The Commission should adopt immediately applicable implementing acts where available evidence reveals that a third country, a territory or a specified sector within

---

[16] Regulation (EC) No 223/2009 of the European Parliament and of the Council of 11 March 2009 on European statistics and repealing Regulation (EC, Euratom) No 1101/2008 of the European Parliament and of the Council on the transmission of data subject to statistical confidentiality to the Statistical Office of the European Communities, Council Regulation (EC) No 322/97 on Community Statistics, and Council Decision 89/382/EEC, Euratom establishing a Committee on the Statistical Programmes of the European Communities (OJ L 87, 31.3.2009, p.164).

that third country, or an international organisation does not ensure an adequate level of protection, and imperative grounds of urgency so require.

(170) Since the objective of this Regulation, namely to ensure an equivalent level of protection of natural persons and the free flow of personal data throughout the Union, cannot be sufficiently achieved by the Member States and can rather, by reason of the scale or effects of the action, be better achieved at Union level, the Union may adopt measures, in accordance with the principle of subsidiarity as set out in Article 5 of the Treaty on European Union (TEU). In accordance with the principle of proportionality as set out in that Article, this Regulation does not go beyond what is necessary in order to achieve that objective.

(171) Directive 95/46/EC should be repealed by this Regulation. Processing already under way on the date of application of this Regulation should be brought into conformity with this Regulation within the period of two years after which this Regulation enters into force. Where processing is based on consent pursuant to Directive 95/46/EC, it is not necessary for the data subject to give his or her consent again if the manner in which the consent has been given is in line with the conditions of this Regulation, so as to allow the controller to continue such processing after the date of application of this Regulation. Commission decisions adopted and authorisations by supervisory authorities based on Directive 95/46/EC remain in force until amended, replaced or repealed.

(172) The European Data Protection Supervisor was consulted in accordance with Article 28(2) of Regulation (EC) No 45/2001 and delivered an opinion on 7 March 2012.[17]

(173) This Regulation should apply to all matters concerning the protection of fundamental rights and freedoms vis-à- vis the processing of personal data which are not subject to specific obligations with the same objective set out in Directive 2002/58/EC of the European Parliament and of the Council,[18] including the obligations on the controller and the rights of natural persons. In order to clarify the relationship between this Regulation and Directive 2002/58/EC, that Directive should be amended accordingly. Once this Regulation is adopted, Directive 2002/58/EC should be reviewed in particular in order to ensure consistency with this Regulation,

HAVE ADOPTED THIS REGULATION:

CHAPTER I – GENERAL PROVISIONS

ARTICLE 1 – SUBJECT-MATTER AND OBJECTIVES

1. This Regulation lays down rules relating to the protection of natural persons with regard to the processing of personal data and rules relating to the free movement of personal data.

2. This Regulation protects fundamental rights and freedoms of natural persons and in particular their right to the protection of personal data.

3. The free movement of personal data within the Union shall be neither restricted nor prohibited for reasons connected with the protection of natural persons with regard to the processing of personal data.

ARTICLE 2 – MATERIAL SCOPE

1. This Regulation applies to the processing of personal data wholly or partly by automated means and to the processing other than by automated means of personal data which form part of a filing system or are intended to form part of a filing system.

---

[17] OJ C 192, 30.6.2012, p.7.
[18] Directive 2002/58/EC of the European Parliament and of the Council of 12 July 2002 concerning the processing of personal data and the protection of privacy in the electronic communications sector (Directive on privacy and electronic communications) (OJ L 201, 31.7.2002, p.37).

2. This Regulation does not apply to the processing of personal data:

(a) in the course of an activity which falls outside the scope of Union law;

(b) by the Member States when carrying out activities which fall within the scope of Chapter 2 of Title V of the TEU;

(c) by a natural person in the course of a purely personal or household activity;

(d) by competent authorities for the purposes of the prevention, investigation, detection or prosecution of criminal offences or the execution of criminal penalties, including the safeguarding against and the prevention of threats to public security.

3. For the processing of personal data by the Union institutions, bodies, offices and agencies, Regulation (EC) No 45/2001 applies. Regulation (EC) No 45/2001 and other Union legal acts applicable to such processing of personal data shall be adapted to the principles and rules of this Regulation in accordance with Article 98.

4. This Regulation shall be without prejudice to the application of Directive 2000/31/EC, in particular of the liability rules of intermediary service providers in Articles 12 to 15 of that Directive.

ARTICLE 3 – TERRITORIAL SCOPE

1. This Regulation applies to the processing of personal data in the context of the activities of an establishment of a controller or a processor in the Union, regardless of whether the processing takes place in the Union or not.

2. This Regulation applies to the processing of personal data of data subjects who are in the Union by a controller or processor not established in the Union, where the processing activities are related to:

(a) the offering of goods or services, irrespective of whether a payment of the data subject is required, to such data subjects in the Union; or

(b) the monitoring of their behaviour as far as their behaviour takes place within the Union.

3. This Regulation applies to the processing of personal data by a controller not established in the Union, but in a place where Member State law applies by virtue of public international law.

ARTICLE 4 – DEFINITIONS

For the purposes of this Regulation:

(1) 'personal data' means any information relating to an identified or identifiable natural person ('data subject'); an identifiable natural person is one who can be identified, directly or indirectly, in particular by reference to an identifier such as a name, an identification number, location data, an online identifier or to one or more factors specific to the physical, physiological, genetic, mental, economic, cultural or social identity of that natural person;

(2) 'processing' means any operation or set of operations which is performed on personal data or on sets of personal data, whether or not by automated means, such as collection, recording, organisation, structuring, storage, adaptation or alteration, retrieval, consultation, use, disclosure by transmission, dissemination or otherwise making available, alignment or combination, restriction, erasure or destruction;

(3) 'restriction of processing' means the marking of stored personal data with the aim of limiting their processing in the future;

(4) 'profiling' means any form of automated processing of personal data consisting of the use of personal data to evaluate certain personal aspects relating to a natural person, in particular to analyse or predict aspects concerning that natural person's performance at work, economic situation, health, personal preferences, interests, reliability, behaviour, location or movements;

(5) 'pseudonymisation' means the processing of personal data in such a manner that the personal data can no longer be attributed to a specific data subject without the use of additional information, provided that such additional information is kept separately and is subject to technical and organisational measures to ensure that the personal data are not attributed to an identified or identifiable natural person;

(6) 'filing system' means any structured set of personal data which are accessible according to specific criteria, whether centralised, decentralised or dispersed on a functional or geographical basis;

(7) 'controller' means the natural or legal person, public authority, agency or other body which, alone or jointly with others, determines the purposes and means of the processing of personal data; where the purposes and means of such processing are determined by Union or Member State law, the controller or the specific criteria for its nomination may be provided for by Union or Member State law;

(8) 'processor' means a natural or legal person, public authority, agency or other body which processes personal data on behalf of the controller;

(9) 'recipient' means a natural or legal person, public authority, agency or another body, to which the personal data are disclosed, whether a third party or not. However, public authorities which may receive personal data in the framework of a particular inquiry in accordance with Union or Member State law shall not be regarded as recipients; the processing of those data by those public authorities shall be in compliance with the applicable data protection rules according to the purposes of the processing;

(10) 'third party' means a natural or legal person, public authority, agency or body other than the data subject, controller, processor and persons who, under the direct authority of the controller or processor, are authorised to process personal data;

(11) 'consent' of the data subject means any freely given, specific, informed and unambiguous indication of the data subject's wishes by which he or she, by a statement or by a clear affirmative action, signifies agreement to the processing of personal data relating to him or her;

(12) 'personal data breach' means a breach of security leading to the accidental or unlawful destruction, loss, alteration, unauthorised disclosure of, or access to, personal data transmitted, stored or otherwise processed;

(13) 'genetic data' means personal data relating to the inherited or acquired genetic characteristics of a natural person which give unique information about the physiology or the health of that natural person and which result, in particular, from an analysis of a biological sample from the natural person in question;

(14) 'biometric data' means personal data resulting from specific technical processing relating to the physical, physiological or behavioural characteristics of a natural person, which allow or confirm the unique identification of that natural person, such as facial images or dactyloscopic data;

(15) 'data concerning health' means personal data related to the physical or mental health of a natural person, including the provision of health care services, which reveal information about his or her health status;

(16) 'main establishment' means:

(a)   as regards a controller with establishments in more than one Member State, the place of its central administration in the Union, unless the decisions on the purposes and means of the processing of personal data are taken in another establishment of the controller in the Union and the latter establishment has the power to have such decisions implemented, in which case the establishment having taken such decisions is to be considered to be the main establishment;

(b)   as regards a processor with establishments in more than one Member State, the place of its central administration in the Union, or, if the processor has no central administration in the Union, the establishment of the processor in the Union where the main processing activities in the context of the activities of an establishment of the processor take place to the extent that the processor is subject to specific obligations under this Regulation;

(17) 'representative' means a natural or legal person established in the Union who, designated by the controller or processor in writing pursuant to Article 27, represents the controller or processor with regard to their respective obligations under this Regulation;

(18) 'enterprise' means a natural or legal person engaged in an economic activity, irrespective of its legal form, including partnerships or associations regularly engaged in an economic activity;

(19) 'group of undertakings' means a controlling undertaking and its controlled undertakings;

(20) 'binding corporate rules' means personal data protection policies which are adhered to by a controller or processor established on the territory of a Member State for transfers or a set of transfers of personal data to a controller or processor in one or more third countries within a group of undertakings, or group of enterprises engaged in a joint economic activity;

(21) 'supervisory authority' means an independent public authority which is established by a Member State pursuant to Article 51;

(22) 'supervisory authority concerned' means a supervisory authority which is concerned by the processing of personal data because:

(a)   the controller or processor is established on the territory of the Member State of that supervisory authority;

(b)   data subjects residing in the Member State of that supervisory authority are substantially affected or likely to be substantially affected by the processing; or

(c)   a complaint has been lodged with that supervisory authority;

(23) 'cross-border processing' means either:

(a)   processing of personal data which takes place in the context of the activities of establishments in more than one Member State of a controller or processor in the Union where the controller or processor is established in more than one Member State; or

(b)   processing of personal data which takes place in the context of the activities of a single establishment of a controller or processor in the Union but which substantially affects or is likely to substantially affect data subjects in more than one Member State.

(24) 'relevant and reasoned objection' means an objection to a draft decision as to whether there is an infringement of this Regulation, or whether envisaged action in relation to the controller or processor complies with this Regulation, which clearly demonstrates the significance of the risks posed by the draft decision as regards the fundamental rights and freedoms of data subjects and, where applicable, the free flow of personal data within the Union;

(25) 'information society service' means a service as defined in point (b) of Article 1(1) of Directive (EU) 2015/1535 of the European Parliament and of the Council[19];

(26) 'international organisation' means an organisation and its subordinate bodies governed by public international law, or any other body which is set up by, or on the basis of, an agreement between two or more countries.

---

[19] Directive (EU) 2015/1535 of the European Parliament and of the Council of 9 September 2015 laying down a procedure for the provision of information in the field of technical regulations and of rules on Information Society services (OJ L 241, 17.9.2015, p.1).

CHAPTER II – PRINCIPLES

ARTICLE 5 – PRINCIPLES RELATING TO PROCESSING OF PERSONAL DATA

1. Personal data shall be:

(a) processed lawfully, fairly and in a transparent manner in relation to the data subject ('lawfulness, fairness and transparency');
(b) collected for specified, explicit and legitimate purposes and not further processed in a manner that is incompatible with those purposes; further processing for archiving purposes in the public interest, scientific or historical research purposes or statistical purposes shall, in accordance with Article 89(1), not be considered to be incompatible with the initial purposes ('purpose limitation');
(c) adequate, relevant and limited to what is necessary in relation to the purposes for which they are processed ('data minimisation');
(d) accurate and, where necessary, kept up to date; every reasonable step must be taken to ensure that personal data that are inaccurate, having regard to the purposes for which they are processed, are erased or rectified without delay ('accuracy');
(e) kept in a form which permits identification of data subjects for no longer than is necessary for the purposes for which the personal data are processed; personal data may be stored for longer periods insofar as the personal data will be processed solely for archiving purposes in the public interest, scientific or historical research purposes or statistical purposes in accordance with Article 89(1) subject to implementation of the appropriate technical and organisational measures required by this Regulation in order to safeguard the rights and freedoms of the data subject ('storage limitation');
(f) processed in a manner that ensures appropriate security of the personal data, including protection against unauthorised or unlawful processing and against accidental loss, destruction or damage, using appropriate technical or organisational measures ('integrity and confidentiality').

2. The controller shall be responsible for, and be able to demonstrate compliance with, paragraph 1 ('accountability').

ARTICLE 6 – LAWFULNESS OF PROCESSING

1. Processing shall be lawful only if and to the extent that at least one of the following applies:

(a) the data subject has given consent to the processing of his or her personal data for one or more specific purposes;
(b) processing is necessary for the performance of a contract to which the data subject is party or in order to take steps at the request of the data subject prior to entering into a contract;
(c) processing is necessary for compliance with a legal obligation to which the controller is subject;
(d) processing is necessary in order to protect the vital interests of the data subject or of another natural person;
(e) processing is necessary for the performance of a task carried out in the public interest or in the exercise of official authority vested in the controller;
(f) processing is necessary for the purposes of the legitimate interests pursued by the controller or by a third party, except where such interests are overridden by the interests or fundamental rights and freedoms of the data subject which require protection of personal data, in particular where the data subject is a child.

Point (f) of the first subparagraph shall not apply to processing carried out by public authorities in the performance of their tasks.

2. Member States may maintain or introduce more specific provisions to adapt the application of the rules of this Regulation with regard to processing for compliance with points (c) and (e) of paragraph 1 by determining more precisely specific requirements for the processing and other measures to ensure lawful and fair processing including for other specific processing situations as provided for in Chapter IX.

3. The basis for the processing referred to in point (c) and (e) of paragraph 1 shall be laid down by:

(a) Union law; or
(b) Member State law to which the controller is subject.

The purpose of the processing shall be determined in that legal basis or, as regards the processing referred to in point (e) of paragraph 1, shall be necessary for the performance of a task carried out in the public interest or in the exercise of official authority vested in the controller. That legal basis may contain specific provisions to adapt the application of rules of this Regulation, inter alia: the general conditions governing the lawfulness of processing by the controller; the types of data which are subject to the processing; the data subjects concerned; the entities to, and the purposes for which, the personal data may be disclosed; the purpose limitation; storage periods; and processing operations and processing procedures, including measures to ensure lawful and fair processing such as those for other specific processing situations as provided for in Chapter IX. The Union or the Member State law shall meet an objective of public interest and be proportionate to the legitimate aim pursued.

4. Where the processing for a purpose other than that for which the personal data have been collected is not based on the data subject's consent or on a Union or Member State law which constitutes a necessary and proportionate measure in a democratic society to safeguard the objectives referred to in Article 23(1), the controller shall, in order to ascertain whether processing for another purpose is compatible with the purpose for which the personal data are initially collected, take into account, inter alia:

(a) any link between the purposes for which the personal data have been collected and the purposes of the intended further processing;
(b) the context in which the personal data have been collected, in particular regarding the relationship between data subjects and the controller;
(c) the nature of the personal data, in particular whether special categories of personal data are processed, pursuant to Article 9, or whether personal data related to criminal convictions and offences are processed, pursuant to Article 10;
(d) the possible consequences of the intended further processing for data subjects;
(e) the existence of appropriate safeguards, which may include encryption or pseudonymisation.

ARTICLE 7 – CONDITIONS FOR CONSENT

1. Where processing is based on consent, the controller shall be able to demonstrate that the data subject has consented to processing of his or her personal data.

2. If the data subject's consent is given in the context of a written declaration which also concerns other matters, the request for consent shall be presented in a manner which is clearly distinguishable from the other matters, in an intelligible and easily accessible form, using clear and plain language. Any part of such a declaration which constitutes an infringement of this Regulation shall not be binding.

3. The data subject shall have the right to withdraw his or her consent at any time. The withdrawal of consent shall not affect the lawfulness of processing based on consent before its withdrawal. Prior to giving consent, the data subject shall be informed thereof. It shall be as easy to withdraw as to give consent.

4. When assessing whether consent is freely given, utmost account shall be taken of whether, inter alia, the performance of a contract, including the provision of a service, is conditional on consent to the processing of personal data that is not necessary for the performance of that contract.

ARTICLE 8 – CONDITIONS APPLICABLE TO CHILD'S CONSENT IN RELATION TO INFORMATION SOCIETY SERVICES

1. Where point (a) of Article 6(1) applies, in relation to the offer of information society services directly to a child, the processing of the personal data of a child shall be lawful where the child is at least 16 years old. Where the child is below the age of 16 years, such processing shall be lawful only if and to the extent that consent is given or authorised by the holder of parental responsibility over the child.

Member States may provide by law for a lower age for those purposes provided that such lower age is not below 13 years.

2. The controller shall make reasonable efforts to verify in such cases that consent is given or authorised by the holder of parental responsibility over the child, taking into consideration available technology.

3. Paragraph 1 shall not affect the general contract law of Member States such as the rules on the validity, formation or effect of a contract in relation to a child.

ARTICLE 9 – PROCESSING OF SPECIAL CATEGORIES OF PERSONAL DATA

1. Processing of personal data revealing racial or ethnic origin, political opinions, religious or philosophical beliefs, or trade union membership, and the processing of genetic data, biometric data for the purpose of uniquely identifying a natural person, data concerning health or data concerning a natural person's sex life or sexual orientation shall be prohibited.

2. Paragraph 1 shall not apply if one of the following applies:

(a) the data subject has given explicit consent to the processing of those personal data for one or more specified purposes, except where Union or Member State law provide that the prohibition referred to in paragraph 1 may not be lifted by the data subject;

(b) processing is necessary for the purposes of carrying out the obligations and exercising specific rights of the controller or of the data subject in the field of employment and social security and social protection law in so far as it is authorised by Union or Member State law or a collective agreement pursuant to Member State law providing for appropriate safeguards for the fundamental rights and the interests of the data subject;

(c) processing is necessary to protect the vital interests of the data subject or of another natural person where the data subject is physically or legally incapable of giving consent;

(d) processing is carried out in the course of its legitimate activities with appropriate safeguards by a foundation, association or any other not-for-profit body with a political, philosophical, religious or trade union aim and on condition that the processing relates solely to the members or to former members of the body or to persons who have regular contact with it in connection with its purposes and that the personal data are not disclosed outside that body without the consent of the data subjects;

(e) processing relates to personal data which are manifestly made public by the data subject;

(f) processing is necessary for the establishment, exercise or defence of legal claims or whenever courts are acting in their judicial capacity;

(g) processing is necessary for reasons of substantial public interest, on the basis of Union or Member State law which shall be proportionate to the aim pursued, respect the essence of the right to data protection and provide for suitable and specific measures to safeguard the fundamental rights and the interests of the data subject;

(h) processing is necessary for the purposes of preventive or occupational medicine, for the assessment of the working capacity of the employee, medical diagnosis, the provision of health or social care or treatment or the management of health or social care systems and services on the basis of Union or Member State law or pursuant to contract with a health professional and subject to the conditions and safeguards referred to in paragraph 3;

(i) processing is necessary for reasons of public interest in the area of public health, such as protecting against serious cross-border threats to health or ensuring high standards of quality and safety of health care and of medicinal products or medical devices, on the basis of Union or Member State law which provides for suitable and specific measures to safeguard the rights and freedoms of the data subject, in particular professional secrecy;

(j) processing is necessary for archiving purposes in the public interest, scientific or historical research purposes or statistical purposes in accordance with Article 89(1) based on Union or Member State law which shall be proportionate to the aim pursued, respect the essence of the right to data protection and provide for suitable and specific measures to safeguard the fundamental rights and the interests of the data subject.

3. Personal data referred to in paragraph 1 may be processed for the purposes referred to in point (h) of paragraph 2 when those data are processed by or under the responsibility of a professional subject to the obligation of professional secrecy under Union or Member State law or rules established by national competent bodies or by another person also subject to an obligation of secrecy under Union or Member State law or rules established by national competent bodies.

4. Member States may maintain or introduce further conditions, including limitations, with regard to the processing of genetic data, biometric data or data concerning health.

ARTICLE 10 – PROCESSING OF PERSONAL DATA RELATING TO CRIMINAL CONVICTIONS AND OFFENCES

Processing of personal data relating to criminal convictions and offences or related security measures based on Article 6(1) shall be carried out only under the control of official authority or when the processing is authorised by Union or Member State law providing for appropriate safeguards for the rights and freedoms of data subjects. Any comprehensive register of criminal convictions shall be kept only under the control of official authority.

ARTICLE 11 – PROCESSING WHICH DOES NOT REQUIRE IDENTIFICATION

1. If the purposes for which a controller processes personal data do not or do no longer require the identification of a data subject by the controller, the controller shall not be obliged to maintain, acquire or process additional information in order to identify the data subject for the sole purpose of complying with this Regulation.

2. Where, in cases referred to in paragraph 1 of this Article, the controller is able to demonstrate that it is not in a position to identify the data subject, the controller shall inform the data subject accordingly, if possible. In such cases, Articles 15 to 20 shall not apply except where the data subject, for the purpose of exercising his or her rights under those articles, provides additional information enabling his or her identification.

CHAPTER III – RIGHTS OF THE DATA SUBJECT

Section 1 – Transparency and modalities

ARTICLE 12 – TRANSPARENT INFORMATION, COMMUNICATION AND MODALITIES FOR THE EXERCISE OF THE RIGHTS OF THE DATA SUBJECT

1. The controller shall take appropriate measures to provide any information referred to in Articles 13 and 14 and any communication under Articles 15 to 22 and 34 relating to processing to the data subject in a concise, transparent, intelligible and easily accessible form, using clear and plain language, in particular for any information addressed specifically to a child. The information shall be provided in writing, or by other means, including, where appropriate, by electronic means. When requested by the data subject, the information may be provided orally, provided that the identity of the data subject is proven by other means.

2. The controller shall facilitate the exercise of data subject rights under Articles 15 to 22. In the cases referred to in Article 11(2), the controller shall not refuse to act on the request of the data subject for exercising his or her rights under Articles 15 to 22, unless the controller demonstrates that it is not in a position to identify the data subject.

3. The controller shall provide information on action taken on a request under Articles 15 to 22 to the data subject without undue delay and in any event within one month of receipt of the request. That period may be extended by two further months where necessary, taking into account the complexity and number of the requests. The controller shall inform the data subject of any such extension within one month of receipt of the request, together with the reasons for the delay. Where the data subject makes the request by electronic form means, the information shall be provided by electronic means where possible, unless otherwise requested by the data subject.

4. If the controller does not take action on the request of the data subject, the controller shall inform the data subject without delay and at the latest within one month of receipt of the request of the reasons for not taking action and on the possibility of lodging a complaint with a supervisory authority and seeking a judicial remedy.

5. Information provided under Articles 13 and 14 and any communication and any actions taken under Articles 15 to 22 and 34 shall be provided free of charge. Where requests from a data subject are manifestly unfounded or excessive, in particular because of their repetitive character, the controller may either:

(a)   charge a reasonable fee taking into account the administrative costs of providing the information or communication or taking the action requested; or
(b)   refuse to act on the request.

The controller shall bear the burden of demonstrating the manifestly unfounded or excessive character of the request.

6. Without prejudice to Article 11, where the controller has reasonable doubts concerning the identity of the natural person making the request referred to in Articles 15 to 21, the controller may request the provision of additional information necessary to confirm the identity of the data subject.

7. The information to be provided to data subjects pursuant to Articles 13 and 14 may be provided in combination with standardised icons in order to give in an easily visible, intelligible and clearly legible manner a meaningful overview of the intended processing. Where the icons are presented electronically they shall be machine-readable.

8. The Commission shall be empowered to adopt delegated acts in accordance with Article 92 for the purpose of determining the information to be presented by the icons and the procedures for providing standardised icons.

Section 2 – *Information and access to personal data*

ARTICLE 13 – INFORMATION TO BE PROVIDED WHERE PERSONAL DATA ARE COLLECTED FROM THE DATA SUBJECT

1. Where personal data relating to a data subject are collected from the data subject, the controller shall, at the time when personal data are obtained, provide the data subject with all of the following information:

(a) the identity and the contact details of the controller and, where applicable, of the controller's representative;

(b) the contact details of the data protection officer, where applicable;

(c) the purposes of the processing for which the personal data are intended as well as the legal basis for the processing;

(d) where the processing is based on point (f) of Article 6(1), the legitimate interests pursued by the controller or by a third party;

(e) the recipients or categories of recipients of the personal data, if any;

(f) where applicable, the fact that the controller intends to transfer personal data to a third country or international organisation and the existence or absence of an adequacy decision by the Commission, or in the case of transfers referred to in Article 46 or 47, or the second subparagraph of Article 49(1), reference to the appropriate or suitable safeguards and the means by which to obtain a copy of them or where they have been made available.

2. In addition to the information referred to in paragraph 1, the controller shall, at the time when personal data are obtained, provide the data subject with the following further information necessary to ensure fair and transparent processing:

(a) the period for which the personal data will be stored, or if that is not possible, the criteria used to determine that period;

(b) the existence of the right to request from the controller access to and rectification or erasure of personal data or restriction of processing concerning the data subject or to object to processing as well as the right to data portability;

(c) where the processing is based on point (a) of Article 6(1) or point (a) of Article 9(2), the existence of the right to withdraw consent at any time, without affecting the lawfulness of processing based on consent before its withdrawal;

(d) the right to lodge a complaint with a supervisory authority;

(e) whether the provision of personal data is a statutory or contractual requirement, or a requirement necessary to enter into a contract, as well as whether the data subject is obliged to provide the personal data and of the possible consequences of failure to provide such data;

(f) the existence of automated decision-making, including profiling, referred to in Article 22(1) and (4) and, at least in those cases, meaningful information about the logic involved, as well as the significance and the envisaged consequences of such processing for the data subject.

3. Where the controller intends to further process the personal data for a purpose other than that for which the personal data were collected, the controller shall provide the data subject prior to that further processing with information on that other purpose and with any relevant further information as referred to in paragraph 2.

4. Paragraphs 1, 2 and 3 shall not apply where and insofar as the data subject already has the information.

ARTICLE 14 – INFORMATION TO BE PROVIDED WHERE PERSONAL DATA HAVE NOT BEEN OBTAINED FROM THE DATA SUBJECT

1. Where personal data have not been obtained from the data subject, the controller shall provide the data subject with the following information:

(a) the identity and the contact details of the controller and, where applicable, of the controller's representative;

(b) the contact details of the data protection officer, where applicable;

(c) the purposes of the processing for which the personal data are intended as well as the legal basis for the processing;

(d) the categories of personal data concerned;

(e) the recipients or categories of recipients of the personal data, if any;

(f) where applicable, that the controller intends to transfer personal data to a recipient in a third country or international organisation and the existence or absence of an adequacy decision by the Commission, or in the case of transfers referred to in Article 46 or 47, or the second subparagraph of Article 49(1), reference to the appropriate or suitable safeguards and the means to obtain a copy of them or where they have been made available.

2. In addition to the information referred to in paragraph 1, the controller shall provide the data subject with the following information necessary to ensure fair and transparent processing in respect of the data subject:

(a) the period for which the personal data will be stored, or if that is not possible, the criteria used to determine that period;

(b) where the processing is based on point (f) of Article 6(1), the legitimate interests pursued by the controller or by a third party;

(c) the existence of the right to request from the controller access to and rectification or erasure of personal data or restriction of processing concerning the data subject and to object to processing as well as the right to data portability;

(d) where processing is based on point (a) of Article 6(1) or point (a) of Article 9(2), the existence of the right to withdraw consent at any time, without affecting the lawfulness of processing based on consent before its withdrawal;

(e) the right to lodge a complaint with a supervisory authority;

(f) from which source the personal data originate, and if applicable, whether it came from publicly accessible sources;

(g) the existence of automated decision-making, including profiling, referred to in Article 22(1) and (4) and, at least in those cases, meaningful information about the logic involved, as well as the significance and the envisaged consequences of such processing for the data subject.

3. The controller shall provide the information referred to in paragraphs 1 and 2:

(a) within a reasonable period after obtaining the personal data, but at the latest within one month, having regard to the specific circumstances in which the personal data are processed;

(b) if the personal data are to be used for communication with the data subject, at the latest at the time of the first communication to that data subject; or

(c) if a disclosure to another recipient is envisaged, at the latest when the personal data are first disclosed.

4. Where the controller intends to further process the personal data for a purpose other than that for which the personal data were obtained, the controller shall provide the data subject prior to that further processing with information on that other purpose and with any relevant further information as referred to in paragraph 2.

5. Paragraphs 1 to 4 shall not apply where and insofar as:

(a) the data subject already has the information;

(b) the provision of such information proves impossible or would involve a disproportionate effort, in particular for processing for archiving purposes in the public interest, scientific or historical research purposes or statistical purposes, subject to the conditions and safeguards referred to in Article 89(1) or in so far as the obligation referred to in paragraph 1 of this Article is likely to render impossible or seriously impair the achievement of the objectives of that processing. In such cases the controller shall take appropriate measures to protect the data subject's rights and freedoms and legitimate interests, including making the information publicly available;

(c) obtaining or disclosure is expressly laid down by Union or Member State law to which the controller is subject and which provides appropriate measures to protect the data subject's legitimate interests; or

(d) where the personal data must remain confidential subject to an obligation of professional secrecy regulated by Union or Member State law, including a statutory obligation of secrecy.

ARTICLE 15 – RIGHT OF ACCESS BY THE DATA SUBJECT

1. The data subject shall have the right to obtain from the controller confirmation as to whether or not personal data concerning him or her are being processed, and, where that is the case, access to the personal data and the following information:

(a) the purposes of the processing;
(b) the categories of personal data concerned;
(c) the recipients or categories of recipient to whom the personal data have been or will be disclosed, in particular recipients in third countries or international organisations;
(d) where possible, the envisaged period for which the personal data will be stored, or, if not possible, the criteria used to determine that period;
(e) the existence of the right to request from the controller rectification or erasure of personal data or restriction of processing of personal data concerning the data subject or to object to such processing;
(f) the right to lodge a complaint with a supervisory authority;
(g) where the personal data are not collected from the data subject, any available information as to their source;
(h) the existence of automated decision-making, including profiling, referred to in Article 22(1) and (4) and, at least in those cases, meaningful information about the logic involved, as well as the significance and the envisaged consequences of such processing for the data subject.

2. Where personal data are transferred to a third country or to an international organisation, the data subject shall have the right to be informed of the appropriate safeguards pursuant to Article 46 relating to the transfer.

3. The controller shall provide a copy of the personal data undergoing processing. For any further copies requested by the data subject, the controller may charge a reasonable fee based on administrative costs. Where the data subject makes the request by electronic means, and unless otherwise requested by the data subject, the information shall be provided in a commonly used electronic form.

4. The right to obtain a copy referred to in paragraph 3 shall not adversely affect the rights and freedoms of others.

Section 3 – Rectification and erasure

ARTICLE 16 – RIGHT TO RECTIFICATION

The data subject shall have the right to obtain from the controller without undue delay the rectification of inaccurate personal data concerning him or her. Taking into account the purposes of the processing, the data subject shall have the right to have incomplete personal data completed, including by means of providing a supplementary statement.

ARTICLE 17 – RIGHT TO ERASURE ('RIGHT TO BE FORGOTTEN')

1. The data subject shall have the right to obtain from the controller the erasure of personal data concerning him or her without undue delay and the controller shall have the obligation to erase personal data without undue delay where one of the following grounds applies:

(a) the personal data are no longer necessary in relation to the purposes for which they were collected or otherwise processed;

(b) the data subject withdraws consent on which the processing is based according to point (a) of Article 6(1), or point (a) of Article 9(2), and where there is no other legal ground for the processing;

(c) the data subject objects to the processing pursuant to Article 21(1) and there are no overriding legitimate grounds for the processing, or the data subject objects to the processing pursuant to Article 21(2);

(d) the personal data have been unlawfully processed;

(e) the personal data have to be erased for compliance with a legal obligation in Union or Member State law to which the controller is subject;

(f) the personal data have been collected in relation to the offer of information society services referred to in Article 8(1).

2. Where the controller has made the personal data public and is obliged pursuant to paragraph 1 to erase the personal data, the controller, taking account of available technology and the cost of implementation, shall take reasonable steps, including technical measures, to inform controllers which are processing the personal data that the data subject has requested the erasure by such controllers of any links to, or copy or replication of, those personal data.

3. Paragraphs 1 and 2 shall not apply to the extent that processing is necessary:

(a) for exercising the right of freedom of expression and information;

(b) for compliance with a legal obligation which requires processing by Union or Member State law to which the controller is subject or for the performance of a task carried out in the public interest or in the exercise of official authority vested in the controller;

(c) for reasons of public interest in the area of public health in accordance with points (h) and (i) of Article 9(2) as well as Article 9(3);

(d) for archiving purposes in the public interest, scientific or historical research purposes or statistical purposes in accordance with Article 89(1) in so far as the right referred to in paragraph 1 is likely to render impossible or seriously impair the achievement of the objectives of that processing; or

(e) for the establishment, exercise or defence of legal claims.

ARTICLE 18 – RIGHT TO RESTRICTION OF PROCESSING

1. The data subject shall have the right to obtain from the controller restriction of processing where one of the following applies:

(a) the accuracy of the personal data is contested by the data subject, for a period enabling the controller to verify the accuracy of the personal data;

(b) the processing is unlawful and the data subject opposes the erasure of the personal data and requests the restriction of their use instead;

(c) the controller no longer needs the personal data for the purposes of the processing, but they are required by the data subject for the establishment, exercise or defence of legal claims;

(d) the data subject has objected to processing pursuant to Article 21(1) pending the verification whether the legitimate grounds of the controller override those of the data subject.

2. Where processing has been restricted under paragraph 1, such personal data shall, with the exception of storage, only be processed with the data subject's consent or for the establishment, exercise or defence of legal claims or for the protection of the rights of another natural or legal person or for reasons of important public interest of the Union or of a Member State.

3. A data subject who has obtained restriction of processing pursuant to paragraph 1 shall be informed by the controller before the restriction of processing is lifted.

ARTICLE 19 – NOTIFICATION OBLIGATION REGARDING RECTIFICATION OR ERASURE OF PERSONAL DATA OR RESTRICTION OF PROCESSING

The controller shall communicate any rectification or erasure of personal data or restriction of processing carried out in accordance with Article 16, Article 17(1) and Article 18 to each recipient to whom the personal data have been disclosed, unless this proves impossible or involves disproportionate effort. The controller shall inform the data subject about those recipients if the data subject requests it.

ARTICLE 20 – RIGHT TO DATA PORTABILITY

1. The data subject shall have the right to receive the personal data concerning him or her, which he or she has provided to a controller, in a structured, commonly used and machine-readable format and have the right to transmit those data to another controller without hindrance from the controller to which the personal data have been provided, where:

(a)   the processing is based on consent pursuant to point (a) of Article 6(1) or point (a) of Article 9(2) or on a contract pursuant to point (b) of Article 6(1); and
(b)   the processing is carried out by automated means.

2. In exercising his or her right to data portability pursuant to paragraph 1, the data subject shall have the right to have the personal data transmitted directly from one controller to another, where technically feasible.

3. The exercise of the right referred to in paragraph 1 of this Article shall be without prejudice to Article 17. That right shall not apply to processing necessary for the performance of a task carried out in the public interest or in the exercise of official authority vested in the controller.

4. The right referred to in paragraph 1 shall not adversely affect the rights and freedoms of others.

Section 4 – Right to object and automated individual decision-making

ARTICLE 21 – RIGHT TO OBJECT

1. The data subject shall have the right to object, on grounds relating to his or her particular situation, at any time to processing of personal data concerning him or her which is based on point (e) or (f) of Article 6(1), including profiling based on those provisions. The controller shall no longer process the personal data unless the controller demonstrates compelling legitimate grounds for the processing which override the interests, rights and freedoms of the data subject or for the establishment, exercise or defence of legal claims.

2. Where personal data are processed for direct marketing purposes, the data subject shall have the right to object at any time to processing of personal data concerning him or her for such marketing, which includes profiling to the extent that it is related to such direct marketing.

3. Where the data subject objects to processing for direct marketing purposes, the personal data shall no longer be processed for such purposes.

4. At the latest at the time of the first communication with the data subject, the right referred to in paragraphs 1 and 2 shall be explicitly brought to the attention of the data subject and shall be presented clearly and separately from any other information.

5. In the context of the use of information society services, and notwithstanding Directive 2002/58/EC, the data subject may exercise his or her right to object by automated means using technical specifications.

6. Where personal data are processed for scientific or historical research purposes or statistical purposes pursuant to Article 89(1), the data subject, on grounds relating to his or her particular situation, shall have the right to object to processing of personal data concerning him or her, unless the processing is necessary for the performance of a task carried out for reasons of public interest.

ARTICLE 22 – AUTOMATED INDIVIDUAL DECISION-MAKING, INCLUDING PROFILING

1. The data subject shall have the right not to be subject to a decision based solely on automated processing, including profiling, which produces legal effects concerning him or her or similarly significantly affects him or her.

2. Paragraph 1 shall not apply if the decision:

(a) is necessary for entering into, or performance of, a contract between the data subject and a data controller;
(b) is authorised by Union or Member State law to which the controller is subject and which also lays down suitable measures to safeguard the data subject's rights and freedoms and legitimate interests; or
(c) is based on the data subject's explicit consent.

3. In the cases referred to in points (a) and (c) of paragraph 2, the data controller shall implement suitable measures to safeguard the data subject's rights and freedoms and legitimate interests, at least the right to obtain human intervention on the part of the controller, to express his or her point of view and to contest the decision.

4. Decisions referred to in paragraph 2 shall not be based on special categories of personal data referred to in Article 9(1), unless point (a) or (g) of Article 9(2) applies and suitable measures to safeguard the data subject's rights and freedoms and legitimate interests are in place.

Section 5 – Restrictions

ARTICLE 23 – RESTRICTIONS

1. Union or Member State law to which the data controller or processor is subject may restrict by way of a legislative measure the scope of the obligations and rights provided for in Articles 12 to 22 and Article 34, as well as Article 5 in so far as its provisions correspond to the rights and obligations provided for in Articles 12 to 22, when such a restriction respects the essence of the fundamental rights and freedoms and is a necessary and proportionate measure in a democratic society to safeguard:

(a) national security;
(b) defence;
(c) public security;
(d) the prevention, investigation, detection or prosecution of criminal offences or the execution of criminal penalties, including the safeguarding against and the prevention of threats to public security;
(e) other important objectives of general public interest of the Union or of a Member State, in particular an important economic or financial interest of the Union or of a Member State, including monetary, budgetary and taxation a matters, public health and social security;
(f) the protection of judicial independence and judicial proceedings;
(g) the prevention, investigation, detection and prosecution of breaches of ethics for regulated professions;
(h) a monitoring, inspection or regulatory function connected, even occasionally, to the exercise of official authority in the cases referred to in points (a) to (e) and (g);

(i)   the protection of the data subject or the rights and freedoms of others;

(j)   the enforcement of civil law claims.

2. In particular, any legislative measure referred to in paragraph 1 shall contain specific provisions at least, where relevant, as to:

(a)   the purposes of the processing or categories of processing;
(b)   the categories of personal data;
(c)   the scope of the restrictions introduced;
(d)   the safeguards to prevent abuse or unlawful access or transfer;
(e)   the specification of the controller or categories of controllers;
(f)   the storage periods and the applicable safeguards taking into account the nature, scope and purposes of the processing or categories of processing;
(g)   the risks to the rights and freedoms of data subjects; and
(h)   the right of data subjects to be informed about the restriction, unless that may be prejudicial to the purpose of the restriction.

CHAPTER IV – CONTROLLER AND PROCESSOR

Section 1 – General obligations

ARTICLE 24 – RESPONSIBILITY OF THE CONTROLLER

1. Taking into account the nature, scope, context and purposes of processing as well as the risks of varying likelihood and severity for the rights and freedoms of natural persons, the controller shall implement appropriate technical and organisational measures to ensure and to be able to demonstrate that processing is performed in accordance with this Regulation. Those measures shall be reviewed and updated where necessary.

2. Where proportionate in relation to processing activities, the measures referred to in paragraph 1 shall include the implementation of appropriate data protection policies by the controller.

3. Adherence to approved codes of conduct as referred to in Article 40 or approved certification mechanisms as referred to in Article 42 may be used as an element by which to demonstrate compliance with the obligations of the controller.

ARTICLE 25 – DATA PROTECTION BY DESIGN AND BY DEFAULT

1. Taking into account the state of the art, the cost of implementation and the nature, scope, context and purposes of processing as well as the risks of varying likelihood and severity for rights and freedoms of natural persons posed by the processing, the controller shall, both at the time of the determination of the means for processing and at the time of the processing itself, implement appropriate technical and organisational measures, such as pseudonymisation, which are designed to implement data-protection principles, such as data minimisation, in an effective manner and to integrate the necessary safeguards into the processing in order to meet the requirements of this Regulation and protect the rights of data subjects.

2. The controller shall implement appropriate technical and organisational measures for ensuring that, by default, only personal data which are necessary for each specific purpose of the processing are processed. That obligation applies to the amount of personal data collected, the extent of their processing, the period of their storage and their accessibility. In particular, such measures shall ensure that by default personal data are not made accessible without the individual's intervention to an indefinite number of natural persons.

3. An approved certification mechanism pursuant to Article 42 may be used as an element to demonstrate compliance with the requirements set out in paragraphs 1 and 2 of this Article.

ARTICLE 26 – JOINT CONTROLLERS

1. Where two or more controllers jointly determine the purposes and means of processing, they shall be joint controllers. They shall in a transparent manner determine their respective responsibilities for compliance with the obligations under this Regulation, in particular as regards the exercising of the rights of the data subject and their respective duties to provide the information referred to in Articles 13 and 14, by means of an arrangement between them unless, and in so far as, the respective responsibilities of the controllers are determined by Union or Member State law to which the controllers are subject. The arrangement may designate a contact point for data subjects.

2. The arrangement referred to in paragraph 1 shall duly reflect the respective roles and relationships of the joint controllers vis-à-vis the data subjects. The essence of the arrangement shall be made available to the data subject.

3. Irrespective of the terms of the arrangement referred to in paragraph 1, the data subject may exercise his or her rights under this Regulation in respect of and against each of the controllers.

ARTICLE 27 – REPRESENTATIVES OF CONTROLLERS OR PROCESSORS NOT ESTABLISHED IN THE UNION

1. Where Article 3(2) applies, the controller or the processor shall designate in writing a representative in the Union.

2. The obligation laid down in paragraph 1 of this Article shall not apply to:

(a)   processing which is occasional, does not include, on a large scale, processing of special categories of data as referred to in Article 9(1) or processing of personal data relating to criminal convictions and offences referred to in Article 10, and is unlikely to result in a risk to the rights and freedoms of natural persons, taking into account the nature, context, scope and purposes of the processing; or
(b)   a public authority or body.

3. The representative shall be established in one of the Member States where the data subjects, whose personal data are processed in relation to the offering of goods or services to them, or whose behaviour is monitored, are.

4. The representative shall be mandated by the controller or processor to be addressed in addition to or instead of the controller or the processor by, in particular, supervisory authorities and data subjects, on all issues related to processing, for the purposes of ensuring compliance with this Regulation.

5. The designation of a representative by the controller or processor shall be without prejudice to legal actions which could be initiated against the controller or the processor themselves.

ARTICLE 28 – PROCESSOR

1. Where processing is to be carried out on behalf of a controller, the controller shall use only processors providing sufficient guarantees to implement appropriate technical and organisational measures in such a manner that processing will meet the requirements of this Regulation and ensure the protection of the rights of the data subject.

2. The processor shall not engage another processor without prior specific or general written authorisation of the controller. In the case of general written authorisation, the processor shall inform the controller of any intended changes concerning the addition or replacement of other processors, thereby giving the controller the opportunity to object to such changes.

3. Processing by a processor shall be governed by a contract or other legal act under Union or Member State law, that is binding on the processor with regard to the controller and that sets out the subject-matter and duration of the processing, the nature and purpose of the processing, the type of personal data and categories of data subjects and the obligations and rights of the controller. That contract or other legal act shall stipulate, in particular, that the processor:

(a) processes the personal data only on documented instructions from the controller, including with regard to transfers of personal data to a third country or an international organisation, unless required to do so by Union or Member State law to which the processor is subject; in such a case, the processor shall inform the controller of that legal requirement before processing, unless that law prohibits such information on important grounds of public interest;

(b) ensures that persons authorised to process the personal data have committed themselves to confidentiality or are under an appropriate statutory obligation of confidentiality;

(c) takes all measures required pursuant to Article 32;

(d) respects the conditions referred to in paragraphs 2 and 4 for engaging another processor;

(e) taking into account the nature of the processing, assists the controller by appropriate technical and organisational measures, insofar as this is possible, for the fulfilment of the controller's obligation to respond to requests for exercising the data subject's rights laid down in Chapter III;

(f) assists the controller in ensuring compliance with the obligations pursuant to Articles 32 to 36 taking into account the nature of processing and the information available to the processor;

(g) at the choice of the controller, deletes or returns all the personal data to the controller after the end of the provision of services relating to processing, and deletes existing copies unless Union or Member State law requires storage of the personal data;

(h) makes available to the controller all information necessary to demonstrate compliance with the obligations laid down in this Article and allow for and contribute to audits, including inspections, conducted by the controller or another auditor mandated by the controller.

With regard to point (h) of the first subparagraph, the processor shall immediately inform the controller if, in its opinion, an instruction infringes this Regulation or other Union or Member State data protection provisions.

4. Where a processor engages another processor for carrying out specific processing activities on behalf of the controller, the same data protection obligations as set out in the contract or other legal act between the controller and the processor as referred to in paragraph 3 shall be imposed on that other processor by way of a contract or other legal act under Union or Member State law, in particular providing sufficient guarantees to implement appropriate technical and organisational measures in such a manner that the processing will meet the requirements of this Regulation. Where that other processor fails to fulfil its data protection obligations, the initial processor shall remain fully liable to the controller for the performance of that other processor's obligations.

5. Adherence of a processor to an approved code of conduct as referred to in Article 40 or an approved certification mechanism as referred to in Article 42 may be used as an element by which to demonstrate sufficient guarantees as referred to in paragraphs 1 and 4 of this Article.

6. Without prejudice to an individual contract between the controller and the processor, the contract or the other legal act referred to in paragraphs 3 and 4 of this Article may be based, in whole or in part, on standard contractual clauses referred to in paragraphs 7 and 8 of this Article, including when they are part of a certification granted to the controller or processor pursuant to Articles 42 and 43.

7. The Commission may lay down standard contractual clauses for the matters referred to in paragraph 3 and 4 of this Article and in accordance with the examination procedure referred to in Article 93(2).

8. A supervisory authority may adopt standard contractual clauses for the matters referred to in paragraph 3 and 4 of this Article and in accordance with the consistency mechanism referred to in Article 63.

9. The contract or the other legal act referred to in paragraphs 3 and 4 shall be in writing, including in electronic form.

10. Without prejudice to Articles 82, 83 and 84, if a processor infringes this Regulation by determining the purposes and means of processing, the processor shall be considered to be a controller in respect of that processing.

ARTICLE 29 – PROCESSING UNDER THE AUTHORITY OF THE CONTROLLER OR PROCESSOR

The processor and any person acting under the authority of the controller or of the processor, who has access to personal data, shall not process those data except on instructions from the controller, unless required to do so by Union or Member State law.

ARTICLE 30 – RECORDS OF PROCESSING ACTIVITIES

1. Each controller and, where applicable, the controller's representative, shall maintain a record of processing activities under its responsibility. That record shall contain all of the following information:

(a) the name and contact details of the controller and, where applicable, the joint controller, the controller's representative and the data protection officer;
(b) the purposes of the processing;
(c) a description of the categories of data subjects and of the categories of personal data;
(d) the categories of recipients to whom the personal data have been or will be disclosed including recipients in third countries or international organisations;
(e) where applicable, transfers of personal data to a third country or an international organisation, including the identification of that third country or international organisation and, in the case of transfers referred to in the second subparagraph of Article 49(1), the documentation of suitable safeguards;
(f) where possible, the envisaged time limits for erasure of the different categories of data;
(g) where possible, a general description of the technical and organisational security measures referred to in Article 32(1).

2. Each processor and, where applicable, the processor's representative shall maintain a record of all categories of processing activities carried out on behalf of a controller, containing:

(a) the name and contact details of the processor or processors and of each controller on behalf of which the processor is acting, and, where applicable, of the controller's or the processor's representative, and the data protection officer;
(b) the categories of processing carried out on behalf of each controller;
(c) where applicable, transfers of personal data to a third country or an international organisation, including the identification of that third country or international organisation and, in the case of transfers referred to in the second subparagraph of Article 49(1), the documentation of suitable safeguards;
(d) where possible, a general description of the technical and organisational security measures referred to in Article 32(1).

3. The records referred to in paragraphs 1 and 2 shall be in writing, including in electronic form.

4. The controller or the processor and, where applicable, the controller's or the processor's representative, shall make the record available to the supervisory authority on request.

5. The obligations referred to in paragraphs 1 and 2 shall not apply to an enterprise or an organisation employing fewer than 250 persons unless the processing it carries out is likely to result in a risk to the rights and freedoms of data subjects, the processing is not occasional, or the processing includes special categories of data as referred to in Article 9(1) or personal data relating to criminal convictions and offences referred to in Article 10.

ARTICLE 31 – COOPERATION WITH THE SUPERVISORY AUTHORITY

The controller and the processor and, where applicable, their representatives, shall cooperate, on request, with the supervisory authority in the performance of its tasks.

Section 2 – Security of personal data

ARTICLE 32 – SECURITY OF PROCESSING

1. Taking into account the state of the art, the costs of implementation and the nature, scope, context and purposes of processing as well as the risk of varying likelihood and severity for the rights and freedoms of natural persons, the controller and the processor shall implement appropriate technical and organisational measures to ensure a level of security appropriate to the risk, including inter alia as appropriate:

(a) the pseudonymisation and encryption of personal data;
(b) the ability to ensure the ongoing confidentiality, integrity, availability and resilience of processing systems and services;
(c) the ability to restore the availability and access to personal data in a timely manner in the event of a physical or technical incident;
(d) a process for regularly testing, assessing and evaluating the effectiveness of technical and organisational measures for ensuring the security of the processing.

2. In assessing the appropriate level of security account shall be taken in particular of the risks that are presented by processing, in particular from accidental or unlawful destruction, loss, alteration, unauthorised disclosure of, or access to personal data transmitted, stored or otherwise processed.

3. Adherence to an approved code of conduct as referred to in Article 40 or an approved certification mechanism as referred to in Article 42 may be used as an element by which to demonstrate compliance with the requirements set out in paragraph 1 of this Article.

4. The controller and processor shall take steps to ensure that any natural person acting under the authority of the controller or the processor who has access to personal data does not process them except on instructions from the controller, unless he or she is required to do so by Union or Member State law.

ARTICLE 33 – NOTIFICATION OF A PERSONAL DATA BREACH TO THE SUPERVISORY AUTHORITY

1. In the case of a personal data breach, the controller shall without undue delay and, where feasible, not later than 72 hours after having become aware of it, notify the personal data breach to the supervisory authority competent in accordance with Article 55, unless the personal data breach is unlikely to result in a risk to the rights and freedoms of natural persons. Where the notification to the supervisory authority is not made within 72 hours, it shall be accompanied by reasons for the delay.

2. The processor shall notify the controller without undue delay after becoming aware of a personal data breach.

3. The notification referred to in paragraph 1 shall at least:

(a) describe the nature of the personal data breach including where possible, the categories and approximate number of data subjects concerned and the categories and approximate number of personal data records concerned;
(b) communicate the name and contact details of the data protection officer or other contact point where more information can be obtained;
(c) describe the likely consequences of the personal data breach;
(d) describe the measures taken or proposed to be taken by the controller to address the personal data breach, including, where appropriate, measures to mitigate its possible adverse effects.

4. Where, and in so far as, it is not possible to provide the information at the same time, the information may be provided in phases without undue further delay.

5. The controller shall document any personal data breaches, comprising the facts relating to the personal data breach, its effects and the remedial action taken. That documentation shall enable the supervisory authority to verify compliance with this Article.

ARTICLE 34 – COMMUNICATION OF A PERSONAL DATA BREACH TO THE DATA SUBJECT

1. When the personal data breach is likely to result in a high risk to the rights and freedoms of natural persons, the controller shall communicate the personal data breach to the data subject without undue delay.

2. The communication to the data subject referred to in paragraph 1 of this Article shall describe in clear and plain language the nature of the personal data breach and contain at least the information and measures referred to in points (b), (c) and (d) of Article 33(3).

3. The communication to the data subject referred to in paragraph 1 shall not be required if any of the following conditions are met:

(a) the controller has implemented appropriate technical and organisational protection measures, and those measures were applied to the personal data affected by the personal data breach, in particular those that render the personal data unintelligible to any person who is not authorised to access it, such as encryption;
(b) the controller has taken subsequent measures which ensure that the high risk to the rights and freedoms of data subjects referred to in paragraph 1 is no longer likely to materialise;
(c) it would involve disproportionate effort. In such a case, there shall instead be a public communication or similar measure whereby the data subjects are informed in an equally effective manner.

4. If the controller has not already communicated the personal data breach to the data subject, the supervisory authority, having considered the likelihood of the personal data breach resulting in a high risk, may require it to do so or may decide that any of the conditions referred to in paragraph 3 are met.

Section 3 – Data protection impact assessment and prior consultation

ARTICLE 35 – DATA PROTECTION IMPACT ASSESSMENT

1. Where a type of processing in particular using new technologies, and taking into account the nature, scope, context and purposes of the processing, is likely to result in a high risk to the rights and freedoms of natural persons, the controller shall, prior to the processing, carry out an assessment of the impact of the envisaged processing operations on the protection of personal data. A single assessment may address a set of similar processing operations that present similar high risks.

2. The controller shall seek the advice of the data protection officer, where designated, when carrying out a data protection impact assessment.

3. A data protection impact assessment referred to in paragraph 1 shall in particular be required in the case of:

(a) a systematic and extensive evaluation of personal aspects relating to natural persons which is based on automated processing, including profiling, and on which decisions are based that produce legal effects concerning the natural person or similarly significantly affect the natural person;

(b) processing on a large scale of special categories of data referred to in Article 9(1), or of personal data relating to criminal convictions and offences referred to in Article 10; or

(c) a systematic monitoring of a publicly accessible area on a large scale.

4. The supervisory authority shall establish and make public a list of the kind of processing operations which are subject to the requirement for a data protection impact assessment pursuant to paragraph 1. The supervisory authority shall communicate those lists to the Board referred to in Article 68.

5. The supervisory authority may also establish and make public a list of the kind of processing operations for which no data protection impact assessment is required. The supervisory authority shall communicate those lists to the Board.

6. Prior to the adoption of the lists referred to in paragraphs 4 and 5, the competent supervisory authority shall apply the consistency mechanism referred to in Article 63 where such lists involve processing activities which are related to the offering of goods or services to data subjects or to the monitoring of their behaviour in several Member States, or may substantially affect the free movement of personal data within the Union.

7. The assessment shall contain at least:

(a) a systematic description of the envisaged processing operations and the purposes of the processing, including, where applicable, the legitimate interest pursued by the controller;

(b) an assessment of the necessity and proportionality of the processing operations in relation to the purposes;

(c) an assessment of the risks to the rights and freedoms of data subjects referred to in paragraph 1; and

(d) the measures envisaged to address the risks, including safeguards, security measures and mechanisms to ensure the protection of personal data and to demonstrate compliance with this Regulation taking into account the rights and legitimate interests of data subjects and other persons concerned.

8. Compliance with approved codes of conduct referred to in Article 40 by the relevant controllers or processors shall be taken into due account in assessing the impact of the processing operations performed by such controllers or processors, in particular for the purposes of a data protection impact assessment.

9. Where appropriate, the controller shall seek the views of data subjects or their representatives on the intended processing, without prejudice to the protection of commercial or public interests or the security of processing operations.

10. Where processing pursuant to point (c) or (e) of Article 6(1) has a legal basis in Union law or in the law of the Member State to which the controller is subject, that law regulates the specific processing operation or set of operations in question, and a data protection impact assessment has already been carried out as part of a general impact assessment in the context of the adoption of that legal basis, paragraphs 1 to 7 shall not apply unless Member States deem it to be necessary to carry out such an assessment prior to processing activities.

11. Where necessary, the controller shall carry out a review to assess if processing is performed in accordance with the data protection impact assessment at least when there is a change of the risk represented by processing operations.

ARTICLE 36 – PRIOR CONSULTATION

1. The controller shall consult the supervisory authority prior to processing where a data protection impact assessment under Article 35 indicates that the processing would result in a high risk in the absence of measures taken by the controller to mitigate the risk.

2. Where the supervisory authority is of the opinion that the intended processing referred to in paragraph 1 would infringe this Regulation, in particular where the controller has insufficiently identified or mitigated the risk, the supervisory authority shall, within period of up to eight weeks of receipt of the request for consultation, provide written advice to the controller and, where applicable to the processor, and may use any of its powers referred to in Article 58. That period may be extended by six weeks, taking into account the complexity of the intended processing. The supervisory authority shall inform the controller and, where applicable, the processor, of any such extension within one month of receipt of the request for consultation together with the reasons for the delay. Those periods may be suspended until the supervisory authority has obtained information it has requested for the purposes of the consultation.

3. When consulting the supervisory authority pursuant to paragraph 1, the controller shall provide the supervisory authority with:

(a) where applicable, the respective responsibilities of the controller, joint controllers and processors involved in the processing, in particular for processing within a group of undertakings;
(b) the purposes and means of the intended processing;
(c) the measures and safeguards provided to protect the rights and freedoms of data subjects pursuant to this Regulation;
(d) where applicable, the contact details of the data protection officer;
(e) the data protection impact assessment provided for in Article 35; and
(f) any other information requested by the supervisory authority.

4. Member States shall consult the supervisory authority during the preparation of a proposal for a legislative measure to be adopted by a national parliament, or of a regulatory measure based on such a legislative measure, which relates to processing.

5. Notwithstanding paragraph 1, Member State law may require controllers to consult with, and obtain prior authorisation from, the supervisory authority in relation to processing by a controller for the performance of a task carried out by the controller in the public interest, including processing in relation to social protection and public health.

Section 4 – Data protection officer

ARTICLE 37 – DESIGNATION OF THE DATA PROTECTION OFFICER

1. The controller and the processor shall designate a data protection officer in any case where:

(a) the processing is carried out by a public authority or body, except for courts acting in their judicial capacity;
(b) the core activities of the controller or the processor consist of processing operations which, by virtue of their nature, their scope and/or their purposes, require regular and systematic monitoring of data subjects on a large scale; or
(c) the core activities of the controller or the processor consist of processing on a large scale of special categories of data pursuant to Article 9 and personal data relating to criminal convictions and offences referred to in Article 10.

2. A group of undertakings may appoint a single data protection officer provided that a data protection officer is easily accessible from each establishment.

3. Where the controller or the processor is a public authority or body, a single data protection officer may be designated for several such authorities or bodies, taking account of their organisational structure and size.

4. In cases other than those referred to in paragraph 1, the controller or processor or associations and other bodies representing categories of controllers or processors may or, where required by Union or Member State law shall, designate a data protection officer. The data protection officer may act for such associations and other bodies representing controllers or processors.

5. The data protection officer shall be designated on the basis of professional qualities and, in particular, expert knowledge of data protection law and practices and the ability to fulfil the tasks referred to in Article 39.

6. The data protection officer may be a staff member of the controller or processor, or fulfil the tasks on the basis of a service contract.

7. The controller or the processor shall publish the contact details of the data protection officer and communicate them to the supervisory authority.

ARTICLE 38 – POSITION OF THE DATA PROTECTION OFFICER

1. The controller and the processor shall ensure that the data protection officer is involved, properly and in a timely manner, in all issues which relate to the protection of personal data.

2. The controller and processor shall support the data protection officer in performing the tasks referred to in Article 39 by providing resources necessary to carry out those tasks and access to personal data and processing operations, and to maintain his or her expert knowledge.

3. The controller and processor shall ensure that the data protection officer does not receive any instructions regarding the exercise of those tasks. He or she shall not be dismissed or penalised by the controller or the processor for performing his tasks. The data protection officer shall directly report to the highest management level of the controller or the processor.

4. Data subjects may contact the data protection officer with regard to all issues related to processing of their personal data and to the exercise of their rights under this Regulation.

5. The data protection officer shall be bound by secrecy or confidentiality concerning the performance of his or her tasks, in accordance with Union or Member State law.

6. The data protection officer may fulfil other tasks and duties. The controller or processor shall ensure that any such tasks and duties do not result in a conflict of interests.

ARTICLE 39 – TASKS OF THE DATA PROTECTION OFFICER

1. The data protection officer shall have at least the following tasks:

(a) to inform and advise the controller or the processor and the employees who carry out processing of their obligations pursuant to this Regulation and to other Union or Member State data protection provisions;

(b) to monitor compliance with this Regulation, with other Union or Member State data protection provisions and with the policies of the controller or processor in relation to the protection of personal data, including the assignment of responsibilities, awareness-raising and training of staff involved in processing operations, and the related audits;

(c) to provide advice where requested as regards the data protection impact assessment and monitor its performance pursuant to Article 35;

(d) to cooperate with the supervisory authority;

(e) to act as the contact point for the supervisory authority on issues relating to processing, including the prior consultation referred to in Article 36, and to consult, where appropriate, with regard to any other matter.

2. The data protection officer shall in the performance of his or her tasks have due regard to the risk associated with processing operations, taking into account the nature, scope, context and purposes of processing.

Section 5 – Codes of conduct and certification

ARTICLE 40 – CODES OF CONDUCT

1. The Member States, the supervisory authorities, the Board and the Commission shall encourage the drawing up of codes of conduct intended to contribute to the proper application of this Regulation, taking account of the specific features of the various processing sectors and the specific needs of micro, small and medium-sized enterprises.

2. Associations and other bodies representing categories of controllers or processors may prepare codes of conduct, or amend or extend such codes, for the purpose of specifying the application of this Regulation, such as with regard to:

(a) fair and transparent processing;
(b) the legitimate interests pursued by controllers in specific contexts;
(c) the collection of personal data;
(d) the pseudonymisation of personal data;
(e) the information provided to the public and to data subjects;
(f) the exercise of the rights of data subjects;
(g) the information provided to, and the protection of, children, and the manner in which the consent of the holders of parental responsibility over children is to be obtained;
(h) the measures and procedures referred to in Articles 24 and 25 and the measures to ensure security of processing referred to in Article 32;
(i) the notification of personal data breaches to supervisory authorities and the communication of such personal data breaches to data subjects;
(j) the transfer of personal data to third countries or international organisations; or
(k) out-of-court proceedings and other dispute resolution procedures for resolving disputes between controllers and data subjects with regard to processing, without prejudice to the rights of data subjects pursuant to Articles 77 and 79.

3. In addition to adherence by controllers or processors subject to this Regulation, codes of conduct approved pursuant to paragraph 5 of this Article and having general validity pursuant to paragraph 9 of this Article may also be adhered to by controllers or processors that are not subject to this Regulation pursuant to Article 3 in order to provide appropriate safeguards within the framework of personal data transfers to third countries or international organisations under the terms referred to in point (e) of Article 46(2). Such controllers or processors shall make binding and enforceable commitments, via contractual or other legally binding instruments, to apply those appropriate safeguards including with regard to the rights of data subjects.

4. A code of conduct referred to in paragraph 2 of this Article shall contain mechanisms which enable the body referred to in Article 41(1) to carry out the mandatory monitoring of compliance with its provisions by the controllers or processors which undertake to apply it, without prejudice to the tasks and powers of supervisory authorities competent pursuant to Article 55 or 56.

5. Associations and other bodies referred to in paragraph 2 of this Article which intend to prepare a code of conduct or to amend or extend an existing code shall submit the draft code, amendment or extension to the supervisory authority which is competent pursuant to Article 55. The supervisory authority shall provide an opinion on whether the draft code,

amendment or extension complies with this Regulation and shall approve that draft code, amendment or extension if it finds that it provides sufficient appropriate safeguards.

6. Where the draft code, or amendment or extension is approved in accordance with paragraph 5, and where the code of conduct concerned does not relate to processing activities in several Member States, the supervisory authority shall register and publish the code.

7. Where a draft code of conduct relates to processing activities in several Member States, the supervisory authority which is competent pursuant to Article 55 shall, before approving the draft code, amendment or extension, submit it in the procedure referred to in Article 63 to the Board which shall provide an opinion on whether the draft code, amendment or extension complies with this Regulation or, in the situation referred to in paragraph 3 of this Article, provides appropriate safeguards.

8. Where the opinion referred to in paragraph 7 confirms that the draft code, amendment or extension complies with this Regulation, or, in the situation referred to in paragraph 3, provides appropriate safeguards, the Board shall submit its opinion to the Commission.

9. The Commission may, by way of implementing acts, decide that the approved code of conduct, amendment or extension submitted to it pursuant to paragraph 8 of this Article have general validity within the Union. Those implementing acts shall be adopted in accordance with the examination procedure set out in Article 93(2).

10. The Commission shall ensure appropriate publicity for the approved codes which have been decided as having general validity in accordance with paragraph 9.

11. The Board shall collate all approved codes of conduct, amendments and extensions in a register and shall make them publicly available by way of appropriate means.

ARTICLE 41 – MONITORING OF APPROVED CODES OF CONDUCT

1. Without prejudice to the tasks and powers of the competent supervisory authority under Articles 57 and 58, the monitoring of compliance with a code of conduct pursuant to Article 40 may be carried out by a body which has an appropriate level of expertise in relation to the subject-matter of the code and is accredited for that purpose by the competent supervisory authority.

2. A body as referred to in paragraph 1 may be accredited to monitor compliance with a code of conduct where that body has:

(a) demonstrated its independence and expertise in relation to the subject-matter of the code to the satisfaction of the competent supervisory authority;

(b) established procedures which allow it to assess the eligibility of controllers and processors concerned to apply the code, to monitor their compliance with its provisions and to periodically review its operation;

(c) established procedures and structures to handle complaints about infringements of the code or the manner in which the code has been, or is being, implemented by a controller or processor, and to make those procedures and structures transparent to data subjects and the public; and

(d) demonstrated to the satisfaction of the competent supervisory authority that its tasks and duties do not result in a conflict of interests.

3. The competent supervisory authority shall submit the draft criteria for accreditation of a body as referred to in paragraph 1 of this Article to the Board pursuant to the consistency mechanism referred to in Article 63.

4. Without prejudice to the tasks and powers of the competent supervisory authority and the provisions of Chapter VIII, a body as referred to in paragraph 1 of this Article shall, subject to appropriate safeguards, take appropriate action in cases of infringement of the

code by a controller or processor, including suspension or exclusion of the controller or processor concerned from the code. It shall inform the competent supervisory authority of such actions and the reasons for taking them.

5. The competent supervisory authority shall revoke the accreditation of a body as referred to in paragraph 1 if the conditions for accreditation are not, or are no longer, met or where actions taken by the body infringe this Regulation.

6. This Article shall not apply to processing carried out by public authorities and bodies.

ARTICLE 42 – CERTIFICATION

1. The Member States, the supervisory authorities, the Board and the Commission shall encourage, in particular at Union level, the establishment of data protection certification mechanisms and of data protection seals and marks, for the purpose of demonstrating compliance with this Regulation of processing operations by controllers and processors. The specific needs of micro, small and medium-sized enterprises shall be taken into account.

2. In addition to adherence by controllers or processors subject to this Regulation, data protection certification mechanisms, seals or marks approved pursuant to paragraph 5 of this Article may be established for the purpose of demonstrating the existence of appropriate safeguards provided by controllers or processors that are not subject to this Regulation pursuant to Article 3 within the framework of personal data transfers to third countries or international organisations under the terms referred to in point (f) of Article 46(2). Such controllers or processors shall make binding and enforceable commitments, via contractual or other legally binding instruments, to apply those appropriate safeguards, including with regard to the rights of data subjects.

3. The certification shall be voluntary and available via a process that is transparent.

4. A certification pursuant to this Article does not reduce the responsibility of the controller or the processor for compliance with this Regulation and is without prejudice to the tasks and powers of the supervisory authorities which are competent pursuant to Article 55 or 56.

5. A certification pursuant to this Article shall be issued by the certification bodies referred to in Article 43 or by the competent supervisory authority, on the basis of criteria approved by that competent supervisory authority pursuant to Article 58(3) or by the Board pursuant to Article 63. Where the criteria are approved by the Board, this may result in a common certification, the European Data Protection Seal.

6. The controller or processor which submits its processing to the certification mechanism shall provide the certification body referred to in Article 43, or where applicable, the competent supervisory authority, with all information and access to its processing activities which are necessary to conduct the certification procedure.

7. Certification shall be issued to a controller or processor for a maximum period of three years and may be renewed, under the same conditions, provided that the relevant requirements continue to be met. Certification shall be withdrawn, as applicable, by the certification bodies referred to in Article 43 or by the competent supervisory authority where the requirements for the certification are not or are no longer met.

8. The Board shall collate all certification mechanisms and data protection seals and marks in a register and shall make them publicly available by any appropriate means.

ARTICLE 43 – CERTIFICATION BODIES

1. Without prejudice to the tasks and powers of the competent supervisory authority under Articles 57 and 58, certification bodies which have an appropriate level of expertise in relation to data protection shall, after informing the supervisory authority in order to allow it to exercise its powers pursuant to point (h) of Article 58(2) where necessary, issue and renew

certification. Member States shall ensure that those certification bodies are accredited by one or both of the following:

(a) the supervisory authority which is competent pursuant to Article 55 or 56;
(b) the national accreditation body named in accordance with Regulation (EC) No 765/2008 of the European Parliament and of the Council[20] in accordance with EN-ISO/IEC 17065/2012 and with the additional requirements established by the supervisory authority which is competent pursuant to Article 55 or 56.

2. Certification bodies referred to in paragraph 1 shall be accredited in accordance with that paragraph only where they have:

(a) demonstrated their independence and expertise in relation to the subject-matter of the certification to the satisfaction of the competent supervisory authority;
(b) undertaken to respect the criteria referred to in Article 42(5) and approved by the supervisory authority which is competent pursuant to Article 55 or 56 or by the Board pursuant to Article 63;
(c) established procedures for the issuing, periodic review and withdrawal of data protection certification, seals and marks;
(d) established procedures and structures to handle complaints about infringements of the certification or the manner in which the certification has been, or is being, implemented by the controller or processor, and to make those procedures and structures transparent to data subjects and the public; and
(e) demonstrated, to the satisfaction of the competent supervisory authority, that their tasks and duties do not result in a conflict of interests.

3. The accreditation of certification bodies as referred to in paragraphs 1 and 2 of this Article shall take place on the basis of criteria approved by the supervisory authority which is competent pursuant to Article 55 or 56 or by the Board pursuant to Article 63. In the case of accreditation pursuant to point (b) of paragraph 1 of this Article, those requirements shall complement those envisaged in Regulation (EC) No 765/2008 and the technical rules that describe the methods and procedures of the certification bodies.

4. The certification bodies referred to in paragraph 1 shall be responsible for the proper assessment leading to the certification or the withdrawal of such certification without prejudice to the responsibility of the controller or processor for compliance with this Regulation. The accreditation shall be issued for a maximum period of five years and may be renewed on the same conditions provided that the certification body meets the requirements set out in this Article.

5. The certification bodies referred to in paragraph 1 shall provide the competent supervisory authorities with the reasons for granting or withdrawing the requested certification.

6. The requirements referred to in paragraph 3 of this Article and the criteria referred to in Article 42(5) shall be made public by the supervisory authority in an easily accessible form. The supervisory authorities shall also transmit those requirements and criteria to the Board. The Board shall collate all certification mechanisms and data protection seals in a register and shall make them publicly available by any appropriate means.

7. Without prejudice to Chapter VIII, the competent supervisory authority or the national accreditation body shall revoke an accreditation of a certification body pursuant to paragraph 1 of this Article where the conditions for the accreditation are not, or are no longer, met or where actions taken by a certification body infringe this Regulation.

8. The Commission shall be empowered to adopt delegated acts in accordance with Article 92 for the purpose of specifying the requirements to be taken into account for the data protection certification mechanisms referred to in Article 42(1).

---

[20] Regulation (EC) No 765/2008 of the European Parliament and of the Council of 9 July 2008 setting out the requirements for accreditation and market surveillance relating to the marketing of products and repealing Regulation (EEC) No 339/93 (OJ L 218, 13.8.2008, p.30).

9. The Commission may adopt implementing acts laying down technical standards for certification mechanisms and data protection seals and marks, and mechanisms to promote and recognise those certification mechanisms, seals and marks. Those implementing acts shall be adopted in accordance with the examination procedure referred to in Article 93(2).

CHAPTER V – TRANSFERS OF PERSONAL DATA TO THIRD COUNTRIES OR INTERNATIONAL ORGANISATIONS

ARTICLE 44 – GENERAL PRINCIPLE FOR TRANSFERS

Any transfer of personal data which are undergoing processing or are intended for processing after transfer to a third country or to an international organisation shall take place only if, subject to the other provisions of this Regulation, the conditions laid down in this Chapter are complied with by the controller and processor, including for onward transfers of personal data from the third country or an international organisation to another third country or to another international organisation. All provisions in this Chapter shall be applied in order to ensure that the level of protection of natural persons guaranteed by this Regulation is not undermined.

ARTICLE 45 – TRANSFERS ON THE BASIS OF AN ADEQUACY DECISION

1. A transfer of personal data to a third country or an international organisation may take place where the Commission has decided that the third country, a territory or one or more specified sectors within that third country, or the international organisation in question ensures an adequate level of protection. Such a transfer shall not require any specific authorisation.

2. When assessing the adequacy of the level of protection, the Commission shall, in particular, take account of the following elements:

(a) the rule of law, respect for human rights and fundamental freedoms, relevant legislation, both general and sectoral, including concerning public security, defence, national security and criminal law and the access of public authorities to personal data, as well as the implementation of such legislation, data protection rules, professional rules and security measures, including rules for the onward transfer of personal data to another third country or international organisation which are complied with in that country or international organisation, case-law, as well as effective and enforceable data subject rights and effective administrative and judicial redress for the data subjects whose personal data are being transferred;

(b) the existence and effective functioning of one or more independent supervisory authorities in the third country or to which an international organisation is subject, with responsibility for ensuring and enforcing compliance with the data protection rules, including adequate enforcement powers, for assisting and advising the data subjects in exercising their rights and for cooperation with the supervisory authorities of the Member States; and

(c) the international commitments the third country or international organisation concerned has entered into, or other obligations arising from legally binding conventions or instruments as well as from its participation in multilateral or regional systems, in particular in relation to the protection of personal data.

3. The Commission, after assessing the adequacy of the level of protection, may decide, by means of implementing act, that a third country, a territory or one or more specified sectors within a third country, or an international organisation ensures an adequate level of protection within the meaning of paragraph 2 of this Article. The implementing act shall provide for a mechanism for a periodic review, at least every four years, which shall take into account all relevant developments in the third country or international organisation. The

implementing act shall specify its territorial and sectoral application and, where applicable, identify the supervisory authority or authorities referred to in point (b) of paragraph 2 of this Article. The implementing act shall be adopted in accordance with the examination procedure referred to in Article 93(2).

4. The Commission shall, on an ongoing basis, monitor developments in third countries and international organisations that could affect the functioning of decisions adopted pursuant to paragraph 3 of this Article and decisions adopted on the basis of Article 25(6) of Directive 95/46/EC.

5. The Commission shall, where available information reveals, in particular following the review referred to in paragraph 3 of this Article, that a third country, a territory or one or more specified sectors within a third country, or an international organisation no longer ensures an adequate level of protection within the meaning of paragraph 2 of this Article, to the extent necessary, repeal, amend or suspend the decision referred to in paragraph 3 of this Article by means of implementing acts without retro-active effect. Those implementing acts shall be adopted in accordance with the examination procedure referred to in Article 93(2).

On duly justified imperative grounds of urgency, the Commission shall adopt immediately applicable implementing acts in accordance with the procedure referred to in Article 93(3).

6. The Commission shall enter into consultations with the third country or international organisation with a view to remedying the situation giving rise to the decision made pursuant to paragraph 5.

7. A decision pursuant to paragraph 5 of this Article is without prejudice to transfers of personal data to the third country, a territory or one or more specified sectors within that third country, or the international organisation in question pursuant to Articles 46 to 49.

8. The Commission shall publish in the *Official Journal of the European Union* and on its website a list of the third countries, territories and specified sectors within a third country and international organisations for which it has decided that an adequate level of protection is or is no longer ensured.

9. Decisions adopted by the Commission on the basis of Article 25(6) of Directive 95/46/EC shall remain in force until amended, replaced or repealed by a Commission Decision adopted in accordance with paragraph 3 or 5 of this Article.

ARTICLE 46 – TRANSFERS SUBJECT TO APPROPRIATE SAFEGUARDS

1. In the absence of a decision pursuant to Article 45(3), a controller or processor may transfer personal data to a third country or an international organisation only if the controller or processor has provided appropriate safeguards, and on condition that enforceable data subject rights and effective legal remedies for data subjects are available.

2. The appropriate safeguards referred to in paragraph 1 may be provided for, without requiring any specific authorisation from a supervisory authority, by:
(a) a legally binding and enforceable instrument between public authorities or bodies;
(b) binding corporate rules in accordance with Article 47;
(c) standard data protection clauses adopted by the Commission in accordance with the examination procedure referred to in Article 93(2);
(d) standard data protection clauses adopted by a supervisory authority and approved by the Commission pursuant to the examination procedure referred to in Article 93(2);
(e) an approved code of conduct pursuant to Article 40 together with binding and enforceable commitments of the controller or processor in the third country to apply the appropriate safeguards, including as regards data subjects' rights; or
(f) an approved certification mechanism pursuant to Article 42 together with binding and enforceable commitments of the controller or processor in the third country to apply the appropriate safeguards, including as regards data subjects' rights.

3. Subject to the authorisation from the competent supervisory authority, the appropriate safeguards referred to in paragraph 1 may also be provided for, in particular, by:

(a) contractual clauses between the controller or processor and the controller, processor or the recipient of the personal data in the third country or international organisation; or
(b) provisions to be inserted into administrative arrangements between public authorities or bodies which include enforceable and effective data subject rights.

4. The supervisory authority shall apply the consistency mechanism referred to in Article 63 in the cases referred to in paragraph 3 of this Article.

5. Authorisations by a Member State or supervisory authority on the basis of Article 26(2) of Directive 95/46/EC shall remain valid until amended, replaced or repealed, if necessary, by that supervisory authority. Decisions adopted by the Commission on the basis of Article 26(4) of Directive 95/46/EC shall remain in force until amended, replaced or repealed, if necessary, by a Commission Decision adopted in accordance with paragraph 2 of this Article.

ARTICLE 47 – BINDING CORPORATE RULES

1. The competent supervisory authority shall approve binding corporate rules in accordance with the consistency mechanism set out in Article 63, provided that they:

(a) are legally binding and apply to and are enforced by every member concerned of the group of undertakings, or group of enterprises engaged in a joint economic activity, including their employees;
(b) expressly confer enforceable rights on data subjects with regard to the processing of their personal data; and
(c) fulfil the requirements laid down in paragraph 2.

2. The binding corporate rules referred to in paragraph 1 shall specify at least:

(a) the structure and contact details of the group of undertakings, or group of enterprises engaged in a joint economic activity and of each of its members;
(b) the data transfers or set of transfers, including the categories of personal data, the type of processing and its purposes, the type of data subjects affected and the identification of the third country or countries in question;
(c) their legally binding nature, both internally and externally;
(d) the application of the general data protection principles, in particular purpose limitation, data minimisation, limited storage periods, data quality, data protection by design and by default, legal basis for processing, processing of special categories of personal data, measures to ensure data security, and the requirements in respect of onward transfers to bodies not bound by the binding corporate rules;
(e) the rights of data subjects in regard to processing and the means to exercise those rights, including the right not to be subject to decisions based solely on automated processing, including profiling in accordance with Article 22, the right to lodge a complaint with the competent supervisory authority and before the competent courts of the Member States in accordance with Article 79, and to obtain redress and, where appropriate, compensation for a breach of the binding corporate rules;
(f) the acceptance by the controller or processor established on the territory of a Member State of liability for any breaches of the binding corporate rules by any member concerned not established in the Union; the controller or the processor shall be exempt from that liability, in whole or in part, only if it proves that that member is not responsible for the event giving rise to the damage;
(g) how the information on the binding corporate rules, in particular on the provisions referred to in points (d), (e) and (f) of this paragraph is provided to the data subjects in addition to Articles 13 and 14;
(h) the tasks of any data protection officer designated in accordance with Article 37 or any other person or entity in charge of the monitoring compliance with the binding

corporate rules within the group of undertakings, or group of enterprises engaged in a joint economic activity, as well as monitoring training and complaint-handling;

(i)   the complaint procedures;

(j)   the mechanisms within the group of undertakings, or group of enterprises engaged in a joint economic activity for ensuring the verification of compliance with the binding corporate rules. Such mechanisms shall include data protection audits and methods for ensuring corrective actions to protect the rights of the data subject. Results of such verification should be communicated to the person or entity referred to in point (h) and to the board of the controlling undertaking of a group of undertakings, or of the group of enterprises engaged in a joint economic activity, and should be available upon request to the competent supervisory authority;

(k)   the mechanisms for reporting and recording changes to the rules and reporting those changes to the supervisory authority;

(l)   the cooperation mechanism with the supervisory authority to ensure compliance by any member of the group of undertakings, or group of enterprises engaged in a joint economic activity, in particular by making available to the supervisory authority the results of verifications of the measures referred to in point (j);

(m)   the mechanisms for reporting to the competent supervisory authority any legal requirements to which a member of the group of undertakings, or group of enterprises engaged in a joint economic activity is subject in a third country which are likely to have a substantial adverse effect on the guarantees provided by the binding corporate rules; and

(n)   the appropriate data protection training to personnel having permanent or regular access to personal data.

3. The Commission may specify the format and procedures for the exchange of information between controllers, processors and supervisory authorities for binding corporate rules within the meaning of this Article. Those implementing acts shall be adopted in accordance with the examination procedure set out in Article 93(2).

ARTICLE 48 – TRANSFERS OR DISCLOSURES NOT AUTHORISED BY UNION LAW

Any judgment of a court or tribunal and any decision of an administrative authority of a third country requiring a controller or processor to transfer or disclose personal data may only be recognised or enforceable in any manner if based on an international agreement, such as a mutual legal assistance treaty, in force between the requesting third country and the Union or a Member State, without prejudice to other grounds for transfer pursuant to this Chapter.

ARTICLE 49 – DEROGATIONS FOR SPECIFIC SITUATIONS

1. In the absence of an adequacy decision pursuant to Article 45(3), or of appropriate safeguards pursuant to Article 46, including binding corporate rules, a transfer or a set of transfers of personal data to a third country or an international organisation shall take place only on one of the following conditions:

(a)   the data subject has explicitly consented to the proposed transfer, after having been informed of the possible risks of such transfers for the data subject due to the absence of an adequacy decision and appropriate safeguards;

(b)   the transfer is necessary for the performance of a contract between the data subject and the controller or the implementation of pre-contractual measures taken at the data subject's request;

(c)   the transfer is necessary for the conclusion or performance of a contract concluded in the interest of the data subject between the controller and another natural or legal person;

(d)   the transfer is necessary for important reasons of public interest;

(e) the transfer is necessary for the establishment, exercise or defence of legal claims;

(f) the transfer is necessary in order to protect the vital interests of the data subject or of other persons, where the data subject is physically or legally incapable of giving consent;

(g) the transfer is made from a register which according to Union or Member State law is intended to provide information to the public and which is open to consultation either by the public in general or by any person who can demonstrate a legitimate interest, but only to the extent that the conditions laid down by Union or Member State law for consultation are fulfilled in the particular case.

Where a transfer could not be based on a provision in Article 45 or 46, including the provisions on binding corporate rules, and none of the derogations for a specific situation referred to in the first subparagraph of this paragraph is applicable, a transfer to a third country or an international organisation may take place only if the transfer is not repetitive, concerns only a limited number of data subjects, is necessary for the purposes of compelling legitimate interests pursued by the controller which are not overridden by the interests or rights and freedoms of the data subject, and the controller has assessed all the circumstances surrounding the data transfer and has on the basis of that assessment provided suitable safeguards with regard to the protection of personal data. The controller shall inform the supervisory authority of the transfer. The controller shall, in addition to providing the information referred to in Articles 13 and 14, inform the data subject of the transfer and on the compelling legitimate interests pursued.

2. A transfer pursuant to point (g) of the first subparagraph of paragraph 1 shall not involve the entirety of the personal data or entire categories of the personal data contained in the register. Where the register is intended for consultation by persons having a legitimate interest, the transfer shall be made only at the request of those persons or if they are to be the recipients.

3. Points (a), (b) and (c) of the first subparagraph of paragraph 1 and the second subparagraph thereof shall not apply to activities carried out by public authorities in the exercise of their public powers.

4. The public interest referred to in point (d) of the first subparagraph of paragraph 1 shall be recognised in Union law or in the law of the Member State to which the controller is subject.

5. In the absence of an adequacy decision, Union or Member State law may, for important reasons of public interest, expressly set limits to the transfer of specific categories of personal data to a third country or an international organisation. Member States shall notify such provisions to the Commission.

6. The controller or processor shall document the assessment as well as the suitable safeguards referred to in the second subparagraph of paragraph 1 of this Article in the records referred to in Article 30.

ARTICLE 50 – INTERNATIONAL COOPERATION FOR THE PROTECTION OF PERSONAL DATA

In relation to third countries and international organisations, the Commission and supervisory authorities shall take appropriate steps to:

(a) develop international cooperation mechanisms to facilitate the effective enforcement of legislation for the protection of personal data;

(b) provide international mutual assistance in the enforcement of legislation for the protection of personal data, including through notification, complaint referral, investigative assistance and information exchange, subject to appropriate safeguards for the protection of personal data and other fundamental rights and freedoms;

(c) engage relevant stakeholders in discussion and activities aimed at furthering international cooperation in the enforcement of legislation for the protection of personal data;

(d) promote the exchange and documentation of personal data protection legislation and practice, including on jurisdictional conflicts with third countries.

CHAPTER VI – INDEPENDENT SUPERVISORY AUTHORITIES

Section 1 – Independent status

ARTICLE 51 – SUPERVISORY AUTHORITY

1. Each Member State shall provide for one or more independent public authorities to be responsible for monitoring the application of this Regulation, in order to protect the fundamental rights and freedoms of natural persons in relation to processing and to facilitate the free flow of personal data within the Union ('supervisory authority').

2. Each supervisory authority shall contribute to the consistent application of this Regulation throughout the Union. For that purpose, the supervisory authorities shall cooperate with each other and the Commission in accordance with Chapter VII.

3. Where more than one supervisory authority is established in a Member State, that Member State shall designate the supervisory authority which is to represent those authorities in the Board and shall set out the mechanism to ensure compliance by the other authorities with the rules relating to the consistency mechanism referred to in Article 63.

4. Each Member State shall notify to the Commission the provisions of its law which it adopts pursuant to this Chapter, by 25 May 2018 and, without delay, any subsequent amendment affecting them.

ARTICLE 52 – INDEPENDENCE

1. Each supervisory authority shall act with complete independence in performing its tasks and exercising its powers in accordance with this Regulation.

2. The member or members of each supervisory authority shall, in the performance of their tasks and exercise of their powers in accordance with this Regulation, remain free from external influence, whether direct or indirect, and shall neither seek nor take instructions from anybody.

3. Member or members of each supervisory authority shall refrain from any action incompatible with their duties and shall not, during their term of office, engage in any incompatible occupation, whether gainful or not.

4. Each Member State shall ensure that each supervisory authority is provided with the human, technical and financial resources, premises and infrastructure necessary for the effective performance of its tasks and exercise of its powers, including those to be carried out in the context of mutual assistance, cooperation and participation in the Board.

5. Each Member State shall ensure that each supervisory authority chooses and has its own staff which shall be subject to the exclusive direction of the member or members of the supervisory authority concerned.

6. Each Member State shall ensure that each supervisory authority is subject to financial control which does not affect its independence and that it has separate, public annual budgets, which may be part of the overall state or national budget.

ARTICLE 53 – GENERAL CONDITIONS FOR THE MEMBERS OF THE SUPERVISORY AUTHORITY

1. Member States shall provide for each member of their supervisory authorities to be appointed by means of a transparent procedure by:

– their parliament;
– their government;
– their head of State; or
– an independent body entrusted with the appointment under Member State law.

2. Each member shall have the qualifications, experience and skills, in particular in the area of the protection of personal data, required to perform its duties and exercise its powers.

3. The duties of a member shall end in the event of the expiry of the term of office, resignation or compulsory retirement, in accordance with the law of the Member State concerned.

4. A member shall be dismissed only in cases of serious misconduct or if the member no longer fulfils the conditions required for the performance of the duties.

ARTICLE 54 – RULES ON THE ESTABLISHMENT OF THE SUPERVISORY AUTHORITY

1. Each Member State shall provide by law for all of the following:

(a) the establishment of each supervisory authority;
(b) the qualifications and eligibility conditions required to be appointed as member of each supervisory authority;
(c) the rules and procedures for the appointment of the member or members of each supervisory authority;
(d) the duration of the term of the member or members of each supervisory authority of no less than four years, except for the first appointment after 24 May 2016, part of which may take place for a shorter period where that is necessary to protect the independence of the supervisory authority by means of a staggered appointment procedure;
(e) whether and, if so, for how many terms the member or members of each supervisory authority is eligible for reappointment;
(f) the conditions governing the obligations of the member or members and staff of each supervisory authority, prohibitions on actions, occupations and benefits incompatible therewith during and after the term of office and rules governing the cessation of employment.

2. The member or members and the staff of each supervisory authority shall, in accordance with Union or Member State law, be subject to a duty of professional secrecy both during and after their term of office, with regard to any confidential information which has come to their knowledge in the course of the performance of their tasks or exercise of their powers. During their term of office, that duty of professional secrecy shall in particular apply to reporting by natural persons of infringements of this Regulation.

Section 2 – Competence, tasks and powers

ARTICLE 55 – COMPETENCE

1. Each supervisory authority shall be competent for the performance of the tasks assigned to and the exercise of the powers conferred on it in accordance with this Regulation on the territory of its own Member State.

2. Where processing is carried out by public authorities or private bodies acting on the basis of point (c) or (e) of Article 6(1), the supervisory authority of the Member State concerned shall be competent. In such cases Article 56 does not apply.

3. Supervisory authorities shall not be competent to supervise processing operations of courts acting in their judicial capacity.

ARTICLE 56 – COMPETENCE OF THE LEAD SUPERVISORY AUTHORITY

1. Without prejudice to Article 55, the supervisory authority of the main establishment or of the single establishment of the controller or processor shall be competent to act as lead supervisory authority for the cross-border processing carried out by that controller or processor in accordance with the procedure provided in Article 60.

2. By derogation from paragraph 1, each supervisory authority shall be competent to handle a complaint lodged with it or a possible infringement of this Regulation, if the subject matter relates only to an establishment in its Member State or substantially affects data subjects only in its Member State.

3. In the cases referred to in paragraph 2 of this Article, the supervisory authority shall inform the lead supervisory authority without delay on that matter. Within a period of three weeks after being informed the lead supervisory authority shall decide whether or not it will handle the case in accordance with the procedure provided in Article 60, taking into account whether or not there is an establishment of the controller or processor in the Member State of which the supervisory authority informed it.

4. Where the lead supervisory authority decides to handle the case, the procedure provided in Article 60 shall apply. The supervisory authority which informed the lead supervisory authority may submit to the lead supervisory authority a draft for a decision. The lead supervisory authority shall take utmost account of that draft when preparing the draft decision referred to in Article 60(3).

5. Where the lead supervisory authority decides not to handle the case, the supervisory authority which informed the lead supervisory authority shall handle it according to Articles 61 and 62.

6. The lead supervisory authority shall be the sole interlocutor of the controller or processor for the cross-border processing carried out by that controller or processor.

ARTICLE 57 – TASKS

1. Without prejudice to other tasks set out under this Regulation, each supervisory authority shall on its territory:
(a) monitor and enforce the application of this Regulation;
(b) promote public awareness and understanding of the risks, rules, safeguards and rights in relation to processing. Activities addressed specifically to children shall receive specific attention;
(c) advise, in accordance with Member State law, the national parliament, the government, and other institutions and bodies on legislative and administrative measures relating to the protection of natural persons' rights and freedoms with regard to processing;
(d) promote the awareness of controllers and processors of their obligations under this Regulation;
(e) upon request, provide information to any data subject concerning the exercise of their rights under this Regulation and, if appropriate, cooperate with the supervisory authorities in other Member States to that end;
(f) handle complaints lodged by a data subject, or by a body, organisation or association in accordance with Article 80, and investigate, to the extent appropriate, the subject matter of the complaint and inform the complainant of the progress and the outcome of the investigation within a reasonable period, in particular if further investigation or coordination with another supervisory authority is necessary;
(g) cooperate with, including sharing information and provide mutual assistance to, other supervisory authorities with a view to ensuring the consistency of application and enforcement of this Regulation;

(h) conduct investigations on the application of this Regulation, including on the basis of information received from another supervisory authority or other public authority;

(i)   monitor relevant developments, insofar as they have an impact on the protection of personal data, in particular the development of information and communication technologies and commercial practices;

(j)   adopt standard contractual clauses referred to in Article 28(8) and in point (d) of Article 46(2);

(k) establish and maintain a list in relation to the requirement for data protection impact assessment pursuant to Article 35(4);

(l)   give advice on the processing operations referred to in Article 36(2);

(m) encourage the drawing up of codes of conduct pursuant to Article 40(1) and provide an opinion and approve such codes of conduct which provide sufficient safeguards, pursuant to Article 40(5);

(n) encourage the establishment of data protection certification mechanisms and of data protection seals and marks pursuant to Article 42(1), and approve the criteria of certification pursuant to Article 42(5);

(o) where applicable, carry out a periodic review of certifications issued in accordance with Article 42(7);

(p) draft and publish the criteria for accreditation of a body for monitoring codes of conduct pursuant to Article 41 and of a certification body pursuant to Article 43;

(q) conduct the accreditation of a body for monitoring codes of conduct pursuant to Article 41 and of a certification body pursuant to Article 43;

(r)   authorise contractual clauses and provisions referred to in Article 46(3);

(s)   approve binding corporate rules pursuant to Article 47;

(t)   contribute to the activities of the Board;

(u) keep internal records of infringements of this Regulation and of measures taken in accordance with Article 58(2); and

(v) fulfil any other tasks related to the protection of personal data.

2. Each supervisory authority shall facilitate the submission of complaints referred to in point (f) of paragraph 1 by measures such as a complaint submission form which can also be completed electronically, without excluding other means of communication.

3. The performance of the tasks of each supervisory authority shall be free of charge for the data subject and, where applicable, for the data protection officer.

4. Where requests are manifestly unfounded or excessive, in particular because of their repetitive character, the supervisory authority may charge a reasonable fee based on administrative costs, or refuse to act on the request. The supervisory authority shall bear the burden of demonstrating the manifestly unfounded or excessive character of the request.

ARTICLE 58 – POWERS

1. Each supervisory authority shall have all of the following investigative powers:

(a) to order the controller and the processor, and, where applicable, the controller's or the processor's representative to provide any information it requires for the performance of its tasks;

(b) to carry out investigations in the form of data protection audits;

(c) to carry out a review on certifications issued pursuant to Article 42(7);

(d) to notify the controller or the processor of an alleged infringement of this Regulation;

(e) to obtain, from the controller and the processor, access to all personal data and to all information necessary for the performance of its tasks;

(f) to obtain access to any premises of the controller and the processor, including to any data processing equipment and means, in accordance with Union or Member State procedural law.

2. Each supervisory authority shall have all of the following corrective powers:

(a) to issue warnings to a controller or processor that intended processing operations are likely to infringe provisions of this Regulation;

(b) to issue reprimands to a controller or a processor where processing operations have infringed provisions of this Regulation;

(c) to order the controller or the processor to comply with the data subject's requests to exercise his or her rights pursuant to this Regulation;

(d) to order the controller or processor to bring processing operations into compliance with the provisions of this Regulation, where appropriate, in a specified manner and within a specified period;

(e) to order the controller to communicate a personal data breach to the data subject;

(f) to impose a temporary or definitive limitation including a ban on processing;

(g) to order the rectification or erasure of personal data or restriction of processing pursuant to Articles 16, 17 and 18 and the notification of such actions to recipients to whom the personal data have been disclosed pursuant to Article 17(2) and Article 19;

(h) to withdraw a certification or to order the certification body to withdraw a certification issued pursuant to Articles 42 and 43, or to order the certification body not to issue certification if the requirements for the certification are not or are no longer met;

(i) to impose an administrative fine pursuant to Article 83, in addition to, or instead of measures referred to in this paragraph, depending on the circumstances of each individual case;

(j) to order the suspension of data flows to a recipient in a third country or to an international organisation.

3. Each supervisory authority shall have all of the following authorisation and advisory powers:

(a) to advise the controller in accordance with the prior consultation procedure referred to in Article 36;

(b) to issue, on its own initiative or on request, opinions to the national parliament, the Member State government or, in accordance with Member State law, to other institutions and bodies as well as to the public on any issue related to the protection of personal data;

(c) to authorise processing referred to in Article 36(5), if the law of the Member State requires such prior authorisation;

(d) to issue an opinion and approve draft codes of conduct pursuant to Article 40(5);

(e) to accredit certification bodies pursuant to Article 43;

(f) to issue certifications and approve criteria of certification in accordance with Article 42(5);

(g) to adopt standard data protection clauses referred to in Article 28(8) and in point (d) of Article 46(2);

(h) to authorise contractual clauses referred to in point (a) of Article 46(3);

(i) to authorise administrative arrangements referred to in point (b) of Article 46(3);

(j) to approve binding corporate rules pursuant to Article 47.

4. The exercise of the powers conferred on the supervisory authority pursuant to this Article shall be subject to appropriate safeguards, including effective judicial remedy and due process, set out in Union and Member State law in accordance with the Charter.

5. Each Member State shall provide by law that its supervisory authority shall have the power to bring infringements of this Regulation to the attention of the judicial authorities and where appropriate, to commence or engage otherwise in legal proceedings, in order to enforce the provisions of this Regulation.

6. Each Member State may provide by law that its supervisory authority shall have additional powers to those referred to in paragraphs 1, 2 and 3. The exercise of those powers shall not impair the effective operation of Chapter VII.

ARTICLE 59 – ACTIVITY REPORTS

Each supervisory authority shall draw up an annual report on its activities, which may include a list of types of infringement notified and types of measures taken in accordance with Article 58(2). Those reports shall be transmitted to the national parliament, the government and other authorities as designated by Member State law. They shall be made available to the public, to the Commission and to the Board.

CHAPTER VII – COOPERATION AND CONSISTENCY

Section 1 – Cooperation

ARTICLE 60 – COOPERATION BETWEEN THE LEAD SUPERVISORY AUTHORITY AND THE OTHER SUPERVISORY AUTHORITIES CONCERNED

1. The lead supervisory authority shall cooperate with the other supervisory authorities concerned in accordance with this Article in an endeavour to reach consensus. The lead supervisory authority and the supervisory authorities concerned shall exchange all relevant information with each other.

2. The lead supervisory authority may request at any time other supervisory authorities concerned to provide mutual assistance pursuant to Article 61 and may conduct joint operations pursuant to Article 62, in particular for carrying out investigations or for monitoring the implementation of a measure concerning a controller or processor established in another Member State.

3. The lead supervisory authority shall, without delay, communicate the relevant information on the matter to the other supervisory authorities concerned. It shall without delay submit a draft decision to the other supervisory authorities concerned for their opinion and take due account of their views.

4. Where any of the other supervisory authorities concerned within a period of four weeks after having been consulted in accordance with paragraph 3 of this Article, expresses a relevant and reasoned objection to the draft decision, the lead supervisory authority shall, if it does not follow the relevant and reasoned objection or is of the opinion that the objection is not relevant or reasoned, submit the matter to the consistency mechanism referred to in Article 63.

5. Where the lead supervisory authority intends to follow the relevant and reasoned objection made, it shall submit to the other supervisory authorities concerned a revised draft decision for their opinion. That revised draft decision shall be subject to the procedure referred to in paragraph 4 within a period of two weeks.

6. Where none of the other supervisory authorities concerned has objected to the draft decision submitted by the lead supervisory authority within the period referred to in paragraphs 4 and 5, the lead supervisory authority and the supervisory authorities concerned shall be deemed to be in agreement with that draft decision and shall be bound by it.

7. The lead supervisory authority shall adopt and notify the decision to the main establishment or single establishment of the controller or processor, as the case may be and inform the other supervisory authorities concerned and the Board of the decision in question, including a summary of the relevant facts and grounds. The supervisory authority with which a complaint has been lodged shall inform the complainant on the decision.

8. By derogation from paragraph 7, where a complaint is dismissed or rejected, the supervisory authority with which the complaint was lodged shall adopt the decision and notify it to the complainant and shall inform the controller thereof.

9. Where the lead supervisory authority and the supervisory authorities concerned agree to dismiss or reject parts of a complaint and to act on other parts of that complaint, a separate decision shall be adopted for each of those parts of the matter. The lead supervisory authority shall adopt the decision for the part concerning actions in relation to the controller, shall notify it to the main establishment or single establishment of the controller or processor on the territory of its Member State and shall inform the complainant thereof, while the supervisory authority of the complainant shall adopt the decision for the part concerning dismissal or rejection of that complaint, and shall notify it to that complainant and shall inform the controller or processor thereof.

10. After being notified of the decision of the lead supervisory authority pursuant to paragraphs 7 and 9, the controller or processor shall take the necessary measures to ensure compliance with the decision as regards processing activities in the context of all its establishments in the Union. The controller or processor shall notify the measures taken for complying with the decision to the lead supervisory authority, which shall inform the other supervisory authorities concerned.

11. Where, in exceptional circumstances, a supervisory authority concerned has reasons to consider that there is an urgent need to act in order to protect the interests of data subjects, the urgency procedure referred to in Article 66 shall apply.

12. The lead supervisory authority and the other supervisory authorities concerned shall supply the information required under this Article to each other by electronic means, using a standardised format.

ARTICLE 61 – MUTUAL ASSISTANCE

1. Supervisory authorities shall provide each other with relevant information and mutual assistance in order to implement and apply this Regulation in a consistent manner, and shall put in place measures for effective cooperation with one another. Mutual assistance shall cover, in particular, information requests and supervisory measures, such as requests to carry out prior authorisations and consultations, inspections and investigations.

2. Each supervisory authority shall take all appropriate measures required to reply to a request of another supervisory authority without undue delay and no later than one month after receiving the request. Such measures may include, in particular, the transmission of relevant information on the conduct of an investigation.

3. Requests for assistance shall contain all the necessary information, including the purpose of and reasons for the request. Information exchanged shall be used only for the purpose for which it was requested.

4. The requested supervisory authority shall not refuse to comply with the request unless:

(a) it is not competent for the subject-matter of the request or for the measures it is requested to execute; or
(b) compliance with the request would infringe this Regulation or Union or Member State law to which the supervisory authority receiving the request is subject.

5. The requested supervisory authority shall inform the requesting supervisory authority of the results or, as the case may be, of the progress of the measures taken in order to respond to the request. The requested supervisory authority shall provide reasons for any refusal to comply with a request pursuant to paragraph 4.

6. Requested supervisory authorities shall, as a rule, supply the information requested by other supervisory authorities by electronic means, using a standardised format.

7. Requested supervisory authorities shall not charge a fee for any action taken by them pursuant to a request for mutual assistance. Supervisory authorities may agree on rules to

indemnify each other for specific expenditure arising from the provision of mutual assistance in exceptional circumstances.

8. Where a supervisory authority does not provide the information referred to in paragraph 5 of this Article within one month of receiving the request of another supervisory authority, the requesting supervisory authority may adopt a provisional measure on the territory of its Member State in accordance with Article 55(1). In that case, the urgent need to act under Article 66(1) shall be presumed to be met and require an urgent binding decision from the Board pursuant to Article 66(2).

9. The Commission may, by means of implementing acts, specify the format and procedures for mutual assistance referred to in this Article and the arrangements for the exchange of information by electronic means between supervisory authorities, and between supervisory authorities and the Board, in particular the standardised format referred to in paragraph 6 of this Article. Those implementing acts shall be adopted in accordance with the examination procedure referred to in Article 93(2).

ARTICLE 62 – JOINT OPERATIONS OF SUPERVISORY AUTHORITIES

1. The supervisory authorities shall, where appropriate, conduct joint operations including joint investigations and joint enforcement measures in which members or staff of the supervisory authorities of other Member States are involved.

2. Where the controller or processor has establishments in several Member States or where a significant number of data subjects in more than one Member State are likely to be substantially affected by processing operations, a supervisory authority of each of those Member States shall have the right to participate in joint operations. The supervisory authority which is competent pursuant to Article 56(1) or (4) shall invite the supervisory authority of each of those Member States to take part in the joint operations and shall respond without delay to the request of a supervisory authority to participate.

3. A supervisory authority may, in accordance with Member State law, and with the seconding supervisory authority's authorisation, confer powers, including investigative powers on the seconding supervisory authority's members or staff involved in joint operations or, in so far as the law of the Member State of the host supervisory authority permits, allow the seconding supervisory authority's members or staff to exercise their investigative powers in accordance with the law of the Member State of the seconding supervisory authority. Such investigative powers may be exercised only under the guidance and in the presence of members or staff of the host supervisory authority. The seconding supervisory authority's members or staff shall be subject to the Member State law of the host supervisory authority.

4. Where, in accordance with paragraph 1, staff of a seconding supervisory authority operate in another Member State, the Member State of the host supervisory authority shall assume responsibility for their actions, including liability, for any damage caused by them during their operations, in accordance with the law of the Member State in whose territory they are operating.

5. The Member State in whose territory the damage was caused shall make good such damage under the conditions applicable to damage caused by its own staff. The Member State of the seconding supervisory authority whose staff has caused damage to any person in the territory of another Member State shall reimburse that other Member State in full any sums it has paid to the persons entitled on their behalf.

6. Without prejudice to the exercise of its rights vis-à-vis third parties and with the exception of paragraph 5, each Member State shall refrain, in the case provided for in paragraph 1, from requesting reimbursement from another Member State in relation to damage referred to in paragraph 4.

7. Where a joint operation is intended and a supervisory authority does not, within one month, comply with the obligation laid down in the second sentence of paragraph 2 of this Article, the other supervisory authorities may adopt a provisional measure on the territory of its Member State in accordance with Article 55. In that case, the urgent need to act under Article 66(1) shall be presumed to be met and require an opinion or an urgent binding decision from the Board pursuant to Article 66(2).

Section 2 – Consistency

ARTICLE 63 – CONSISTENCY MECHANISM

In order to contribute to the consistent application of this Regulation throughout the Union, the supervisory authorities shall cooperate with each other and, where relevant, with the Commission, through the consistency mechanism as set out in this Section.

ARTICLE 64 – OPINION OF THE BOARD

1. The Board shall issue an opinion where a competent supervisory authority intends to adopt any of the measures below. To that end, the competent supervisory authority shall communicate the draft decision to the Board, when it:

(a) aims to adopt a list of the processing operations subject to the requirement for a data protection impact assessment pursuant to Article 35(4);
(b) concerns a matter pursuant to Article 40(7) whether a draft code of conduct or an amendment or extension to a code of conduct complies with this Regulation;
(c) aims to approve the criteria for accreditation of a body pursuant to Article 41(3) or a certification body pursuant to Article 43(3);
(d) aims to determine standard data protection clauses referred to in point (d) of Article 46(2) and in Article 28(8);
(e) aims to authorise contractual clauses referred to in point (a) of Article 46(3); or
(f) aims to approve binding corporate rules within the meaning of Article 47.

2. Any supervisory authority, the Chair of the Board or the Commission may request that any matter of general application or producing effects in more than one Member State be examined by the Board with a view to obtaining an opinion, in particular where a competent supervisory authority does not comply with the obligations for mutual assistance in accordance with Article 61 or for joint operations in accordance with Article 62.

3. In the cases referred to in paragraphs 1 and 2, the Board shall issue an opinion on the matter submitted to it provided that it has not already issued an opinion on the same matter. That opinion shall be adopted within eight weeks by simple majority of the members of the Board. That period may be extended by a further six weeks, taking into account the complexity of the subject matter. Regarding the draft decision referred to in paragraph 1 circulated to the members of the Board in accordance with paragraph 5, a member which has not objected within a reasonable period indicated by the Chair, shall be deemed to be in agreement with the draft decision.

4. Supervisory authorities and the Commission shall, without undue delay, communicate by electronic means to the Board, using a standardised format any relevant information, including as the case may be a summary of the facts, the draft decision, the grounds which make the enactment of such measure necessary, and the views of other supervisory authorities concerned.

5. The Chair of the Board shall, without undue, delay inform by electronic means:

(a) the members of the Board and the Commission of any relevant information which has been communicated to it using a standardised format. The secretariat of the Board shall, where necessary, provide translations of relevant information; and

(b) the supervisory authority referred to, as the case may be, in paragraphs 1 and 2, and the Commission of the opinion and make it public.

6. The competent supervisory authority shall not adopt its draft decision referred to in paragraph 1 within the period referred to in paragraph 3.

7. The supervisory authority referred to in paragraph 1 shall take utmost account of the opinion of the Board and shall, within two weeks after receiving the opinion, communicate to the Chair of the Board by electronic means whether it will maintain or amend its draft decision and, if any, the amended draft decision, using a standardised format.

8. Where the supervisory authority concerned informs the Chair of the Board within the period referred to in paragraph 7 of this Article that it does not intend to follow the opinion of the Board, in whole or in part, providing the relevant grounds, Article 65(1) shall apply.

ARTICLE 65 – DISPUTE RESOLUTION BY THE BOARD

1. In order to ensure the correct and consistent application of this Regulation in individual cases, the Board shall adopt a binding decision in the following cases:

(a) where, in a case referred to in Article 60(4), a supervisory authority concerned has raised a relevant and reasoned objection to a draft decision of the lead authority or the lead authority has rejected such an objection as being not relevant or reasoned. The binding decision shall concern all the matters which are the subject of the relevant and reasoned objection, in particular whether there is an infringement of this Regulation;
(b) where there are conflicting views on which of the supervisory authorities concerned is competent for the main establishment;
(c) where a competent supervisory authority does not request the opinion of the Board in the cases referred to in Article 64(1), or does not follow the opinion of the Board issued under Article 64. In that case, any supervisory authority concerned or the Commission may communicate the matter to the Board.

2. The decision referred to in paragraph 1 shall be adopted within one month from the referral of the subject-matter by a two-thirds majority of the members of the Board. That period may be extended by a further month on account of the complexity of the subject-matter. The decision referred to in paragraph 1 shall be reasoned and addressed to the lead supervisory authority and all the supervisory authorities concerned and binding on them.

3. Where the Board has been unable to adopt a decision within the periods referred to in paragraph 2, it shall adopt its decision within two weeks following the expiration of the second month referred to in paragraph 2 by a simple majority of the members of the Board. Where the members of the Board are split, the decision shall by adopted by the vote of its Chair.

4. The supervisory authorities concerned shall not adopt a decision on the subject matter submitted to the Board under paragraph 1 during the periods referred to in paragraphs 2 and 3.

5. The Chair of the Board shall notify, without undue delay, the decision referred to in paragraph 1 to the supervisory authorities concerned. It shall inform the Commission thereof. The decision shall be published on the website of the Board without delay after the supervisory authority has notified the final decision referred to in paragraph 6.

6. The lead supervisory authority or, as the case may be, the supervisory authority with which the complaint has been lodged shall adopt its final decision on the basis of the decision referred to in paragraph 1 of this Article, without undue delay and at the latest by one month after the Board has notified its decision. The lead supervisory authority or, as the case may be, the supervisory authority with which the complaint has been lodged, shall inform the Board of the date when its final decision is notified respectively to the controller or the processor and to the data subject. The final decision of the supervisory authorities concerned shall be

adopted under the terms of Article 60(7), (8) and (9). The final decision shall refer to the decision referred to in paragraph 1 of this Article and shall specify that the decision referred to in that paragraph will be published on the website of the Board in accordance with paragraph 5 of this Article. The final decision shall attach the decision referred to in paragraph 1 of this Article.

ARTICLE 66 – URGENCY PROCEDURE

1. In exceptional circumstances, where a supervisory authority concerned considers that there is an urgent need to act in order to protect the rights and freedoms of data subjects, it may, by way of derogation from the consistency mechanism referred to in Articles 63, 64 and 65 or the procedure referred to in Article 60, immediately adopt provisional measures intended to produce legal effects on its own territory with a specified period of validity which shall not exceed three months. The supervisory authority shall, without delay, communicate those measures and the reasons for adopting them to the other supervisory authorities concerned, to the Board and to the Commission.

2. Where a supervisory authority has taken a measure pursuant to paragraph 1 and considers that final measures need urgently be adopted, it may request an urgent opinion or an urgent binding decision from the Board, giving reasons for requesting such opinion or decision.

3. Any supervisory authority may request an urgent opinion or an urgent binding decision, as the case may be, from the Board where a competent supervisory authority has not taken an appropriate measure in a situation where there is an urgent need to act, in order to protect the rights and freedoms of data subjects, giving reasons for requesting such opinion or decision, including for the urgent need to act.

4. By derogation from Article 64(3) and Article 65(2), an urgent opinion or an urgent binding decision referred to in paragraphs 2 and 3 of this Article shall be adopted within two weeks by simple majority of the members of the Board.

ARTICLE 67 – EXCHANGE OF INFORMATION

The Commission may adopt implementing acts of general scope in order to specify the arrangements for the exchange of information by electronic means between supervisory authorities, and between supervisory authorities and the Board, in particular the standardised format referred to in Article 64.

Those implementing acts shall be adopted in accordance with the examination procedure referred to in Article 93(2).

Section 3 – European data protection board

ARTICLE 68 – EUROPEAN DATA PROTECTION BOARD

1. The European Data Protection Board (the 'Board') is hereby established as a body of the Union and shall have legal personality.

2. The Board shall be represented by its Chair.

3. The Board shall be composed of the head of one supervisory authority of each Member State and of the European Data Protection Supervisor, or their respective representatives.

4. Where in a Member State more than one supervisory authority is responsible for monitoring the application of the provisions pursuant to this Regulation, a joint representative shall be appointed in accordance with that Member State's law.

5. The Commission shall have the right to participate in the activities and meetings of the Board without voting right. The Commission shall designate a representative. The Chair of the Board shall communicate to the Commission the activities of the Board.

6. In the cases referred to in Article 65, the European Data Protection Supervisor shall have voting rights only on decisions which concern principles and rules applicable to the Union institutions, bodies, offices and agencies which correspond in substance to those of this Regulation.

ARTICLE 69 – INDEPENDENCE

1. The Board shall act independently when performing its tasks or exercising its powers pursuant to Articles 70 and 71.

2. Without prejudice to requests by the Commission referred to in point (b) of Article 70(1) and in Article 70(2), the Board shall, in the performance of its tasks or the exercise of its powers, neither seek nor take instructions from anybody.

ARTICLE 70 – TASKS OF THE BOARD

1. The Board shall ensure the consistent application of this Regulation. To that end, the Board shall, on its own initiative or, where relevant, at the request of the Commission, in particular:

(a) monitor and ensure the correct application of this Regulation in the cases provided for in Articles 64 and 65 without prejudice to the tasks of national supervisory authorities;

(b) advise the Commission on any issue related to the protection of personal data in the Union, including on any proposed amendment of this Regulation;

(c) advise the Commission on the format and procedures for the exchange of information between controllers, processors and supervisory authorities for binding corporate rules;

(d) issue guidelines, recommendations, and best practices on procedures for erasing links, copies or replications of personal data from publicly available communication services as referred to in Article 17(2);

(e) examine, on its own initiative, on request of one of its members or on request of the Commission, any question covering the application of this Regulation and issue guidelines, recommendations and best practices in order to encourage consistent application of this Regulation;

(f) issue guidelines, recommendations and best practices in accordance with point (e) of this paragraph for further specifying the criteria and conditions for decisions based on profiling pursuant to Article 22(2);

(g) issue guidelines, recommendations and best practices in accordance with point (e) of this paragraph for establishing the personal data breaches and determining the undue delay referred to in Article 33(1) and (2) and for the particular circumstances in which a controller or a processor is required to notify the personal data breach;

(h) issue guidelines, recommendations and best practices in accordance with point (e) of this paragraph as to the circumstances in which a personal data breach is likely to result in a high risk to the rights and freedoms of the natural persons referred to in Article 34(1).

(i) issue guidelines, recommendations and best practices in accordance with point (e) of this paragraph for the purpose of further specifying the criteria and requirements for personal data transfers based on binding corporate rules adhered to by controllers and binding corporate rules adhered to by processors and on further necessary requirements to ensure the protection of personal data of the data subjects concerned referred to in Article 47;

(j) issue guidelines, recommendations and best practices in accordance with point (e) of this paragraph for the purpose of further specifying the criteria and requirements for the personal data transfers on the basis of Article 49(1);

(k) draw up guidelines for supervisory authorities concerning the application of measures referred to in Article 58(1), (2) and (3) and the setting of administrative fines pursuant to Article 83;

(l) review the practical application of the guidelines, recommendations and best practices referred to in points (e) and (f);

(m) issue guidelines, recommendations and best practices in accordance with point (e) of this paragraph for establishing common procedures for reporting by natural persons of infringements of this Regulation pursuant to Article 54(2);

(n) encourage the drawing-up of codes of conduct and the establishment of data protection certification mechanisms and data protection seals and marks pursuant to Articles 40 and 42;

(o) carry out the accreditation of certification bodies and its periodic review pursuant to Article 43 and maintain a public register of accredited bodies pursuant to Article 43(6) and of the accredited controllers or processors established in third countries pursuant to Article 42(7);

(p) specify the requirements referred to in Article 43(3) with a view to the accreditation of certification bodies under Article 42;

(q) provide the Commission with an opinion on the certification requirements referred to in Article 43(8);

(r) provide the Commission with an opinion on the icons referred to in Article 12(7);

(s) provide the Commission with an opinion for the assessment of the adequacy of the level of protection in a third country or international organisation, including for the assessment whether a third country, a territory or one or more specified sectors within that third country, or an international organisation no longer ensures an adequate level of protection. To that end, the Commission shall provide the Board with all necessary documentation, including correspondence with the government of the third country, with regard to that third country, territory or specified sector, or with the international organisation.

(t) issue opinions on draft decisions of supervisory authorities pursuant to the consistency mechanism referred to in Article 64(1), on matters submitted pursuant to Article 64(2) and to issue binding decisions pursuant to Article 65, including in cases referred to in Article 66;

(u) promote the cooperation and the effective bilateral and multilateral exchange of information and best practices between the supervisory authorities;

(v) promote common training programmes and facilitate personnel exchanges between the supervisory authorities and, where appropriate, with the supervisory authorities of third countries or with international organisations;

(w) promote the exchange of knowledge and documentation on data protection legislation and practice with data protection supervisory authorities worldwide.

(x) issue opinions on codes of conduct drawn up at Union level pursuant to Article 40(9); and

(y) maintain a publicly accessible electronic register of decisions taken by supervisory authorities and courts on issues handled in the consistency mechanism.

2. Where the Commission requests advice from the Board, it may indicate a time limit, taking into account the urgency of the matter.

3. The Board shall forward its opinions, guidelines, recommendations, and best practices to the Commission and to the committee referred to in Article 93 and make them public.

4. The Board shall, where appropriate, consult interested parties and give them the opportunity to comment within a reasonable period. The Board shall, without prejudice to Article 76, make the results of the consultation procedure publicly available.

ARTICLE 71 – REPORTS

1. The Board shall draw up an annual report regarding the protection of natural persons with regard to processing in the Union and, where relevant, in third countries and international organisations. The report shall be made public and be transmitted to the European Parliament, to the Council and to the Commission.

2. The annual report shall include a review of the practical application of the guidelines, recommendations and best practices referred to in point (l) of Article 70(1) as well as of the binding decisions referred to in Article 65.

ARTICLE 72 – PROCEDURE

1. The Board shall take decisions by a simple majority of its members, unless otherwise provided for in this Regulation.

2. The Board shall adopt its own rules of procedure by a two-thirds majority of its members and organise its own operational arrangements.

ARTICLE 73 – CHAIR

1. The Board shall elect a chair and two deputy chairs from amongst its members by simple majority.

2. The term of office of the Chair and of the deputy chairs shall be five years and be renewable once.

ARTICLE 74 – TASKS OF THE CHAIR

1. The Chair shall have the following tasks:
(a) to convene the meetings of the Board and prepare its agenda;
(b) to notify decisions adopted by the Board pursuant to Article 65 to the lead supervisory authority and the supervisory authorities concerned;
(c) to ensure the timely performance of the tasks of the Board, in particular in relation to the consistency mechanism referred to in Article 63.

2. The Board shall lay down the allocation of tasks between the Chair and the deputy chairs in its rules of procedure.

ARTICLE 75 – SECRETARIAT

1. The Board shall have a secretariat, which shall be provided by the European Data Protection Supervisor.

2. The secretariat shall perform its tasks exclusively under the instructions of the Chair of the Board.

3. The staff of the European Data Protection Supervisor involved in carrying out the tasks conferred on the Board by this Regulation shall be subject to separate reporting lines from the staff involved in carrying out tasks conferred on the European Data Protection Supervisor.

4. Where appropriate, the Board and the European Data Protection Supervisor shall establish and publish a Memorandum of Understanding implementing this Article, determining the terms of their cooperation, and applicable to the staff of the European Data Protection Supervisor involved in carrying out the tasks conferred on the Board by this Regulation.

5. The secretariat shall provide analytical, administrative and logistical support to the Board.

6. The secretariat shall be responsible in particular for:

(a)   the day-to-day business of the Board;
(b)   communication between the members of the Board, its Chair and the Commission;
(c)   communication with other institutions and the public;
(d)   the use of electronic means for the internal and external communication;
(e)   the translation of relevant information;
(f)   the preparation and follow-up of the meetings of the Board;
(g)   the preparation, drafting and publication of opinions, decisions on the settlement of disputes between supervisory authorities and other texts adopted by the Board.

ARTICLE 76 – CONFIDENTIALITY

1. The discussions of the Board shall be confidential where the Board deems it necessary, as provided for in its rules of procedure.

2. Access to documents submitted to members of the Board, experts and representatives of third parties shall be governed by Regulation (EC) No 1049/2001 of the European Parliament and of the Council.[21]

CHAPTER VIII – REMEDIES, LIABILITY AND PENALTIES

ARTICLE 77 – RIGHT TO LODGE A COMPLAINT WITH A SUPERVISORY AUTHORITY

1. Without prejudice to any other administrative or judicial remedy, every data subject shall have the right to lodge a complaint with a supervisory authority, in particular in the Member State of his or her habitual residence, place of work or place of the alleged infringement if the data subject considers that the processing of personal data relating to him or her infringes this Regulation.

2. The supervisory authority with which the complaint has been lodged shall inform the complainant on the progress and the outcome of the complaint including the possibility of a judicial remedy pursuant to Article 78.

ARTICLE 78 – RIGHT TO AN EFFECTIVE JUDICIAL REMEDY AGAINST A SUPERVISORY AUTHORITY

1. Without prejudice to any other administrative or non-judicial remedy, each natural or legal person shall have the right to an effective judicial remedy against a legally binding decision of a supervisory authority concerning them.

2. Without prejudice to any other administrative or non-judicial remedy, each data subject shall have the right to a an effective judicial remedy where the supervisory authority which is competent pursuant to Articles 55 and 56 does not handle a complaint or does not inform the data subject within three months on the progress or outcome of the complaint lodged pursuant to Article 77.

3. Proceedings against a supervisory authority shall be brought before the courts of the Member State where the supervisory authority is established.

4. Where proceedings are brought against a decision of a supervisory authority which was preceded by an opinion or a decision of the Board in the consistency mechanism, the supervisory authority shall forward that opinion or decision to the court.

---

[21] Regulation (EC) No 1049/2001 of the European Parliament and of the Council of 30 May 2001 regarding public access to European Parliament, Council and Commission documents (OJ L 145, 31.5.2001, p.43).

ARTICLE 79 – RIGHT TO AN EFFECTIVE JUDICIAL REMEDY AGAINST A CONTROLLER OR PROCESSOR

1. Without prejudice to any available administrative or non-judicial remedy, including the right to lodge a complaint with a supervisory authority pursuant to Article 77, each data subject shall have the right to an effective judicial remedy where he or she considers that his or her rights under this Regulation have been infringed as a result of the processing of his or her personal data in non-compliance with this Regulation.

2. Proceedings against a controller or a processor shall be brought before the courts of the Member State where the controller or processor has an establishment. Alternatively, such proceedings may be brought before the courts of the Member State where the data subject has his or her habitual residence, unless the controller or processor is a public authority of a Member State acting in the exercise of its public powers.

ARTICLE 80 – REPRESENTATION OF DATA SUBJECTS

1. The data subject shall have the right to mandate a not-for-profit body, organisation or association which has been properly constituted in accordance with the law of a Member State, has statutory objectives which are in the public interest, and is active in the field of the protection of data subjects' rights and freedoms with regard to the protection of their personal data to lodge the complaint on his or her behalf, to exercise the rights referred to in Articles 77, 78 and 79 on his or her behalf, and to exercise the right to receive compensation referred to in Article 82 on his or her behalf where provided for by Member State law.

2. Member States may provide that any body, organisation or association referred to in paragraph 1 of this Article, independently of a data subject's mandate, has the right to lodge, in that Member State, a complaint with the supervisory authority which is competent pursuant to Article 77 and to exercise the rights referred to in Articles 78 and 79 if it considers that the rights of a data subject under this Regulation have been infringed as a result of the processing.

ARTICLE 81 – SUSPENSION OF PROCEEDINGS

1. Where a competent court of a Member State has information on proceedings, concerning the same subject matter as regards processing by the same controller or processor, that are pending in a court in another Member State, it shall contact that court in the other Member State to confirm the existence of such proceedings.

2. Where proceedings concerning the same subject matter as regards processing of the same controller or processor are pending in a court in another Member State, any competent court other than the court first seized may suspend its proceedings.

3. Where those proceedings are pending at first instance, any court other than the court first seized may also, on the application of one of the parties, decline jurisdiction if the court first seized has jurisdiction over the actions in question and its law permits the consolidation thereof.

ARTICLE 82 – RIGHT TO COMPENSATION AND LIABILITY

1. Any person who has suffered material or non-material damage as a result of an infringement of this Regulation shall have the right to receive compensation from the controller or processor for the damage suffered.

2. Any controller involved in processing shall be liable for the damage caused by processing which infringes this Regulation. A processor shall be liable for the damage caused by processing only where it has not complied with obligations of this Regulation specifically directed to processors or where it has acted outside or contrary to lawful instructions of the controller.

3. A controller or processor shall be exempt from liability under paragraph 2 if it proves that it is not in any way responsible for the event giving rise to the damage.

4. Where more than one controller or processor, or both a controller and a processor, are involved in the same processing and where they are, under paragraphs 2 and 3, responsible for any damage caused by processing, each controller or processor shall be held liable for the entire damage in order to ensure effective compensation of the data subject.

5. Where a controller or processor has, in accordance with paragraph 4, paid full compensation for the damage suffered, that controller or processor shall be entitled to claim back from the other controllers or processors involved in the same processing that part of the compensation corresponding to their part of responsibility for the damage, in accordance with the conditions set out in paragraph 2.

6. Court proceedings for exercising the right to receive compensation shall be brought before the courts competent under the law of the Member State referred to in Article 79(2).

ARTICLE 83 – GENERAL CONDITIONS FOR IMPOSING ADMINISTRATIVE FINES

1. Each supervisory authority shall ensure that the imposition of administrative fines pursuant to this Article in respect of infringements of this Regulation referred to in paragraphs 4, 5 and 6 shall in each individual case be effective, proportionate and dissuasive.

2. Administrative fines shall, depending on the circumstances of each individual case, be imposed in addition to, or instead of, measures referred to in points (a) to (h) and (j) of Article 58(2). When deciding whether to impose an administrative fine and deciding on the amount of the administrative fine in each individual case due regard shall be given to the following:

(a) the nature, gravity and duration of the infringement taking into account the nature scope or purpose of the processing concerned as well as the number of data subjects affected and the level of damage suffered by them;
(b) the intentional or negligent character of the infringement;
(c) any action taken by the controller or processor to mitigate the damage suffered by data subjects;
(d) the degree of responsibility of the controller or processor taking into account technical and organisational measures implemented by them pursuant to Articles 25 and 32;
(e) any relevant previous infringements by the controller or processor;
(f) the degree of cooperation with the supervisory authority, in order to remedy the infringement and mitigate the possible adverse effects of the infringement;
(g) the categories of personal data affected by the infringement;
(h) the manner in which the infringement became known to the supervisory authority, in particular whether, and if so to what extent, the controller or processor notified the infringement;
(i) where measures referred to in Article 58(2) have previously been ordered against the controller or processor concerned with regard to the same subject-matter, compliance with those measures;
(j) adherence to approved codes of conduct pursuant to Article 40 or approved certification mechanisms pursuant to Article 42; and
(k) any other aggravating or mitigating factor applicable to the circumstances of the case, such as financial benefits gained, or losses avoided, directly or indirectly, from the infringement.

3. If a controller or processor intentionally or negligently, for the same or linked processing operations, infringes several provisions of this Regulation, the total amount of the administrative fine shall not exceed the amount specified for the gravest infringement.

4. Infringements of the following provisions shall, in accordance with paragraph 2, be subject to administrative fines up to 10 000 000 EUR, or in the case of an undertaking, up to 2% of the total worldwide annual turnover of the preceding financial year, whichever is higher:

(a) the obligations of the controller and the processor pursuant to Articles 8, 11, 25 to 39 and 42 and 43;
(b) the obligations of the certification body pursuant to Articles 42 and 43;
(c) the obligations of the monitoring body pursuant to Article 41(4).

5. Infringements of the following provisions shall, in accordance with paragraph 2, be subject to administrative fines up to 20 000 000 EUR, or in the case of an undertaking, up to 4% of the total worldwide annual turnover of the preceding financial year, whichever is higher:

(a) the basic principles for processing, including conditions for consent, pursuant to Articles 5, 6, 7 and 9;
(b) the data subjects' rights pursuant to Articles 12 to 22;
(c) the transfers of personal data to a recipient in a third country or an international organisation pursuant to Articles 44 to 49;
(d) any obligations pursuant to Member State law adopted under Chapter IX;
(e) non-compliance with an order or a temporary or definitive limitation on processing or the suspension of data flows by the supervisory authority pursuant to Article 58(2) or failure to provide access in violation of Article 58(1).

6. Non-compliance with an order by the supervisory authority as referred to in Article 58(2) shall, in accordance with paragraph 2 of this Article, be subject to administrative fines up to 20 000 000 EUR, or in the case of an undertaking, up to 4 % of the total worldwide annual turnover of the preceding financial year, whichever is higher.

7. Without prejudice to the corrective powers of supervisory authorities pursuant to Article 58(2), each Member State may lay down the rules on whether and to what extent administrative fines may be imposed on public authorities and bodies established in that Member State.

8. The exercise by the supervisory authority of its powers under this Article shall be subject to appropriate procedural safeguards in accordance with Union and Member State law, including effective judicial remedy and due process.

9. Where the legal system of the Member State does not provide for administrative fines, this Article may be applied in such a manner that the fine is initiated by the competent supervisory authority and imposed by competent national courts, while ensuring that those legal remedies are effective and have an equivalent effect to the administrative fines imposed by supervisory authorities. In any event, the fines imposed shall be effective, proportionate and dissuasive. Those Member States shall notify to the Commission the provisions of their laws which they adopt pursuant to this paragraph by 25 May 2018 and, without delay, any subsequent amendment law or amendment affecting them.

ARTICLE 84 – PENALTIES

1. Member States shall lay down the rules on other penalties applicable to infringements of this Regulation in particular for infringements which are not subject to administrative fines pursuant to Article 83, and shall take all measures necessary to ensure that they are implemented. Such penalties shall be effective, proportionate and dissuasive.

2. Each Member State shall notify to the Commission the provisions of its law which it adopts pursuant to paragraph 1, by 25 May 2018 and, without delay, any subsequent amendment affecting them.

CHAPTER IX – PROVISIONS RELATING TO SPECIFIC PROCESSING SITUATIONS

ARTICLE 85 – PROCESSING AND FREEDOM OF EXPRESSION AND INFORMATION

1. Member States shall by law reconcile the right to the protection of personal data pursuant to this Regulation with the right to freedom of expression and information, including processing for journalistic purposes and the purposes of academic, artistic or literary expression.

2. For processing carried out for journalistic purposes or the purpose of academic artistic or literary expression, Member States shall provide for exemptions or derogations from Chapter II (principles), Chapter III (rights of the data subject), Chapter IV (controller and processor), Chapter V (transfer of personal data to third countries or international organisations), Chapter VI (independent supervisory authorities), Chapter VII (cooperation and consistency) and Chapter IX (specific data processing situations) if they are necessary to reconcile the right to the protection of personal data with the freedom of expression and information.

3. Each Member State shall notify to the Commission the provisions of its law which it has adopted pursuant to paragraph 2 and, without delay, any subsequent amendment law or amendment affecting them.

ARTICLE 86 – PROCESSING AND PUBLIC ACCESS TO OFFICIAL DOCUMENTS

Personal data in official documents held by a public authority or a public body or a private body for the performance of a task carried out in the public interest may be disclosed by the authority or body in accordance with Union or Member State law to which the public authority or body is subject in order to reconcile public access to official documents with the right to the protection of personal data pursuant to this Regulation.

ARTICLE 87 – PROCESSING OF THE NATIONAL IDENTIFICATION NUMBER

Member States may further determine the specific conditions for the processing of a national identification number or any other identifier of general application. In that case the national identification number or any other identifier of general application shall be used only under appropriate safeguards for the rights and freedoms of the data subject pursuant to this Regulation.

ARTICLE 88 – PROCESSING IN THE CONTEXT OF EMPLOYMENT

1. Member States may, by law or by collective agreements, provide for more specific rules to ensure the protection of the rights and freedoms in respect of the processing of employees' personal data in the employment context, in particular for the purposes of the recruitment, the performance of the contract of employment, including discharge of obligations laid down by law or by collective agreements, management, planning and organisation of work, equality and diversity in the workplace, health and safety at work, protection of employer's or customer's property and for the purposes of the exercise and enjoyment, on an individual or collective basis, of rights and benefits related to employment, and for the purpose of the termination of the employment relationship.

2. Those rules shall include suitable and specific measures to safeguard the data subject's human dignity, legitimate interests and fundamental rights, with particular regard to the

transparency of processing, the transfer of personal data within a group of undertakings, or a group of enterprises engaged in a joint economic activity and monitoring systems at the work place.

3. Each Member State shall notify to the Commission those provisions of its law which it adopts pursuant to paragraph 1, by 25 May 2018 and, without delay, any subsequent amendment affecting them.

ARTICLE 89 – SAFEGUARDS AND DEROGATIONS RELATING TO PROCESSING FOR ARCHIVING PURPOSES IN THE PUBLIC INTEREST, SCIENTIFIC OR HISTORICAL RESEARCH PURPOSES OR STATISTICAL PURPOSES

1. Processing for archiving purposes in the public interest, scientific or historical research purposes or statistical purposes, shall be subject to appropriate safeguards, in accordance with this Regulation, for the rights and freedoms of the data subject. Those safeguards shall ensure that technical and organisational measures are in place in particular in order to ensure respect for the principle of data minimisation. Those measures may include pseudonymisation provided that those purposes can be fulfilled in that manner. Where those purposes can be fulfilled by further processing which does not permit or no longer permits the identification of data subjects, those purposes shall be fulfilled in that manner.

2. Where personal data are processed for scientific or historical research purposes or statistical purposes, Union or Member State law may provide for derogations from the rights referred to in Articles 15, 16, 18 and 21 subject to the conditions and safeguards referred to in paragraph 1 of this Article in so far as such rights are likely to render impossible or seriously impair the achievement of the specific purposes, and such derogations are necessary for the fulfilment of those purposes.

3. Where personal data are processed for archiving purposes in the public interest, Union or Member State law may provide for derogations from the rights referred to in Articles 15, 16, 18, 19, 20 and 21 subject to the conditions and safeguards referred to in paragraph 1 of this Article in so far as such rights are likely to render impossible or seriously impair the achievement of the specific purposes, and such derogations are necessary for the fulfilment of those purposes.

4. Where processing referred to in paragraphs 2 and 3 serves at the same time another purpose, the derogations shall apply only to processing for the purposes referred to in those paragraphs.

ARTICLE 90 – OBLIGATIONS OF SECRECY

1. Member States may adopt specific rules to set out the powers of the supervisory authorities laid down in points (e) and (f) of Article 58(1) in relation to controllers or processors that are subject, under Union or Member State law or rules established by national competent bodies, to an obligation of professional secrecy or other equivalent obligations of secrecy where this is necessary and proportionate to reconcile the right of the protection of personal data with the obligation of secrecy. Those rules shall apply only with regard to personal data which the controller or processor has received as a result of or has obtained in an activity covered by that obligation of secrecy.

2. Each Member State shall notify to the Commission the rules adopted pursuant to paragraph 1, by 25 May 2018 and, without delay, any subsequent amendment affecting them.

ARTICLE 91 – EXISTING DATA PROTECTION RULES OF CHURCHES AND RELIGIOUS ASSOCIATIONS

1. Where in a Member State, churches and religious associations or communities apply, at the time of entry into force of this Regulation, comprehensive rules relating to the protection of natural persons with regard to processing, such rules may continue to apply, provided that they are brought into line with this Regulation.

2. Churches and religious associations which apply comprehensive rules in accordance with paragraph 1 of this Article shall be subject to the supervision of an independent supervisory authority, which may be specific, provided that it fulfils the conditions laid down in Chapter VI of this Regulation.

CHAPTER X – DELEGATED ACTS AND IMPLEMENTING ACTS

ARTICLE 92 – EXERCISE OF THE DELEGATION

1. The power to adopt delegated acts is conferred on the Commission subject to the conditions laid down in this Article.

2. The delegation of power referred to in Article 12(8) and Article 43(8) shall be conferred on the Commission for an indeterminate period of time from 24 May 2016.

3. The delegation of power referred to in Article 12(8) and Article 43(8) may be revoked at any time by the European Parliament or by the Council. A decision of revocation shall put an end to the delegation of power specified in that decision. It shall take effect the day following that of its publication in the *Official Journal of the European Union* or at a later date specified therein. It shall not affect the validity of any delegated acts already in force.

4. As soon as it adopts a delegated act, the Commission shall notify it simultaneously to the European Parliament and to the Council.

5. A delegated act adopted pursuant to Article 12(8) and Article 43(8) shall enter into force only if no objection has been expressed by either the European Parliament or the Council within a period of three months of notification of that act to the European Parliament and the Council or if, before the expiry of that period, the European Parliament and the Council have both informed the Commission that they will not object. That period shall be extended by three months at the initiative of the European Parliament or of the Council.

ARTICLE 93 – COMMITTEE PROCEDURE

1. The Commission shall be assisted by a committee. That committee shall be a committee within the meaning of Regulation (EU) No 182/2011.

2. Where reference is made to this paragraph, Article 5 of Regulation (EU) No 182/2011 shall apply.

3. Where reference is made to this paragraph, Article 8 of Regulation (EU) No 182/2011, in conjunction with Article 5 thereof, shall apply.

CHAPTER XI – FINAL PROVISIONS

ARTICLE 94 – REPEAL OF DIRECTIVE 95/46/EC

1. Directive 95/46/EC is repealed with effect from 25 May 2018.

2. References to the repealed Directive shall be construed as references to this Regulation. References to the Working Party on the Protection of Individuals with regard to the

Processing of Personal Data established by Article 29 of Directive 95/46/EC shall be construed as references to the European Data Protection Board established by this Regulation.

ARTICLE 95 – RELATIONSHIP WITH DIRECTIVE 2002/58/EC

This Regulation shall not impose additional obligations on natural or legal persons in relation to processing in connection with the provision of publicly available electronic communications services in public communication networks in the Union in relation to matters for which they are subject to specific obligations with the same objective set out in Directive 2002/58/EC.

ARTICLE 96 – RELATIONSHIP WITH PREVIOUSLY CONCLUDED AGREEMENTS

International agreements involving the transfer of personal data to third countries or international organisations which were concluded by Member States prior to 24 May 2016, and which comply with Union law as applicable prior to that date, shall remain in force until amended, replaced or revoked.

ARTICLE 97 – COMMISSION REPORTS

1. By 25 May 2020 and every four years thereafter, the Commission shall submit a report on the evaluation and review of this Regulation to the European Parliament and to the Council. The reports shall be made public.

2. In the context of the evaluations and reviews referred to in paragraph 1, the Commission shall examine, in particular, the application and functioning of:

(a) Chapter V on the transfer of personal data to third countries or international organisa- tions with particular regard to decisions adopted pursuant to Article 45(3) of this Regulation and decisions adopted on the basis of Article 25(6) of Directive 95/46/EC;
(b) Chapter VII on cooperation and consistency.

3. For the purpose of paragraph 1, the Commission may request information from Member States and supervisory authorities.

4. In carrying out the evaluations and reviews referred to in paragraphs 1 and 2, the Commission shall take into account the positions and findings of the European Parliament, of the Council, and of other relevant bodies or sources.

5. The Commission shall, if necessary, submit appropriate proposals to amend this Regula- tion, in particular taking into account of developments in information technology and in the light of the state of progress in the information society.

ARTICLE 98 – REVIEW OF OTHER UNION LEGAL ACTS ON DATA PROTECTION

The Commission shall, if appropriate, submit legislative proposals with a view to amending other Union legal acts on the protection of personal data, in order to ensure uniform and consistent protection of natural persons with regard to processing. This shall in particular concern the rules relating to the protection of natural persons with regard to processing by Union institutions, bodies, offices and agencies and on the free movement of such data.

ARTICLE 99 – ENTRY INTO FORCE AND APPLICATION

1. This Regulation shall enter into force on the twentieth day following that of its publica- tion in the *Official Journal of the European Union*.

2. It shall apply from 25 May 2018.

This Regulation shall be binding in its entirety and directly applicable in all Member States.

Done at Brussels, 27 April 2016.

For the European Parliament
The President
M. SCHULZ

For the Council
The President
J.A. HENNIS-PLASSCHAERT

INDEX